XSLT 2.0
web development

The Charles F. Goldfarb Definitive XML Series

Holman
Definitive XSLT and XPath

Walmsley
Definitive XML Schema

Garshol
Definitive XML Application Development

Hocek and Cuddihy
Definitive VoiceXML™

Holman
Definitive XSL-FO

Goldfarb and Prescod
Charles F. Goldfarb's XML Handbook™ Fifth Edition

Goldfarb and Walmsley
XML in Office 2003: *Information Sharing with Desktop XML*

Kirsanov
XSLT 2.0 Web Development

Walmsley
Definitive XQuery

Titles in this series are produced using XML, SGML, and/or XSL. XSL-FO documents are rendered into PDF by the *XEP Rendering Engine* from RenderX: www.renderx.com.

About the Series Editor
Charles F. Goldfarb is the father of XML technology. He invented SGML, the Standard Generalized Markup Language on which both XML and HTML are based. You can find him on the Web at: www.xmlbooks.com.

About the Series Logo
The rebus is an ancient literary tradition, dating from 16th century Picardy, and is especially appropriate to a series involving fine distinctions between markup and text, metadata and data. The logo is a rebus incorporating the series name within a stylized XML comment declaration.

XSLT 2.0
web development

Dmitry Kirsanov

PRENTICE HALL
Professional Technical Reference
Upper Saddle River, NJ 07458
www.phptr.com

A Cataloging-in-Publication Data record for this book can be obtained from the Library of Congress.

Editorial/Production Supervisor: *Faye Gemmellaro*
Editor in Chief: *Mark L. Taub*
Editorial Assistant: *Noreen Regina*
Marketing Manager: *Chanda Leary-Coutu*
Manufacturing Manager: *Alexis R. Heydt-Long*
Manufacturing Buyer: *Maura Zaldivar*
Cover Designer: *Dmitry Kirsanov*
Cover Design Director: *Jerry Votta*
Book Interior Design: *Dmitry Kirsanov*

Prentice Hall PTR offers discounts on this book when ordered in quantity for bulk purchases or special sales. For more information, please contact: U.S. Corporate and Government Sales, 1–800–382–3419, corpsales@pearsontechgroup.com. For sales outside of the United States, please contact: International Sales, 1–317–581–3793, international@pearsontechgroup.com.

Printed in the United States of America

Second printing

Text printed on recycled paper

ISBN 0–13–140635–3

Pearson Education LTD.
Pearson Education Australia PTY, Limited
Pearson Education Singapore, Pte. Ltd.
Pearson Education North Asia Ltd.
Pearson Education Canada, Ltd.
Pearson Educación de Mexico, S.A. de C.V.
Pearson Education—Japan
Pearson Education Malaysia, Ptd. Ltd.

Overview

Contents

chapter 3 *Elements of a web site* **89**

chapter **5** *The XSLT stylesheet* 183

Focusing on what's important • *Not only XSLT*

chapter 6 *XML software* **279**

A no monster zone • *Bang for the buck* • *Standards compliance*

chapter **7** *XML on the server*   357

List of figures

List of examples

Foreword

O, what a tangled web we weave . . .

You may claim that Sir Walter Scott didn't write that line about *your* website and you would be correct — but only because he didn't have the ability to "View Source"!

The fact is that most websites today — however well organized they may appear in a browser — are horribly tangled below the surface. Their documents are a maintenance nightmare in which data, styling, and implementation code are hopelessly intermingled. And as the Web becomes increasingly dynamic and data-driven, the tangle worsens.

The fundamental problem is the lack of a consistent, media-independent, semantic representation of content. XML is the solution, and the key to applying XML to Web development has always been XSLT transformations. Now XSLT 2.0 has added powerful new facilities, capable of dealing with the increasing dynamism of the Web.

Dmitry Kirsanov is a professional Web developer, both a graphic artist and a programmer. He knows how to use XML and XSLT and he has the proven ability to share that knowledge with you. His *WebReference* series, *Dmitry's Design Lab*, was launched in 1997 and is still a fixture at `www.webreference.com/dlab`. His three books on Web design and the Internet have sold over 65,000 copies in his native Russia.

Scott's complete thought was

O, what a tangled web we weave,
When first we practice to deceive!

Developers are deceiving themselves by thinking that today's Web can be built and maintained with yesterday's outmoded tangle of HTML, scripts, and styles. *XSLT 2.0 Web Development* will show you how XML and XSLT 2.0 can — literally! — transform your website.

Charles F. Goldfarb
Saratoga, CA
February 2004

Introduction

Why this book is needed

"I am left with the feeling that all of the sites I have created are 50% elegance, and 50% nasty kludge."

This quote from a recent Slashdot[1] discussion on PHP development resonated with the audience. Indeed, as many would attest, a web site usually starts simple but quickly grows into a complex, convoluted mess — where you are afraid of making a change for fear of breaking something else.

Why should a web site so quickly become a nightmare of unmaintainable code, visual and semantic inconsistencies, and outright errors embarrassingly visible to the whole world? Many reasons could be quoted, from limitations specific to the particular web development platforms (such as PHP, ASP, or Perl) to fundamental drawbacks of the "web site as an application" paradigm.

---

1. www.slashdot.org

This book is devoted to one very important way in which the majority of today's web sites are broken — and, of course, to the technology which (if correctly applied) can mend this breakage. The problem I'm speaking about is the lack of a consistently semantic and media-independent representation of web site content; the technology that can help you solve this problem is XML; and the key to applying it in web development is XSLT transformations.

Say what you mean. XML is no panacea. It won't magically make your sites self-maintaining or error-proof. But it will give you a critical advantage: Just as a good programming language allows you to freely express your algorithms, XML makes it possible to actually *say what you mean* in content markup.

The word *content* is the key. XML is actually more important for web development than any programming language — simply because you can have a web site without a dynamic engine of any kind, but there cannot exist a web site without content.

In fact, a lot of the approaches in this book apply not only to web sites but to any XML-based document workflows, such as books or technical documentation. XML stimulates thinking about content *as such*, abstracting it not only from its presentation but from any processing requirements as well.

What you will find in this book

This is not a general XML book; it is a book on one specific application of XML. What you'll find here is as much XML and XSLT as is necessary for a sequence of very practical tasks:

- structuring your web site content into cleanly separated semantic layers;

- developing a custom XML markup vocabulary for each layer;

- automatically validating both markup and structure of content;

- transforming content from source XML to browser-ready HTML using XSLT (optionally with generation of images and other non-HTML objects); and

- integrating the content markup and transformation system with existing web development frameworks and other software.

Building the backbone. The point of using XML in web design is to separate *content* from *presentation*; the above items cover the complete transition from the former to the latter. Simply put, we focus on developing the best source markup for your content and programming the most efficient transformation into your chosen presentation style.

An XML web site may include other components, such as a database, a dynamic engine, or a maintenance back-end. There is a wide range of auxiliary tools and architectures compatible with an XML-based web site. Many of them are mentioned in this book, and a few are explored in detail (notably Cocoon, Chapter 7). However, the content-to-presentation assembly line is the backbone of any XML web site and our main focus of attention in this book.

Usability and portability. In a web development context, the term *usability* normally refers to how easy to use a web site is for a visitor. In this book, however, I would like to redefine this term by focusing on a different aspect of usability that is too often ignored — usability of a web site for its developers, authors, editors, and maintainers. With the Web growing more and more collaborative, this aspect is becoming critical.

Using semantic XML for content markup is already a big step toward liberating web authors from worrying about things they don't need to worry about. But semantic XML is only an idea; how you implement this idea will seriously affect the "authorability" and "maintainability" of your site. This is where this book, with its pervasive ideas of simplification, abbreviation, and readability, might be useful.

Another important theme of the book is *portability*. Again, this term usually describes a web site's viewability and functionality across browsers and platforms. It's not less important, however, that before

a web site gets to your browser, it must be developed and authored —
often in different environments and on different platforms. We touch
on this server-side aspect of portability with regard to the XML/XSLT
workflow.

Who this book is for

Everyone interested in web development or in practical XML/XSLT
should find this book interesting. It will be especially useful for web
designers, web developers, project managers, as well as webmasters
and web site administrators. Whether you are building a modest personal home page or a large dynamic site, learning the XML way of
doing things will transform your outlook even if you don't plan to use
(all of) this book's techniques.

You need to have a basic knowledge of XML to read and enjoy this
book. For most chapters, understanding of XML syntax and common
XML-related terms[2] will be enough, but for Chapter 5 you will want
to know some XSLT and especially XPath. Expert knowledge of
HTML is neither required nor offered. Some familiarity with web
development concepts and jargon might be useful but is not necessary.

How this book is organized

Perhaps you've already thumbed through the book, so you might have
noticed that it breaks into three main parts. The first part is composed
mostly of text and diagrams; the second features lots of example
code; the last displays a number of screenshots. This sequence
metaphorically reflects the path that we'll follow from manipulating
abstract notions, to writing practical markup and code, to launching
and maintaining a final working web site.

----

2. Excluding the syntax and terminology of XML DTDs which (with a few
exceptions) are intentionally ignored in favor of more powerful and modern
schema languages.

- **Chapter 1** is mostly theoretical; we'll spend some time discussing the basic premises of XML and its applicability to web development. It is recommended that you read this chapter carefully, for its concepts and terminology are used throughout the book. No real harm will be done, however, if you poke into the book's code examples first and return to Chapter 1 later.

   The topics of this chapter include the principles behind using XML with web sites, an overview of relevant XML standards, and a classification of the possible ways to set up an XML web site. Special attention is paid to the dynamic web sites and the approaches to combining XML processing with a dynamic engine.

- **Chapter 2** is dedicated to the foundation of an XML web site — its *source definition*. This includes schemas for all document types used by the web site's XML source plus all the rules and regulations that may be impossible to express in a schema language but that the source must satisfy in order to smoothly transform into a correct web site.

   In this chapter, we'll look at different schema languages and discuss the implementation options for those parts of the source definition that a schema cannot handle. We will also examine the common generic markup constructs, the best approaches to their schematization, and a number of corresponding pitfalls. For instance, in this chapter you'll find insights into the eternal "child elements vs. attributes" dilemma.

- **Chapter 3** is the practical complement to the previous chapter. Here, we'll use the approaches of Chapter 2 to mark up some real web site source documents. Most common elements of web pages, such as text blocks, headings, links, and images, are considered. In most cases, existing standardized vocabularies that you can borrow from are mentioned.

   Some important concepts of the book, such as abbreviating addresses, are introduced in this chapter. This is also the chapter where markup examples start appearing in large numbers, so if you prefer to learn by looking at examples, you might want to start your reading from this chapter. The last section of the chapter presents summary examples of a page document, a master document, and a Schematron schema that validates both types of documents.

- **Chapter 4** is the first of the two XSLT chapters. It is an introduction aimed at a developer who has had some experience with XSLT 1.0. Here, we'll discuss some of the new stuff that is being introduced in XSLT 2.0 and XPath 2.0 as well as the existing XSLT extensions. A detailed analysis is devoted to the important issue of adapting traditional algorithms to XSLT, which is a functional language without an assignment operator.

- **Chapter 5** is the core of the book — the practical XSLT chapter and the largest of all of them. Lots of XSLT code examples show all aspects of an XML-to-HTML transformation, from setting up the environment and building the page layout to low-level text processing. We'll also revisit our Schematron schema to add some exciting new checks made possible by XPath 2.0.

  This chapter not only uses but extends XSLT. We'll see how a few simple Java classes may drastically advance the capabilities of an XSLT stylesheet. These extensions are used in Chapter 5 for all kinds of tasks, from generating bitmap images via SVG to batch processing all page documents of a site. Again, a section with complete listings of the stylesheet and related bits of code summarizes this chapter.

- **Chapter 6** is where the screenshots are. It is devoted to all kinds of software that will help you run your XML web site after the core validation and transformation components are ready. The focus here is not on specific programs but on classifying the functionality of XML software and the approaches to various practical problems.

  Sections of this chapter discuss the existing XML authoring paradigms and the principles of converting other formats into XML. Also reviewed are various tools and utilities for handling

XML, XSLT, and XPath. The last section explores the use of build tools, such as the `make` utility, in XML web site projects.

- **Chapter 7** is concerned with integrating the XML/XSLT system into a web server setup. We'll briefly discuss using an XSLT processor as a servlet, but the bulk of this chapter is devoted to Apache Cocoon, which crowns the chapter and the book. After learning the principles of building Cocoon web sites, we'll revisit our sample web site from previous chapters to see what it takes to adapt it to run under Cocoon.

Typographic conventions

Designing your own book is a mindbending experience (something that songwriters who author both music and lyrics would probably agree with). In my book, I tried to make the text look rich but consistent, pleasantly dense but varied. Some of the solutions that I came up with may deserve a few words.

Running in from aside. Three levels of numbered headings are used within each chapter. In addition, unnumbered bold run-in headings are often used (as in this paragraph) to break the text into even smaller, manageable pieces.

Semantically, the run-ins are closer to margin notes than headings; usually their goal is not to state the subject but to provide a remark, an aside, a metaphor related to the topic of discussion. Hopefully these run-in headings are memorable enough to serve as landmarks facilitating navigation.

Small but not least. Some paragraphs, with or without run-in headings, are set in a smaller type. They present material that may be skipped in the first reading without any damage to understanding. You can treat the smaller-type fragments as extended footnotes or sidebars.

Cross-references. Bold gray numbers (such as 3.9) refer to numbered sections of the book. The running headers and footers should make it easy to find the referenced sections; however, for references that jump especially far, page numbers are also provided.

Syntax coloring without colors. Unlike most computer books with code listings, this one makes use of a concept that has long been commonplace in text editors: syntax coloring. Of course, a black-and-white book page is not really capable of color (except for shades of gray), but instead it can freely use font faces that usually look nicer on paper than on a computer screen. Thus, I have attempted to make code in the book at least as readable as it is in a good text editor by consistently "coloring" syntactic constructions with different font faces.

Essential URLs. All web addresses are given in footnotes in an abbreviated form without `http://`, `index.html`, or trailing slashes.

Slash what? I use forward slashes (/) and not backslashes (\) as directory separators for *both* Windows and Unix (the latter including Mac OS X). The rationale is simple: Forward slashes are standard on Unix and in URLs, and most Windows tools understand both kinds of slashes anyway.

Notes on terminology

The terminology used in the book is basically standard. Sometimes I simplify the accepted terminology in order to make it more accessible, or I use my own terms instead of those used in authoritative sources; all such cases are noted. Some important terms that may appear confusing or are often misunderstood are commented on below.

Element type, element, or tag? When speaking of XML, many people fail to differentiate between an *element* and an *element type*. Sometimes, a *tag* is also confused with an *element*. For example, this fragment

```
<foo> <foo/> </foo>
```

has *three* tags but *two* elements belonging to *one* element type (and having one *element type name*, `foo`). Note that an element cannot have a name — only an element type can; still, we can refer to an element by its element type name if we identify *which* of the elements of this type is in question (for example, "in the first `foo` element"). In the XSLT context, an element from the XSLT namespace (e.g., `xsl:template`) is often called an *instruction*.

Stylesheet or transformation? The word *stylesheet* may be misleading when applied to an XSLT program that transforms one XML document into another; the word *transformation* would be more appropriate. (Note that `xsl:stylesheet` and `xsl:transform` are both acceptable as the root element of an XSLT stylesheet.) Still, backed by tradition, I mostly use "stylesheet" or, sometimes, "transformation stylesheet" when referring to the XSLT component of a web site setup.

Stylesheet or style sheet? To avoid confusion with XSLT *stylesheets*, CSS *style sheets* are always spelled thus; this is conformant with both XSLT and CSS specifications.

Document, instance, page, or file? *Document* is a generic term, but I use it only to refer to XML documents, while HTML documents are usually called *pages*. *Instance* is another term often used in XML (it refers to a document being an instance of its document type), but I will stick to "documents" as more familiar. Neither "document" nor "instance" are synonymous with *file*; a document is not necessarily stored in a file at all. Therefore, "file" is used only when real files, handled by the operating system, are involved.

Document element or root element? The XSLT specification uses the term *document element* with the meaning of *root element*. I use the latter term as more descriptive, even though it may be slightly confusing from an XSLT viewpoint because the "root node" of XPath (`/`) is the parent of the node corresponding to the "root element" (e.g., `/page`).

XML Schema or XSDL? *XML Schema* is the W3C recommendation for a schema language. Unfortunately, its name is way too generic for its own good. Even the capital S in "Schema" cannot prevent confusion when you have to speak about XML Schema among other schema languages for XML, and especially when you refer to specific schemas written in that language. So, in conformance with other books in this series, I use the abbreviation *XSDL* (XML Schema Definition

Language) to refer to the language itself and *XSDL schemas* to refer to specific schema definitions.

Yet another abbreviation you may have seen used for the same language is WXS, standing for W3C XML Schema.

URI or URL? This one may confuse even experts at times. *URI* is a more general term than *URL*, but the difference between them — i.e., those URIs that are not URLs — is so insignificant that for practical purposes, these terms are interchangeable. See RFC 2396[3] for more details.

HTML or XHTML? Since this book views HTML mostly as a result of an XSLT transformation, what I mean when speaking of HTML may actually be either HTML or XHTML (any versions). With XSLT, you can output both formats, and modern browsers do not have any problems with either. When there's a meaningful distinction between HTML and XHTML, this is noted.

"Data is" or "data are"? Formally, *data* is the plural of *datum*. In modern English, however, using "data" as singular is more common, as evidenced by statistics reported by Internet search engines. In this book "data" is used as singular.

How this book was created

"Practice what you preach." "Eat your own dogfood." One way or the other, this book itself uses many of the techniques it describes.

The text of the book was written directly in XML using a custom schema inspired by HTML, DocBook, and Charles F. Goldfarb's DTD that is used by many books in this Definitive XML Series. An XSLT transformation stylesheet written by Alina Kirsanova translated the source into XSL-FO and performed all necessary processing, such as importing code examples (stored separately), special character substitutions (**5.4.2.2**), compiling the Index and TOC, and generating cross-references.

....

3. www.ietf.org/rfc/rfc2396.txt

The design for the book was also created by me, with elements borrowed from the other books in the series that we worked on using the same XML/XSLT/XSL-FO technology. The final rendering of XSL-FO into PDF was done by XEP[4] from RenderX.

Code examples (in a total of 11 different formats and XML vocabularies) were parsed by XEmacs + PSGML (**6.1.1.2**) with custom syntax coloring regexps and then saved into XHTML using `htmlize.el`[5] by Hrvoje Nikšić. The resulting files were then translated by a simple stylesheet into a vocabulary understood by the book's main transformation stylesheet.

Acknowledgments

This book could be much worse (all the way down to the point of nonexistence) without the help of the following people to whom I am deeply indebted:

Charles F. Goldfarb, for inventing SGML before I was born, for persuading me that the book project is realistic, and for a detailed review of the manuscript.

Mark Taub, for managing the project and tirelessly pushing me ahead despite my tendency to procrastinate.

G. Ken Holman, for pointing out some finer points of XSLT and catching many ambiguities and outright errors.

Daniel Smith, for useful comments on writing style and presentation of the material.

Vadim Penzin, for useful discussions of database terminology.

Ilya Oussov, for help with Java extension functions.

Alina, for everything.

----

4. `xep.xattic.com`
5. `fly.srk.fer.hr/~hniksic/emacs/htmlize.el`

Origins of this book

Perhaps the best thing about this book is that it is based on, and in fact was born out of, the author's real-world projects. Since 1998, Dmitry Kirsanov Studio[6] has created web sites for customers around the world. In recent years all the web sites we do are based on XML and XSLT. This book is a snapshot of our current XML experience.

I am a technical writer, freelance XML/XSLT expert, and graphic designer. The book also draws on the magazine and online articles and books I've written. Among these are Dmitry's Design Lab,[7] a monthly column (1997–1999) devoted to exploring creative as well as technical issues pertaining to web design, and *Dmitry Kirsanov's Web Design Book*[8] (1999, in Russian), which has become one of the most influential Russian-language books on web design.

Feedback

I will be grateful for comments, corrections, criticism, or any other form of feedback on this book and its ideas and approaches. Please write me at dmitry@kirsanov.com.[9]

An online companion for this book is available.[10] It provides the book's errata, the complete source code of the examples, and other material.

---

6. www.kirsanov.com

7. www.webreference.com/dlab

8. www.kirsanov.com/web.design

9. I'm relieved that I can, for once, give my email address in plain text — fortunately, spam bots are unable to spider books (yet?) . . . the only downside is that it's not clickable.

10. authors.phptr.com/Kirsanov and www.kirsanov.com/xsltwd

XML and the Web

And what if all of animated nature
Be but organic Harps diversely fram'd,
That tremble into thought, as o'er them sweeps
Plastic and vast, one intellectual breeze,
At once the Soul of each, and God of all?

SAMUEL TAYLOR COLERIDGE, *The Æolian Harp*

I
XML and the Web

XML itself, once you get used to its syntax and terminology, is surprisingly simple. It sounds suspiciously like common sense: *When you see something you can name, do it*. The basic rules for writing these names can be taught to a six year old. How can such a simple thing precipitate such a powerful revolution?

Yet the revolution is raging, fueled in part by XML's simplicity and accessibility. Decades-old speculations about "programming languages of the future" totally missed the point: The modern computing landscape is shaped not by some radically new programming language but by a simple and flexible common data format, XML. Indeed, XML is revolutionary — not in what it offers but in what it lets you do without.

The simpler a thing is, the more dependent it is on interpretation. And interpretations are plenty. The simple XML root underlies an already huge and explosively growing tree of standards, technologies, tools, and lore. Each XML book must begin by charting its own course in this brave new world.

In this chapter, we touch on a wide range of subjects, all of which are important for understanding the techniques described in the rest of the book. It's not your typical XML intro; I cover only those concepts that bubble up every day in practical XML work, and therefore those I can say something useful (and, hopefully, nontrivial) about. Actually, this chapter was the *last* to be written, but it does make sense to read it first.

1.1 Content, presentation, structure

If you ask around, "What is the main problem that XML is supposed to solve?" of those who can answer this question most people will probably speak about "separating content from presentation." This is correct, but invites another interesting question: How come this is a problem at all? Was it a problem before XML? Or before computers?

Generally, our ability to discern concepts is directly related to our language's ability to tell them apart. Linguists know that primitive languages are often characterized by their inability to express abstract or generalized ideas; such a language may have a single word for a "high wind" while lacking more general words for "just wind" or "just high."

We can therefore be sure that the idea of style as something separate from content could not have appeared before the first written document was authored. And for a long time, such separation didn't offer anything useful for practical handling of documents, remaining a purely philosophical speculation. Thus, publishers have long used "tags" to mark up authors' manuscripts for typesetting, but these tags did not tell the typesetter what each fragment of text *is*, only *what font face* to use for it — which means that style and content were always commingled.

Computer as a language.   All this changed with the advent of computers. A computer can be compared to a well-developed human language; both are created by humans (even though the latter is much less "artificial" than the former), and both can represent and communicate any type of information by using special notations.

Not surprisingly, very early in the history of computerized document processing, the idea of separating presentation from content was conceived. As far back as 1969, the Generalized Markup Language (GML) was created at IBM out of the necessity to store and process different kinds of documents in order to integrate multiple applications in a mainframe-based publishing system. The language was later standardized by ISO as SGML (Standard Generalized Markup Language). Starting in 1996, a simplified and streamlined version of SGML called XML[1] has been developed by the W3C.

It thus became possible (and necessary!) to *imagine* the different aspects of a document apart only because computers made it possible to *say* them discernibly. A computer is a tool not only for expressing ideas, but also — and more importantly — for setting them to work. That's how computers, probably for the first time in history, made philosophy an applied science.

1.1.1 The stairway of abstractions

The word "abstraction" may sound vague, but it is an important and very practical concept. When you are developing and later applying an XML markup vocabulary, what you are doing is exactly this — *abstracting out* various aspects of the document and tagging them as you go. Let's look at this process in detail.

There are many different ways in which a document could be represented in the computer. It is natural to order all these representations in such a way that a next one can be obtained from the previous, but not vice versa, in a completely automatic and reliable fashion.[2]

---

1. www.w3.org/XML
2. In fact, any such conversion will still include certain manual components. An accurate definition of a "completely automatic conversion" would be, "A conversion where the amount of manual work does not depend on the size of the document being converted."

For example, a TEX document can be translated into PostScript automatically. This works for all correct TEX documents and, once you've tested the conversion on a few samples, can be run unattended. A reverse conversion, however, is not doable with standard tools. You can try to automate some components of this backward conversion, but it will always require manual checks and fixes, and will always be unreliable and not universal.

We will therefore say that a TEX document is at a higher *level of abstraction* than a PostScript document. Similarly, PostScript is higher than a bitmap representation of the same document (e.g., a JPEG image of the page),[3] while TEX is lower than LaTEX. If two representations can be automatically converted both ways, they are said to be at the same level of abstraction.

1.1.2 Document oppositions

All computerized document formats thus make a giant *stairway of abstractions* that stretches all the way from least to most abstract representations. Your work as a document engineer consists of building the most abstract representation appropriate for your documents and programming the most flexible, robust, and fast descents to the target low-abstraction representations. Going up the stairway is highly unnatural and must be avoided if at all possible.

To help you get a coherent picture of this stairway of abstractions, here are the most important oppositions that characterize documents at its different steps:

- **Convertibility.** By definition, the higher a document is on the abstractions stairway, the wider is the choice of other formats it can be converted into by moving downward. The formats at the bottom are thus dead ends only suitable for direct perusal; those at the top are best for authoring, storage, exchange, and analysis.

---

3. A bitmap is an abstraction too, even though a very low-level one. There are no pixels on paper, so we had to abstract them when representing a paper page in the computer.

- **Style separation.** The amount of "in-place" style information that is embedded into the document to control its presentation decreases as you ascend the stairway.

  - Low-level representations (e.g., bitmap images or PostScript) specify exactly each tiny detail of a page, and you cannot separate *what* is being said from *how* it is being said. Even exporting a document into the style-less plain text format is often not trivial.

  - Mid-level representations (e.g., HTML) simplify and generalize style information into instructions that need to be *interpreted* to yield a page image. Sometimes, style information is separated from the document itself (e.g., into a CSS style sheet), and in most cases, you can reliably export the document into plain text.

  - Finally, high-level abstractions do away with style altogether. Such documents are not for viewing at all, and even before you can attach any style to them, they usually must undergo some transformation and/or aggregation.

An example of a high-level document representation is *semantic XML* — the sort of XML markup that we will develop in this book for source documents of a web site. *Semantic* means "related to the meaning" or, in our terms, "content-only and style-less." Actually, being semantic is only one of the properties of a web site's XML source, but it is the most important one.

In practice, the line between style and content is not always easy to draw. The definition of the abstractions stairway, however, gives you a simple key: If you can derive some of the document's information automatically (based on the rest of the document or on external data such as a style sheet), then this information is style, not content. Numbers in numbered headings give an example of such a "seemingly content but actually style" bit of a document.

- **Richness of structure.** Documents steadily become more varied in structure as you ascend the stairway. Low-level representations use long rows of elements belonging to a handful of types, while high-level ones may have a huge variety of possible element types but only a few element instances per document. Thus, a bitmap image has only one "element type," pixel; PostScript has dozens of primitives; a high-level semantic XML vocabulary such as DocBook may have hundreds of element types.

- **Modularity.** Low-level representations tend to be monolithic — usually one big file includes all the text, images, styles, fonts, and everything else. High-level representations are more often modular, with components of a document residing in separate files and (explicitly or implicitly) linked from some "root" document that often contains only the textual part of the document content.

- As a direct consequence of the previous points, **size** of documents decreases as the level of abstraction increases. After all, the very idea of abstraction is reducing the real-world variety to a few generic principles — and of course, these principles don't need as much storage space as the real thing. Bitmap representations are the largest; PostScript files may be quite sizeable too; the top of the line, semantic XML, is usually the smallest representation of a document.

1.1.3 The role of XML

It is important to understand that by itself, XML is not an abstraction; it is just a *notation for structured data*. Since all computer data, including document representations, is structured, in principle XML can be successfully used on *any* step of the stairway. In other words, XML does not necessarily have to be semantic.

Indeed, it is possible to devise, for example, an XML-based bitmap format where each pixel is represented by an XML element. Another example of a nonsemantic XML vocabulary is XSL-FO (**5.5.3.2**). However, any such formats tend to be awkward and bulky,[4] which

----

4. This book's chapters in XSL-FO are slightly larger than in PDF, even though PDF is at a lower level of abstraction.

suggests that the true usefulness of XML is on the higher steps of the stairway.

Remember that XML is

- **human-readable:** this is more important for the higher steps of the stairway, as documents there are more often authored by humans;

- **arbitrarily rich:** you can easily create vocabularies of any breadth and depth, which, again, is more important for abstract document representations;

- **rather bulky:**[5] this may be a disadvantage for low-abstraction formats, as they are more often processed automatically and are therefore more efficiency-sensitive.

This book is not about XML or XSLT for their own sakes; it is about building highly abstracted semantic representations of web site documents and programming their transformation into a lower-level browser-viewable representation. We just use XML and XSLT as very convenient tools for these jobs.

1.1.4 The role of HTML

As for the target representation that we are interested in, it is not something we have much choice about. The only format that is reliably displayed by all modern browsers and is sufficiently rich for the interface of modern web sites is HTML.

What you can and cannot do with HTML. HTML is a mid-level document format. It can implement a very simple semantic markup (with external CSS style sheets) and is sufficiently compact to be sent over the network. It is also partially modular in that images and some other types of objects are stored separately and referenced from within HTML code.

....

5. One of the XML design goals states, "Terseness in XML markup is of minimal importance."

On the other hand, HTML is not suitable for richly structured documents, since its vocabulary of element types is limited and not extensible. Its modularity is also limited: It can only factor out non-HTML data, but there's no easy mechanism to break into parts and reassemble an HTML document itself (other than by using an external scripting layer).

Besides, the amount of control over presentation offered by the latest version of CSS alone is hardly sufficient for practical web site interfaces. As a result, the real-world HTML today — with its embedded scripts, cross-browser workarounds, layout tables, spacer images, and other presentation-related stuff — is quite messy and not at all semantic.

Even though originally, HTML was designed as an SGML-based semantic markup language, most web authors and browser creators viewed it as an equivalent of some annoyingly poor and old-fashioned word processor format. HTML was thus forced onto a wrong step of the abstractions stairway, which could not but result in gross misuse and all sorts of structural problems. The advance of CSS has stopped the trend of HTML degradation but has failed to reverse it.

This is why a high-level abstract representation, using a semantic XML vocabulary, is such a good idea — for web pages as well as for most other kinds of documents. Authoring and editing is done much more naturally and conveniently in semantic XML; when the source XML documents are ready, they are automatically translated by an XSLT stylesheet into the target format (such as HTML). Figure 1.1 schematically depicts this process, and the rest of the book describes it in detail.

Other target formats. No techniques described in this book cover browser-specific HTML. You know what I'm speaking about: one version for MSIE, another for Netscape . . . luckily, you can now leave this ugly stuff behind forever (unless you target some very old or very weird browsers). Instead, if you are willing to sacrifice universal accessibility for something else (presumably more important to you), you can write an XSLT stylesheet to generate almost any other document format in place of HTML: WML, PDF, SVG, even RTF or Flash. While generating binary formats requires using some

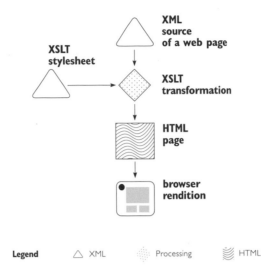

XSLT
stylesheet

XML
source
of a web page

XSLT
transformation

HTML
page

browser
rendition

Legend   △ XML   Processing   HTML

Figure 1.1   An XSLT transformation, controlled by a stylesheet, converts an XML source of a page into HTML which is then displayed by the browser.

additional software (**5.5.2**), at the XSLT side of things, nothing really changes as compared to generating HTML.

Visualizing XML.   Still another way to present a document to the user is by transforming it from the semantic source XML into another, more low-level XML vocabulary reflecting the visual structure of the web page. This low-level XML can then be viewed by an XML-capable browser using an external CSS style sheet (Figure 1.2). The advantage of this method is that the presentation-oriented XML may be more elegant and more useful than the equivalent HTML; the big disadvantage is, of course, the need for the software at the user end to support the XML+CSS combination (**1.4.3**). Another problem is the limited capabilities of CSS (**6.1.5**, page 312) that make this scheme suitable only for simple documents.

1.1.5   The Semantic Web

The level of abstraction attainable with web pages or any other Internet resources cannot be higher than that of the document format they use, which is most often HTML. This makes today's Web predominantly *visual*; you can easily (and even automatically) obtain

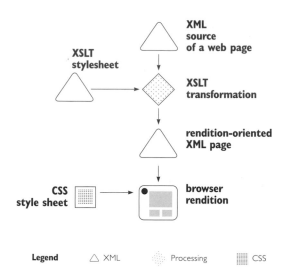

Figure 1.2   A variation of Figure 1.1: Instead of HTML, a combination of presentation-oriented XML and a CSS style sheet renders the page in a browser.

a visible image of any web page, but you cannot extract and codify what it *means to say* unless you, or someone you hire, reads and analyzes it.

In a *Semantic Web*,[6] by contrast, all resources have an easily accessible and consistently expressed semantic aspect. Today, you can read a web page and extract its meaning, but your computer cannot; in a Semantic Web, computers will be able to effectively "understand" resources and do various meaningful things with them (such as intelligent search, comparison, aggregation, compiling digests, etc.).

The vision of the Semantic Web was a driving force behind the initiative to simplify and promote the use of SGML on the Web, which in 1996 resulted in launching of the XML project by the W3C. Today, the Semantic Web is one of the *activities*[7] of the W3C centered around the language called RDF (Resource Description Framework).[8]

6. The term was coined by Tim Berners-Lee, the inventor of the World Wide Web.
7. www.w3.org/2001/sw
8. www.w3.org/RDF

The Extensible Meaning Language. XML is a metalanguage that allows you to describe the *structure* of documents but is agnostic about their *meaning*. This is understandable, since it is hard to imagine a formalism that would be able to express any possible kind of meaning in a form accessible to modern computers.[9] *Some* aspects of meaning, however, can be formalized — which is where RDF comes into play.

An RDF statement (*triple*) connects some resource (*subject*), one of its properties (*predicate*), and the value of that property (*object*). Each of these three components can be identified by a URI. A triple is thus equivalent to a natural language sentence (such as *Bob loves Mary*, where *Bob* is the subject, *loves* is the predicate, and *Mary* is the object) and can therefore express meanings — provided the "words" it uses have some meanings to begin with.

Just as XML is the base of a great many languages that use it to describe various data structures, there exist languages that use the RDF formalism to define various semantic areas (*ontologies*). For example, the FOAF (Friend Of A Friend) standard[10] defines terms, properties, and relationships that can be used to build an RDF description covering all aspects of a person (such as the person's name, nickname, email address, depiction, and even a DNA checksum).

1.2 Data and documents

There are two kinds of data that occur in XML documents: the transactional data that usually resides in databases ("database data") and the human-created kind that is commonly associated with documents ("publishing data"). The distinction can affect any aspect of an XML system, but especially the processing. Let's look at the characteristics of the two.

Database data is regular and has fixed depth. Databases allow rapid access and processing, which is accomplished by restricting the structure of the data. Typically, a database consists of relational tables, each table storing a sequence of records (composite values), each record containing a fixed set of fields (atomic values).

---

9. Without AI, that is.
10. `www.xmlns.com/foaf/0.1`

Fields can link to records in other tables to represent deeper levels of nesting. However, the full set of tables is fixed in the database schema and cannot be modified dynamically. Therefore a given database has a fixed depth.

Database-like XML documents are strongly predictable. In order for an XML document (or any single element of a document) to represent database data, its structure must map easily into the relational table model. We say it must be *strongly predictable*. That is, each element must be constrained to contain either a fixed sequence of element types (such as quantity, item-number, description, price, etc.), data characters only, or nothing at all.

Strongly predictable elements can easily be visualized as forms. A business transaction document, such as a purchase order, is more likely to be strongly predictable than a memo.

Publishing data is freeform. XML data in general may be far less predictable than database data. Even when constrained by a DTD or schema, sufficient variation may be allowed that the data can be considered *freeform*.

For example, an element type's content model may allow several different subelement types to occur multiple times in any order. Because the subelements can be of different types, the depth of the structure is unpredictable. The content model might even allow character data to be intermixed with the subelements (which the XML specification calls *mixed content*).

An example of mixed content is a paragraph where some of the words are marked up for emphasis, or as references, or as other types of inline elements. From the validation viewpoint, mixed content is special because you can only control *what* types of elements are used within another element, not how many or in what order. From the XSLT standpoint, mixed content is somewhat inconvenient to handle because an element with mixed content has *several* child text nodes, each fragment of textual data between inline elements being a separate node (see also **5.4.2.2**).

Looking ahead. One of the strengths of XML is that a document can contain both database data and publishing data, and that both document processing and data processing can be performed on it. Although a web site is primarily concerned with publishing data, there is also a need to deal with database data, particularly in dynamic sites. As we move through the book, we will see that some of the XML techniques work better for one kind of data than for the other.

1.3 Components of an XML web site

This section describes the major components of a working XML-based web site. You already know the role of the source documents and the XSLT transformation stylesheet (Figure 1.1); now let's look at how they fit together and what other data and software you'll need.

1.3.1 Source documents

In your own tongue. There is no single accepted standard of XML vocabulary for source documents of a web site. This is not surprising, given the extreme diversity of topics and structures of web sites.

In this book, therefore, we focus on creating your own custom source vocabulary suitable for your unique document types and web site requirements. Compared to reusing an existing vocabulary, this approach has many advantages — a much simpler structure, names that are more intuitive (at least *for you*), and complete freedom in developing the vocabulary further in any direction and at any time as needed. Chapter 2 lays the foundation, and Chapter 3 builds a robust and convenient source vocabulary on it.

Master and slaves. Source XML documents of a web site not only must abstract out the pure content of the pages; they also need to be structured differently than the target HTML pages. As we'll see in **2.1.2.1**, information that is common to more than one page must be removed into a different document that we will call the *master document* of the web site. In a simple web site, all other documents are *page documents* — leaves of the source tree that have one-to-one correspondence with the web pages.

1.3.2 Validation

Validation is what sets SGML and XML apart from most other data and document formats. Having a complete and self-contained specification of what constitutes a valid document — and being able to automatically check documents against this specification before they go into processing — is becoming critical as information systems grow more complex and more distributed.

The choice of a schema language to use for validation is important, but may be difficult. SGML first standardized DTDs (document type definitions) for validation, but today the choice of schema languages implementing different approaches is much wider. A part of Chapter 2 analyzes the major approaches to validation and the features of existing schema languages.

Schematron rules. In that analysis, rule-based schema languages come out at the top as most convenient for a flexible validation layer that grows as you develop your markup vocabulary and adapts to the requirements of web site maintainers. Of rule-based schema languages, Schematron is the most developed; it also has the big advantage of sharing its XPath component with XSLT. Basics of Schematron are given in Chapter 2, a simple schema for our web site documents is at the end of Chapter 3, and some more advanced Schematron techniques are covered in Chapter 5.

1.3.3 Transformation stylesheet

The XSLT transformation stylesheet is the kernel of an XML web site, and mastering XSLT and XPath is therefore the key to the efficient use of XML. Chapter 4 gives an overview, focusing on the new features of XSLT 2.0 and XPath 2.0 as well as the existing XSLT extensions.

The stylesheet we'll be writing throughout Chapter 5 actually does much more than just translate XML into HTML. Here's a list of the stylesheet components that are discussed (some of them must be present in any stylesheet, while others are optional):

- **Variables, parameters, and functions** are defined once and used many times throughout the stylesheet. In the sample setup described in the book, this code is separated into a shared XSLT library (**5.1.1**) that is imported by both the stylesheet and the Schematron schema allowing the latter to use some of the values and algorithms of the stylesheet for a more meaningful validation.

- **Trunk templates** and **branch templates** (**4.5.1**) are the two kinds of templates controlling the XML-to-HTML transformation; this is where the snippets of HTML code are stored and output in response to the source XML constructs. Trunk templates create the top-level constructs of a page, such as menu and layout; branch templates are responsible for processing textual data, links, and other elements at the lower levels of the source tree.

- **Extension Java classes** optionally allow you to program any functions absent in XSLT and then call them from your stylesheet. We will use this facility for all sorts of useful tasks, such as accessing directories (**5.3.2.1**), querying graphic files (**5.5.1**), running external applications (**5.5.2.7**), and processing text (**5.4.2.2**). The Java classes given in the book will work with most Java-based XSLT processors (they were tested with Saxon), but you can use a similar approach for extending other processors as well.

- **Batch processing** (**5.6**) is another optional component that enables the stylesheet to process not one but all of the site's source XML documents in one go. The good thing about this is that you don't have to prepare a separate list of the files to process — the stylesheet itself will retrieve this list from the site's master document. Thus, a single list of pages in the master can be used for different tasks, such as creating menus, resolving internal links, and batch processing. Programming batch processing in XSLT is only one of the ways to automate site updates; other approaches are possible (**6.5**) that are external with regard to the stylesheet.

1.3.4 Static objects

Another component of a web site, *static objects*, includes everything that goes from the web designer directly to the server without being involved in XSLT processing in any way. Most static objects are images — logos, decorations, backgrounds, and so on — as well as other non-HTML objects such as Flash animations and Java applets.

However, the line between the static and nonstatic objects is not the same as between non-HTML and HTML. Some of the HTML pages whose content *and* design will never change (e.g., a 404 error page) can be static. On the other hand, graphic files (**5.5.2**) and other binary objects (**5.5.3**) can and should be generated by the stylesheet if their content is linked to that of the web pages or is otherwise changeable.

1.3.5 Integration

After the XML/XSLT core of the web site is ready, you must integrate it with other software. If you visualize the sequence of transformations that stretches all the way from the author to the user, then the XML-to-HTML transformation stage, occupying the very end of that sequence, is the most interesting for us. There are, however, other tools that come onto the scene before (or sometimes during) that stage.

Thus, to put your information into XML, you need to use at least a text editor, or a specialized XML editor, or a converter from some other document format. Writing the stylesheet may be assisted by various kinds of XSLT and XPath software. Finally, separate classes of software may be used to control building the site offline and integrating it with a server-side dynamic engine. These tools are the subject of the two last chapters of the book.

1.4 Setting up an XML web site

The two main components of an XML web site, as we've just seen, are the source XML documents and the XSLT transformation stylesheet. Viewed from another angle, on their way from the author to the user, web pages have to go through three distinct environments:

- the *authoring environment* is where web site authoring and maintenance takes place;

- the *web server* is sitting on the Internet, answering requests from clients (typically web browsers); and

- the *user environment* is where a web browser displays the page.

Correspondingly, there are three possible ways to set up an XML-based web site, differing in which of the three above environments hosts the XSLT stylesheet and performs the XML-to-HTML transformation. We will now discuss these three setups in turn.

1.4.1 XML offline

The first setup (Figure 1.3) restricts XSLT processing to the authoring environment. In this scenario, neither source documents nor the stylesheet are ever put on the server; the entire cycle of creating, editing, and transforming XML is performed by site authors and maintainers offline on their own systems. Only the end result of this — HTML pages and graphics — are uploaded to the web server.

The advantages of this approach are obvious:

- **Works with existing servers and clients.** Neither server nor browser software need to be changed in any way. The server will serve HTML and graphics as it always did, and users may never suspect that the web pages they are viewing were produced from XML. Thus, you can use your current hosting providers and target the current browser generation — and still use XML, without placing the burden of supporting it on anyone but yourself.

- **Server performance is optimal.** A direct consequence of the previous point is that in this setup, there is no negative impact on server performance. Serving static files, without processing of any kind, is the easiest and fastest thing to do for any server; if this setup involves dynamic processing on the server (**1.5.2.2**), it is the same as would be without XML.

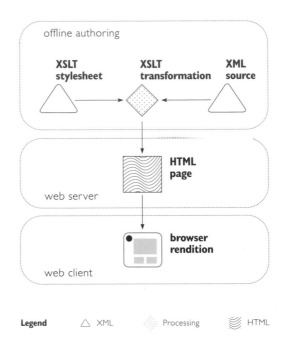

Figure 1.3 XML offline: XSLT transformation is done in the authoring environment, while the web server and web client both deal with HTML pages.

- **Use any software for XML processing.** Since you run your own transformation engine, you have complete control over its features. You are not limited by the XSLT processor, extensions, or auxiliary tools installed on a third-party system; you can install and/or program whatever you please. It's only in this setup that certain advanced (and sometimes time-consuming) tricks are possible — such as generating images (**5.5.2**), which is too slow for the two other setups. You can still benefit from some degree of portability, of course, since you may want to run the same XSLT transformation on different computers and different platforms within your organization.

Now let's turn these advantages upside down to see what problems they correspond to:

- **Not for dynamic sites.** The offline setup works only for static sites. More precisely (**1.5.2.2**), you *can* combine offline XSLT transformation with a dynamic engine on a web server (such as an online store or a forum), but this combination is rather awkward and can only be used as a last resort. Therefore, if your site will contain significant dynamic components, you should instead consider one of the other two XML setups discussed below.

- **Offline updates may be slow.** As with traditional static sites, content updates with an offline XML site are not particularly fast. Editing the source XML document, running offline transformation, and uploading the result to the server may take some time.

- **Limited use of XML.** Since there's no XML on the web server nor in the user's browser, only the site author can take advantage of it. Therefore, the server cannot index its content in XML, search or process it, or convert it into a format different from HTML.

Summarizing, the offline setup is the best way to start experimenting with XML-based web site architecture and may be perfectly adequate for any static or mostly static web site, such as a small corporate site. Once you get an offline XML web site up and running, you can always migrate it to one of the more advanced setups.

1.4.2 XML on the server

In the second setup (Figure 1.4), the web server stores the source XML documents for all web pages and transforms them into HTML on the fly. This means the web site author only has to deal with XML documents, while web clients get the pages in HTML as usual; the conversion from the former to the latter is done in the middle of the road.

Once again, let's see first what is good about this approach:

- **Dynamic sites are OK.** Unlike the offline setup, this one is well suited for dynamic web sites. This is because normally, XSLT transformation must come *after* dynamic processing and data retrieval (**1.5.2.1**). Since the dynamic engine is always on the

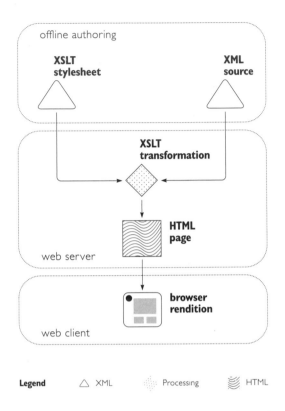

Figure 1.4   XML on the server: XSLT transformation is done on the web server; a client receives an HTML page.

server, the XSLT processor must also reside on the server in order to process the XML data produced by the dynamic engine. Using XML with a database-driven dynamic web site makes it possible to cleanly separate the site's content, style, and programming logic (**7.2.1**, page 363).

• **No special clients required.** Typical web servers do not support XML out of the box, so you'll have to spend some time installing and configuring XML software on your web server (Chapter 7). However, web *clients* (browsers) do not require an upgrade, as what they receive from the server is the same good ol' HTML.

This makes this setup only a bit less practical in today's circumstances than "XML offline."

- **Set up your server as necessary.** If you control your web server, you can install any auxiliary software or extensions on it if it is necessary for XSLT processing — just as you would install it offline in your authoring environment. The only limitations of this setup are security and performance: Whatever you run on the server to process a page must be secure against attacks and must work fast, or the user experience will suffer.[11]

- **More benefit from XML.** Even though normally, an XML-enabled web server sends out web pages in HTML, the fact that it stores them internally in XML makes it possible to use the XML source for other purposes, such as indexing. XML-capable web browsers can also request XML versions of pages to transform them for presentation locally using their own stylesheets.

Naturally, there are some downsides to the "XML on the server" setup as well:

- **Server performance may suffer.** The most critical issue is of course the server performance. Running the XSLT processor for each requested page may have a significant impact on the server's response time. Caching transformed pages may reduce this effect but not eliminate it, because a dynamic page whose content is generated on the fly still has to be transformed every time it is served.

- **Server setup may be complicated.** You'll have to install quite a bunch of additional software on your web server to make it XML-capable. Apart from the performance considerations, this also has possible security implications: The more software is involved in processing a request, the bigger are the chances of vulnerabilities.

....

11. The security and performance requirements are related: A server that spends too much resources serving each page is more vulnerable to a denial-of-service attack.

- **Separate testing of pages is necessary.** Before you upload a modified XML document onto the server, you need to make sure it is not broken. On a live site, posting a page that does not transform or results in a malformed HTML is unacceptable. Pre-upload validation with a schema may catch most errors (especially with a rule-based schema language, **2.2.1.2**), but only running the actual transformation and examining the resulting HTML pages may give you a guarantee. There are two possible approaches to handling this problem:

    - You can run a test transformation in your authoring environment before uploading modified documents to the server. This amounts to combining the "XML offline" and "XML on the server" setups and thus undoes one of the advantages of the latter, namely the relative simplicity of the authoring environment.

    - You can set up a separate protected staging area on your web server. Powered by the same XSLT environment as the public site, it will allow you to check your pages in an area that only you can see. Once you verify that everything is all right, you can re-upload the same document to the public web site.

Overall, this setup seems to be the most viable in the mid-term and the logical next step after you outgrow "XML offline." It is easy both on web authors (no XSLT software to install and learn) and, more importantly, on users (no special XML-capable browsers to access the site). The performance issue will likely become less pressing over time as faster XSLT processors and more powerful server hardware appear.

1.4.3 XML in the browser

The last setup (Figure 1.5) moves XSLT processing further down the road: Now it is the software on the user's system that, upon receiving both the XML source of a page and its XSLT stylesheet, must do the transformation and display the result. After our discussion of the two other setups, the advantages of this method should be clear:

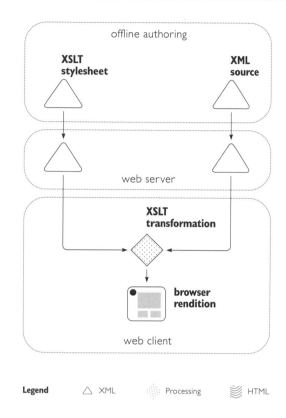

Figure 1.5   XML in the browser: XSLT transformation is done in a web client.

- **Power to the users.** The most important benefit of this setup is users' complete control over XML processing. Given full access to the XML source of a page, you can instruct your browser to use either the stylesheet supplied by the site or any other stylesheet. Moreover, you are no longer limited to HTML; you can, for example, render web pages into PDF via XSL-FO (5.5.3.2).

  Due to the lack of a standardized vocabulary for the markup of web pages,[12] this freedom may not be immediately useful for most

---

12. It is hardly conceivable that any *one* vocabulary will ever be able to cover the entire breadth of information on the Net.

people. Still, it is conceivable that the evolution of the Web toward "XML in the browser" will one day free us from the dependence on HTML.

- **XML is accessible from the server.** Just as in the previous setup, the XML source of the pages can not only be sent to the clients but indexed, searched, and linked to on the server. As more and more web sites adopt this setup, parts of the Web will crystallize into XML-only semantic clusters.

At the moment, however, the disadvantages of this approach outweigh its advantages:

- **XML support in the client is required.** The largest obstacle to implementing this scheme is the need for XML and XSLT support in the browser. Latest versions of Mozilla and MSIE do offer XSLT support, but you definitely cannot rely on it being available to all visitors to your web site. The only workaround is creating a "best viewed with" type of web site that only offers an XML version of its pages to XML-capable browsers but serves regular HTML to all others, which makes the whole idea impractical.

- **Server-side transformation is still necessary.** Another reason that this approach is less than practical is the difference between the original XML vocabulary used for source markup and the vocabulary that is optimal for rendering in the browser. If nothing else, client-side transformation requires a single source document, while the server may store the information pertaining to one page in more than one source document. This means that an XSLT transformation or some other XML processing engine must still be run on the server for each page sent to the client.

- **XSLT extensibility is limited.** Client-side XSLT processing has serious limitations. For security reasons, no XSLT stylesheet can be allowed to read or write any files on the client system — it can only work as a simple XML-to-HTML converter with one input and one output. Also, it can only use standard XSLT without any extensions. These limitations make many of the advanced techniques of Chapter 5 impossible with this setup.

- **Viewing performance may suffer.** Just as sever-side XSLT processing slows down the server, the user's XML web browser will have to spend extra time transforming each page it views. This problem may become serious for large web pages viewed on less capable systems.

The bottom line is that the "XML in the browser" setup, although compelling as the logical next step after the two other scenarios we discussed, is not quite practical at this time. It may become viable in the future as older browsers with limited or no XSLT support are phased out. However, for this setup to really take off, it also requires that a common XML vocabulary for web pages is standardized and an array of client-side tools emerges, enabling people to do something useful with XML web pages in this vocabulary (other than just viewing them).

And what about us? This book covers the first two setups, "XML offline" and "XML on the server," as the most practical for today's web sites. Of them, offline XSLT processing is our focus during most of Chapter 5, since it's the easiest to set up and experiment with. It will also allow us to explore some techniques that are difficult or impossible to implement on the server. In Chapter 7, we'll see how our offline setup can be adapted to run on an XML-capable web server.

1.5 XML and dynamic sites

A *dynamic* web page differs from a *static* one in that some of the information it displays is not stored in files (be it XML documents or files in any other format), but is retrieved from a database and/or calculated on the fly. A dynamic page may also collect data from the user and store it into a database. Database interaction and calculations are done on the web server in response to a page request coming from a client (e.g., a web browser). These days, the majority of web sites contain at least a few dynamic pages.

This section's material will not be needed for most of the book where we deal with the basics of a static XML-based web site; we will return to the dynamic issues only in Chapter 7. So, you can now skip forward to Chapter 2 unless you are specifically interested in combining the XML/XSLT techniques with a dynamic web site engine.

1.5.1   The two sources

Two sources of information are combined by a dynamic web site engine to produce the final browser-viewable web pages. The first source is the dynamic content, usually stored in a database. It tends to be well granularized, that is, broken into final unbreakable atoms — *dynamic values* such as a heading, date, or story text. These dynamic values may change upon each serving of a page to the user.

The second source is static (although it, too, can be stored in a database). It supplies the *templates* into which the dynamic values are inserted. These change only if the site's designer decides to change them, but remain the same throughout the normal update cycle of the site.

1.5.1.1   Dynamic values

Dynamic values, stored in a database or calculated on the fly, can be *atomic* (a single data object, e.g., a string or number) or *composite* (a mix of various objects, e.g., the text of a story that may contain paragraphs, emphasis, links, and other elements).

Self-typing atoms. Atomic values rarely exist outside a database or a program that generated them, so they usually don't require XML for tagging. In other words, there's no need to associate a name and a data type with each atomic value, as these properties are intrinsic for them.

Mixed-content composites.   Composite values with their mixed content (1.2) are another matter. They are typically marked up using HTML or some other regular markup convention, such as Wiki,[13] to be translated to HTML by the dynamic engine. This is not really a

---

13. www.c2.com/cgi/wiki?TextFormattingRules

good idea; a piece of text with some HTML markup is *not* a complete HTML document and as such cannot be validated, which may lead to markup errors in the final served pages that are hard to track. Also, HTML markup makes these composites unsuitable for any other use except generating HTML pages.

A much better solution is defining an XML document type for each distinct type of a composite dynamic value. By using XML markup, you can make your composite values complete, self-describing, and validated.

1.5.1.2   Static templates

In the simplest case, a template is an HTML file with some of its content replaced by scripts that produce actual content (from a database or from calculations) when the page is about to be served (Figure 1.6). Such templates are usually quite messy (as are any big chunks of HTML) and hard to maintain — it is really a mixup of what would better be kept apart!

Many sites rectify the situation a little by removing the code bits from the templates. In this approach, instead of being envelopes for actual code, templates are stored and used as data. The dynamic engine retrieves the templates and the corresponding dynamic values at the same time and merges them, using certain markers within the templates as clues for where to insert the dynamic data.

Other sites go even further by assembling templates on the fly from separate fragments, such as a menu template, a sidebar template, a footer template, etc. (Figure 1.7). The problem with this approach is the same: Template fragments are non-validatable, messy HTML that is very fragile — it is difficult to edit each fragment so that it still fits into its place and the final assemblage is working as designed.

1.5.1.3   Do you need XML?

Some developers tend to think that since a dynamic site separates a static template (i.e., formatting) from what will be inserted into that template (i.e., content), it can deliver the same benefits as an

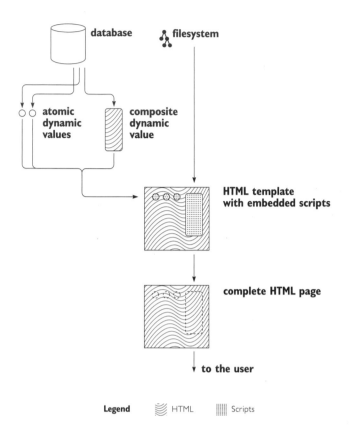

Figure 1.6   A simple dynamic web page: Note that while some of the atomic dynamic values are drawn from the database, others may be calculated by the page's embedded script.

XML-based web site architecture. To some extent, this is true. However, XML offers much more than the simple "template/content" model, and you can get extra benefits by combining a dynamic engine and an XML/XSLT engine in one site.

The problem with most dynamic sites is that the boundary between their static and dynamic components is drawn where it is convenient for the programmer, not necessarily where it is best from the semantic viewpoint. You can think of it this way: A programmer of a dynamic web site takes static, HTML-only pages drafted by the web designer,

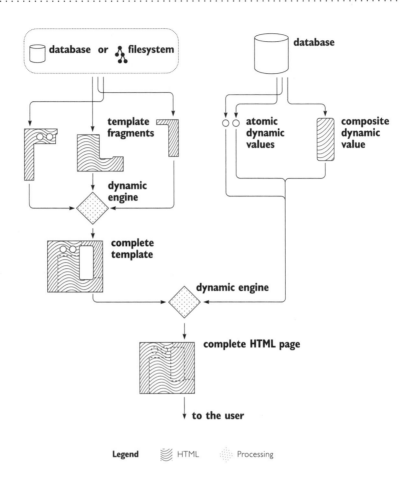

Figure 1.7   A more complex dynamic web page: The program code is removed from the template, and the template is constructed from separate fragments.

tracks down whatever HTML snippets will be changing on those pages, replaces these snippets with some PHP or ASP code pulling data from a database, debugs the whole thing — and voilà, a brand new dynamic web site is up and running.

This has little to do with proper semantic analysis (**2.3**) as performed for XML. I'm not saying that programmers of dynamic web sites fail in their job; it's just that the job of an XML web developer is very different — but not less necessary.

It is important to understand that XML is not just another technology for implementing dynamic sites. Moreover, it turns out that XML is largely orthogonal to the template/content distinction in that it can be meaningfully applied to both static templates and dynamic values.

1.5.2 The two scenarios

Logically, the first step toward a dynamic web site with XML is separating the information on where to insert each value from the information on how to format the whole thing. Templates or template fragments must be stripped of any formatting details and converted into a lean, semantic XML vocabulary whose only goal is to define what pieces of content are present on the page and what structural role is assigned to each piece.

Starting from here, two different scenarios of combining the XML/XSLT engine and the dynamic engine are possible. We will now discuss these scenarios in turn.

1.5.2.1 Compile, then transform

This scenario, illustrated by Figure 1.8, attempts to do as much as possible in XML and only transforms the final result into HTML at the very last stage of the process. This is the most natural approach, although not always optimal.

At first, XML template fragments (stored either in a database or in static files) are assembled into a complete static template that includes both page-specific static content and site-wide metadata. Since the template is not going to change often, you can perform this aggregation step offline and upload the finished template on the server.

Next, dynamic values are inserted into the template. Of course, composite dynamic values are also marked up with a semantic XML vocabulary; for example, they can use the schema of the template fragments or a subset thereof. This second step is normally performed on the server. Finally, the fully assembled XML document is transformed into HTML.

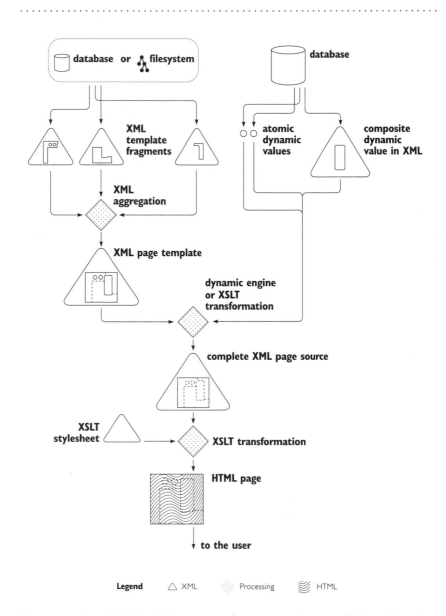

Figure 1.8   Incorporating XML/XSLT into a dynamic web site: "Compile, then transform."

Note that each of the triangular XML documents shown in Figure 1.8, as well as the final complete XML page source, may have its own schema and go through its own validation stage. Usually, however, it is more convenient to have a single schema that allows certain variation and thus accommodates all kinds of objects participating in the process. Similarly, the three distinct diamond-shaped processing blocks may be separate, but they can just as well be combined into one XSLT stylesheet that compiles the template, inserts dynamic values (possibly using extensions to access or calculate them), and finally produces the HTML page.

Before this is possible. There are a couple of obvious prerequisites for this scenario. First, since the entire process of database retrieval, processing, and assembling data is performed in XML, the dynamic engine itself must be XML-aware. You'll have to teach it how to store, search, and extract XML documents instead of plain text or HTML fragments it may have dealt with before. Therefore, native XML databases exist that make storing and reusing XML objects transparent.

Second, the dynamic engine is normally located on the web server so it can retrieve and serve data on the fly. And since the XML-to-HTML transformation comes after the dynamic engine, it must also be installed on the server and perform transformation in real time, in response to each request. As a result, this scenario can only work with the "XML on the server" setup (**1.4.2**, Chapter 7).

"Compile, then transform" scorecard. The benefits of this approach are:

- The formatting layer is abstracted out from many different templates into one stylesheet. Thus, you can make automatic changes to the presentation of not only all pages produced from one template, but all pages produced from different templates. This may even include static pages (those that do not use any dynamic values), as it is only natural to store them using the same XML vocabulary and transform them using the same stylesheet as dynamic pages.

- A direct result of the above is better modularization of the site's infrastructure. Your site's content staff, design staff, and programming staff can all work independently without much risk of obstructing each other's efforts.

• The site's dynamic engine can be made more generic in its design and therefore usable in almost any dynamic web site application so long as the data is in XML. Recently, a number of such generic XML-based web site engines emerged implementing the "compile, then transform" scenario (notably Cocoon, **7.2**). On the other hand, many if not all functions of a dynamic engine such as that in Figure 1.8 can be performed by XSLT stylesheets.

• Besides being a natural fit for "XML on the server," this scenario is as close as you can get to "XML in the browser" (**1.4.3**). Indeed, if it ever becomes practical to serve XML+XSLT from your web site instead of HTML, all you have to do is remove the last transformation stage — everything else remains untouched. Your investment into the XML infrastructure is thus truly long term, as it may outlast the current HTML-centric Web.

Sometimes, however, the requirement that everything is installed on the server may make the uncompromising "compile, then transform" scenario impractical. As we'll see in Chapter 7, installing new software on a web server may be a complex task, or the server may be completely out of your control (e.g., if you use outsourced hosting). Therefore, you might need to look for other, less drastic scenarios that will combine traditional dynamic engines, such as PHP or Perl scripting available from most hosting providers, with offline (**1.4.1**) XML processing.

Compile and transform offline.   Not all dynamic data needs to be produced the moment the page is requested. Quite often, a reasonably delayed update (e.g., once a day) is acceptable. This means that you can take the entire setup depicted in Figure 1.8 and implement it locally, without worrying about web server setup or performance.

Then, all you have to do is set up your system to run the aggregation and transformation periodically and upload the resulting HTML pages to the sever — and you're done. You can also implement a "watch" script that runs the transformation in response to a change in your dynamic data, or simply run the transformation manually. The best way to do that will of course depend on the nature of your data and your web site.

This "offline but dynamic" setup may be a good first step toward implementing the completely dynamic server-side setup of Figure 1.8. It will let you test your source definition and the stylesheet before you start setting up an XML-enabled web server.

1.5.2.2   Transform, then compile

The second scenario, illustrated by Figure 1.9, is a straightforward combination of a simple dynamic site (such as that in Figure 1.6) with offline XSLT transformation producing HTML templates with embedded code. You program your stylesheet to generate an HTML page complete with embedded scripts, upload the resulting template on the server, and let its scripts work exactly as they would in any other HTML page — retrieving dynamic data and inserting it into the page as it is served.

Obviously, to get any advantages from XML's content/formatting separation, we must restrict the dynamic data to atomic (i.e., structureless) values only. This way, all formatting is stored in the stylesheet, and the main difference from the previous scenario is that instead of inserting dynamic values into XML, we insert opaque objects (scripts) into HTML.

This approach works best for mostly static sites that only need a few simple dynamic bits here and there. For example, it is perfectly adequate for a registration form or a feedback collection page that only writes user data into a database but never extracts it back for display.

However, this scenario may work for complex sites too, if you take time to carefully disassemble your dynamic values into atoms (no mixed content allowed) and write robust scriptlets to access these atoms. In return, you will enjoy the first two benefits of the previous scenario (all formatting code is in one place; content, design, and programming jobs are largely independent).

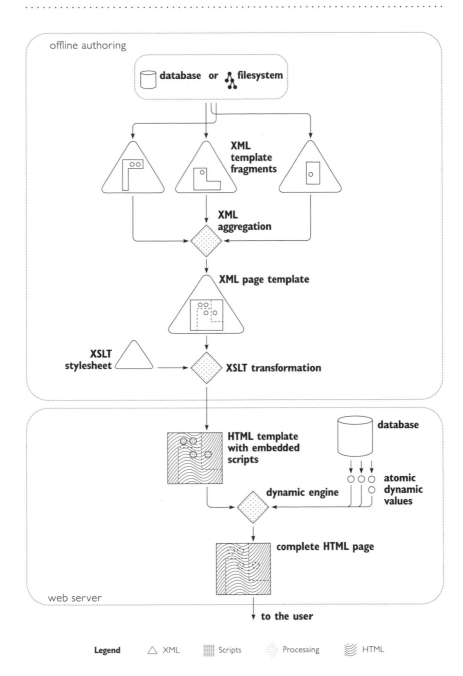

Figure 1.9   Another way to combine XML/XSLT with a dynamic engine: "Transform, then compile." Composite dynamic values are best avoided in this scenario.

2

The source definition

You break ashore and back
        you go silently.
For sea is what you flee
and what you are is sea.

ELIZABETH MOORE, *The Wave*

2

The source definition

This chapter will get you started with developing a custom markup system for your XML-based web site. You'll learn what is involved in defining your own XML language that best suits your site's requirements and what options exist for automatic validation of your source documents.

This chapter should give you a good idea of the capabilities and limitations of modern schema languages as well as the possible approaches to building your complete source definition (which, to be useful, will have to include more than just a schema).

If you are primarily interested in the practical markup of a web site's XML source, you need only read **2.1**, which explains the general architecture of a site's source definition. After that, you can skip to Chapter 3, "Elements of a web site," where we'll look at the typical elements of web pages and discuss their representation in XML.

2.1 The big picture

Defining the definition.   What this chapter's title, "The source definition," refers to is a detailed specification listing all the element types and attributes you will use in your XML, the rules of structuring these units within source documents, and various constraints on their values. All parts of this specification must be in place before you can translate your content into XML.

Some of the source definition rules may be stored in a special document called a *schema definition*, or simply a *schema*. Schemas enable automatic validation; that is, you can feed your documents and a corresponding schema to a validator program and get a list of all errors found. A common type of schema is a document type definition (DTD). However, a complete source definition is likely to include more than just a schema.

Vocabulary alert.   Another common term, *vocabulary*, refers to a set of element types and attributes used in an XML document. Therefore, its chief difference from a *schema* is that a vocabulary does not imply a formalized description in any schema language. On the other hand, depending on the schema language, a schema may be anything from a vocabulary with simple rules for its use (a DTD) to an almost complete source definition (a Schematron schema).

The ways of being correct.   The point of creating a source definition is to ensure that conformant documents are transformed successfully by the stylesheet and yield web pages that are *correct*, in a broad sense. Here are just a few of the requirements that a set of correct web pages must satisfy:[1]

- all visible and invisible components of each page must be in their proper places;

- there must be no missing or wrong page components;

- there must be no missing pages or orphaned links;

---

1. What no source definition can guarantee is the meaningfulness and relevance of your web site *content* — this is why *you* are here, after all.

- all pages must be correctly linked up by the site's navigation system; and so on.

You can add your own requirements or limitations of almost any kind that the site's pages (or parts thereof) must meet. In most cases, the site's source definition is the best place to formally express — and thus enforce — these requirements.

After design but before implementation. A conformant source must, of course, match the site's transformation stylesheet (**1.3.3**). However, usually you create your source definition first and write a corresponding stylesheet later. What you *do* need to have before starting to work on a source definition is a detailed plan of what the final pages will look like and what they will contain. This means that your project must be well past the stages of *content design* (deciding what to put up on your web site and how to distribute the material across pages) and *visual design* (deciding how to present the material graphically).

In the real world, all of these stages tend to overlap. You may find it necessary to make design and content adjustments while working on source definition, then modify the source definition while writing and debugging the stylesheet, and finally polish all of these components both before and after the launch of the site.

2.1.1 Two-tier architecture

As we've just seen, a source definition is more than simply an inventory of the element types and attributes that you can use in your XML documents. It makes sense to subdivide the source definition into two layers: the *document layer* and the *super-document layer*.

Document layer. The document layer is where you declare what can be used within individual source documents. This includes declarations of element types and attributes, as well as the rules for what data types are allowed for them and how these structural units must be laid out in the source. The document layer of the source definition is further subdivided into *document types* (for example, one for the site's front page and another for the subpages). Each document type may have its own hierarchy of element types and enforce its own structure rules.

Often, each document type is described by a separate schema that can be written in the DTD notation or in any other schema language (**2.2.1**). The most valuable aspect of a schema is that it allows you to automatically *validate* your documents using corresponding validator software. For example, with a DTD, a validating XML parser such as Xerces[2] can validate a document during parsing, so any errors will be reported as soon as you attempt an XSLT transformation (as it requires that your source document be parsed first).

Super-document layer.   A complete source definition will likely include a number of rules that cannot be placed into any single document type. These rules involve relations among *different* XML documents or their parts, so I will call them collectively the super-document layer of the source definition. This layer's rules might control

- **information distribution:** what data to store in what source documents;

- **file conventions:** how to name the source documents (this often defines the URIs of the resulting HTML pages after the transformation) and in what directories to put them;

- **file-to-file correspondences:** rules of the type "if you add a page document, you must provide an image file for that page's heading photo";

- **file-to-element correspondences:** rules of the type "if you add a page document, you must add a corresponding page element to the site's master document (**2.1.2.1**)."

Depending on your site's requirements, you may not need all of the above rule types, but you may just as well need others. Not all super-document rules are equally important. Some of them are just recommendations or accepted conventions whose breach will cause no easily

----

2. `xml.apache.org/xerces2-j`

identifiable consequences. Breaking other rules, however, may result in more obvious and unpleasant problems, such as a missing menu item, a wrong image, or a broken link.

Implementing the super-document rules

Unfortunately, the DTD notation, as well as most other schema languages, is unable to express the super-document rules of a source definition. DTDs or XSDL schemas can only control (to various degrees) the XML markup within a document, not connections or dependencies between different documents.

On the other hand, a system of rules is only useful when there are ways to *enforce* these rules — preferably automatically. What are our options for implementing the super-document layer of a source definition?

- **Human-readable instructions.** These may take the form of standalone documentation or comments embedded either in the schema or in the source templates (2.2.3). For example, if you want to ensure that a photo is provided for each section page's heading, you can write down a human-readable rule to this effect in whatever place is the most convenient for the site's editors (in the schema, in the section page template, or on a separate reference sheet printed out and glued to the wall).

  This approach works best with qualified permanent maintenance staff and cannot guarantee automatic conformance. Still, documenting your source definition in some form is necessary in any case, and for simple sites or small teams, it may also suffice for all of your super-document definition needs.

- **Back-end scripting.** You can program the super-document rules into your back-end — the part of the system responsible for interacting with the site's editor. With this approach, checks are made right when a source document is changed and before the stylesheet is run.

  Your back-end may be anything from a simple text editor in which you touch up your XML sources, to a specialized XML editor (6.1), to a complete local or distributed content management system (CMS). Obviously, the scripting capabilities of your back-end and its ability to rise from the currently edited document to the super-document context may vary widely. Some rules may be simple to enforce, while others may require writing external programs to be called from within the back-end. Form-based XML editors (**6.1.3**) make especially good back-end scripting hosts; in them, checks may be activated not only when the entire document is completed but when a particular field is filled in.

While using a "smart" back-end may be convenient, this approach has several disadvantages. First, not all web sites need a complex, scriptable back-end. Many projects will run just fine from a set of static XML sources manually editable with a text or XML editor with limited, if any, scripting capabilities. Second, this solution forces all site maintainers to use the same back-end, which may be suboptimal. Finally, source validation implemented in one back-end may not be easily portable to another.

- **Build layer checks.** You can also program your super-document checks into the build framework that controls stylesheet execution. For example, the `make` utility is often used to perform for programming projects what is a close analog of super-document checks (verifying file existence, checking file dates, etc.) — and, as we'll see (**6.5.1**), `make` can be successfully used for building an XML-based web site.

  Obviously, this approach and the back-end scripting described above share disadvantages. Not all projects and not all developers within a project need to use a separate build layer, and checks created for one build system (e.g., `make`) are not easily portable to another (e.g., Apache Ant).

- **Stylesheet checks.** Your site's XSLT transformation stylesheet can use the `document()` function to access any available XML documents (even those stored remotely). Any data from these external documents can be used in arbitrary calculations or comparisons. Also, extension functions (**5.3.2**) can be called from

XSLT to perform other types of checks, such as verifying the presence of files and directories, determining image sizes and formats, etc. Any errors found by the stylesheet are reported during transformation.

This is perhaps the most natural approach to implementing super-document checks. Once set up, validation is automatic in that the checks are guaranteed to be made before you upload your web-ready files onto the server. Error reports can be arbitrarily long and detailed, and can in effect serve as a sort of on-demand documentation for specific rules. Also, this option does not require that you write a separate subsystem for the sole purpose of source validation; you can (and are encouraged to) add checking and reporting as you implement the corresponding stylesheet logic.

The big problem with this method is that it mixes up what should really be kept apart — source semantics and presentation algorithms. For example, imagine you want to render the same source documents in a different format (e.g., PDF or WML). Instead of writing a completely independent new stylesheet for this, you'll end up borrowing the super-document checks from your original stylesheet — because these checks are actually part of the complete source definition that you are reusing, not part of the presentation algorithms that you are rewriting for the new format. Such duplication of code across stylesheets is prone to errors and difficult to maintain.

- **Schematron schemas.** Schematron[3] is one schema language that stands apart from others in that it uses XPath expressions for defining arbitrary constraints on the structure and data of an XML document. As a result, Schematron allows you to implement all the same checks that are possible with an XSLT stylesheet: arbitrary calculations with XML data, both within one source document and across documents, and practically unlimited checks of non-XML data using extension functions.

---

3. www.ascc.net/xml/resource/schematron/schematron.html

In other words, Schematron provides all the benefits of the stylesheet checks — but without their downsides. The validation layer implemented as a Schematron schema is completely orthogonal to the stylesheet logic[4] and is reusable across applications. In fact, with Schematron, the distinction between the document and super-document layers becomes largely irrelevant, since you can elegantly implement all necessary rules and constraints in one schema.

Greet the winner. Summarizing, Schematron comes very close to being the ideal solution for implementing the entire source definition, including both document and super-document layer rules. The only disadvantage to it is that due to its rule-based nature, expressing entire grammars in Schematron may not be as straightforward as with other schema languages (see **2.2.1** for more on this). In the examples in the following chapters, we'll focus on the Schematron source validation techniques.

Do not forget to super-document. Although combining different super-document enforcement techniques is not usually a good idea, the first of the options described above (human-readable documentation) must accompany any other approach you are using. All the super-document layer rules (as well as the most important document layer rules) must be fully documented so that authors can produce valid documents without having to go through too many trial-and-error iterations.

2.1.2   Organizing source documents

The most obvious approach to translating a web site into XML is, "one XML source document maps to one HTML page." However, following this path pedantically would mean placing *all* of a web page's information into one XML source document. This is demonstrably wrong; even if present on a particular web page, some bits of information may logically belong elsewhere.

---

4. It may, however, share some code with the stylesheet (**5.1.1**).

Master document

Even in the simplest web site setup, we need at least *two* source XML documents for each web page. One is the *page document* storing the material specific to this particular page: text, links, image references, and so on. The other document, which we will call the *master document*, provides material that is common to more than one page: navigation, logos, copyrights, disclaimers, some of the metadata (such as keywords and descriptions that apply to the entire site or section), parent sections' titles and links, etc.

Certain bits of master document data may be used on all pages of the site, while others may apply only to a section within a site. You can therefore further subdivide your master document into several documents (one for the site and one for each section), or you can still store all information in a single master document. In the latter case, the markup of the master document should make it easy for the stylesheet to locate data corresponding to each section.

Find it on the map. Figure 2.1 depicts the process of transforming a sequence of page documents in XML into a sequence of HTML pages and the place of the master document in this process. Note that the page documents and the master document are validated before being fed to the XSLT processor controlled by the transformation stylesheet.

Site directory. The most important data in a master document is a description of the structure of the site, listing all its pages — a *site directory* in XML. Individual pages use this information to figure out their place in the context of the site and build their navigation accordingly. A site map page, often found on complex sites, can be generated by the stylesheet directly from the master.

It may make sense, just to be logical, to separate the master file into a site directory document and a metadata document holding the rest of the site-wide metadata. However, for most projects, such separation holds little advantage by itself.

What it is not. The master document is not to be confused with the site's front page; no matter how different is the latter from the rest of the pages, it is still just a page that is generated from its own source

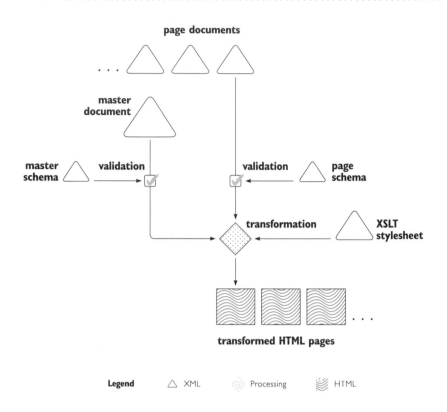

page documents

master document

master schema **validation** **validation** **page schema**

transformation **XSLT stylesheet**

transformed HTML pages

Legend   △ XML   ⣿ Processing   〰 HTML

Figure 2.1 The page documents and the master document are fed to the transformation stylesheet that produces HTML pages.

document. A master document's role is not to generate any specific page but to provide the site directory, common content, and metadata for all pages of the site.

Those familiar with Cocoon (**7.2**) might wonder how a Cocoon sitemap compares to the master document of a site. They have little in common: The sitemap defines the processing patterns of a site, while the master document is part of the site's content.

A sample master document is examined in Chapter 3 (Example 3.2, page 143).

Orthogonal content

Apart from the master document, other source documents — leaves of the source tree — normally correspond one-to-one to the final pages of the site. However, this is not always true. Certain pieces of content may be *orthogonal* to the site's hierarchy — that is, they may appear on more than one page regardless of those pages' place in the tree and sometimes even regardless of their content.

Examples of orthogonal content include news blocks (except those that are the main content of their pages), advertisements, sidebars, featured links, "quotes of the day," etc. Some of it borders on metadata, whose proper place is in the master document; however, unlike metadata, orthogonal content is meaningful even outside of its web site context and is usually updated regularly. It can be organized into its own hierarchy, which is usually independent of (but may be in some aspects parallel to) the main site hierarchy.

Compared to the information they are neighboring with on the final web pages, these orthogonal content units may be maintained by different people, obey different update rules, and even use a different markup vocabulary. This last difference, however, should be avoided because it may be quite costly in terms of complexity of the validation and stylesheet code.

Referencing orthogonals. It makes sense to store orthogonal content in separate source documents. To specify what orthogonal units should go to what site pages, you can use any of the following methods.

- You can hard-code this into the stylesheet. For example, if you want the same sidebar to appear on *all* pages of the site except the front page, it is straightforward to program your stylesheet so it retrieves the sidebar source, formats it, and places it on all subpages it generates. Also, this is the only method that works whenever the logic of placement of orthogonal information cannot be expressed declaratively but is algorithmic.

  For example, if you want each page to automatically display a textual ad block most closely related to its content (which may change often), static XML cannot express that. Only the code that actually builds the page can dynamically implement this algorithm, for example, by searching each page for keywords and matching these to the keywords from an orthogonal pool of ad blocks.

• You can link orthogonal pieces to the main site hierarchy via the master document. For example, you can add an attribute to the elements that represent pages in your master document's tree, specifying the source of the orthogonal unit(s) to be placed on the corresponding page. This is perhaps the most logical approach; it works for an arbitrarily complex (but static) distribution of orthogonal content, making it easy to overview and maintain.

• Finally, you can extend your source markup vocabulary to include an element or attribute that, when encountered in a page document, triggers the inclusion of orthogonal information. This approach may be the first to come to your mind, but it is not necessarily optimal: It contaminates your source with low-relevance information (after all, orthogonal content is so called exactly because it has little direct relation to the other content on the page) and makes the structure of the site more difficult to update by decentralizing connections between pages.

Still another solution is to combine the two last approaches from the above list. You could use the master document to associate some unique identifiers with orthogonal content units stored elsewhere, and then reference these identifiers in page documents to incorporate those units. This gives you both centralized control (you can update all pages that use some unit simply by changing its identifier association in the master) and editing convenience (you only have to edit *one* page document when you want to add or remove some predefined orthogonal units on that page). This is the approach that we will use in the following chapters (see examples in **3.10**, page 140).

Not where it appears to be. When adding an orthogonal reference to a page document, don't try to position it to correspond to the physical position of the orthogonal block on the formatted page. Remember that the structures of the XML page source and its visual rendition cannot be parallel — if only because one is hierarchical while the other is two-dimensional.

Usually, an attribute or a direct child (first or last) of a page document's root element is a good enough place for linking up orthogonal content. The stylesheet will decide what is the best position for the block on the final page. Only in cases when this visual positioning is excessively difficult to calculate in the stylesheet, or when your pages will display orthogonal content intermingled with native content, should the orthogonal references in the source be moved to a place somehow corresponding to the positions of the formatted orthogonal blocks on the web page.

External entities are not for linking. XML provides external parsed entities (**2.2.4.4**) to embed externally stored components of a document. This is not a link between two documents: The entity is treated as an intrinsic part of the document, just as if it were physically part of it.

Parsing, validation, and processing take place after entity references are resolved. They should make no distinction between a document that is stored in a single piece, and the same document with components stored in external parsed entities.

For example, in book projects, entities may be used to store some chapters separately for convenient editing. When the book is parsed and processed, however, the chapters are seen as part of the book, regardless of whether they are physically present or accessed by resolving entity references.

Don't even think about using entity references as the equivalent of links. Link elements exist at the semantic level and the processing for them can vary from one application to another. In our approach to web site design, orthogonal content and site-wide metadata should be handled with links.

Note that some parsers, although DTD-aware, do not support external parsed entities.

2.1.2.3   Storing auxiliary data in the stylesheet

Some of the site's material can also be stored in the transformation stylesheet. This is only advisable for data that does not really belong in the source of the site. That is, if you can create a different (but fully adequate) rendition of the same source without some bits of its content, chances are these bits are not really part of the source proper but may need to be stored in the stylesheet.

Boil-down analysis. For example, suppose your site features a graphic button reading "portfolio." The same button displays a floating tooltip when the mouse pointer is hovering over it, reading "click here to view portfolio." Apparently, this web site element is comprised of three components: the "portfolio" label, a reference to an image file (for example, `img/portfolio.png`), and the text of the tooltip.

Of these three components, only the bare text of the button ("portfolio") clearly deserves to be called its *source* (and to be stored in the source XML document). The image reference, as well as the image file itself, should ideally be generated by the stylesheet from the label (**5.5.2**); however, if this is not possible, the reference to a prefabricated image file can be stored in the source. As for the tooltip, the most effective approach is to also generate it from the button label by automatically prefixing the latter with "click here to view." Store the tooltip text in the source XML only if this automation does not work for all labels, or if you want to reword some labels into the tooltips to make them more descriptive. (Remember, however, that "click here" is meaningless outside of HTML — e.g., if the same material is rendered as a VoiceXML interface.)

2.1.2.4   Other approaches

Everything in one chunk. A different approach to source organization is, "one XML source document maps to many HTML pages." Actually, you can store the source of *all* pages as well as all site metadata in one big document. The stylesheet can easily extract all necessary data from this source repository and generate all pages of the site from it. This also makes some of the super-document checks possible even with those schema languages that cannot go outside of the current document. However, such a monolithic storage unit is not very convenient to update and maintain, especially if more than one person will be working on the site.

Objects in a database. When you have to manage a lot of source documents, it might make sense to store them not in files but in a native XML database, such as Xindice.[5] This will make access to your

---

5. `xml.apache.org/xindice`

data much faster, especially in search operations, and let you do some impressive tricks (e.g., evaluate an XPath expression against many documents at once). However, each object in such a database still represents a self-contained XML document, so everything we discussed above regarding organization of source files still applies.

Reusing existing infrastructure. The web site requirements are your primary starting point, but you must also take into account your organization's established electronic document workflow. Converting other formats to XML is discussed in **6.2**, but if all of the documents around you are in some XML vocabulary, this will have direct consequences for developing the site's source definition and organizing source documents.

2.2 Practical schematization

There are two levels of correctness of an XML document. The lower level is syntactic and structural: End tags must match their start tags, elements must nest properly, all quotes must be closed, all special characters must be properly escaped, and so on. The XML specification terms such documents *well-formed*. Fortunately, you don't have to do anything special to ensure well-formedness: Any XML parser (used in transformation or even built into your XML authoring tool, **6.1**) will report well-formedness errors immediately.

It is only at the higher level — the level of *semantic* correctness — that a well-formed document has to be validated against a source definition. As we saw in the previous section, a typical source definition may include a number of document types and be subdivided into the document and super-document layers (**2.1.1**). At the implementation level, the core of a source definition is one or more schema documents written in a schema language. This section examines the existing schema languages and discusses various issues related to schema design and implementation.

2.2.1   Choosing the language

One of the first decisions you face is the choice of the schema language to use. Once limited, this choice is now quite wide and keeps getting wider.

Besides the old and proven DTDs, you can use any of the numerous other languages capable of formally defining the structure and content of XML documents. The best known of these is W3C's XML Schema Definition Language[6] (often called simply "XML Schema" but abbreviated XSDL in this book). However, there are other schema languages that are no less deserving of your attention. Below we'll look at the main issues to consider when choosing a schema language for your project.

2.2.1.1   Languages for building grammars

All schema languages could be divided into two major groups. The first group encompasses *grammar-based* languages such as DTD, XSDL, and RELAX NG.[7] A *grammar* of a language is its formal description that aims to cover the entire language; if a document has a feature not covered by the grammar, this is because either the grammar is incomplete or the document is invalid. In either case, an error is reported.

Grammar descriptions work "downward"; that is, they start from the most global structural units and proceed to the local constructs defining everything in between. Therefore, a grammar is often similar in structure to the document it describes; for example, an element type declaration in XSDL may have the declarations for its descendants laid out exactly as are the real descendant elements in a valid document.

Grammar limitations. Defining XML vocabularies through grammars is very natural, and the resulting schemas are usually straightforward to read and write. However, it is only in theory that this

---

6. www.w3.org/XML/Schema
7. www.oasis-open.org/committees/relax-ng

approach works perfectly; for many practical scenarios, it is too rigid and inflexible. One of the problems is that many practical types of constraints are impossible to define in grammar-based schema languages. More importantly, in practice you may want to use only a subset of validation rules.

For example, you may want to validate first the structure of a newly created document without checking attribute values or element content, and only go for full validation at a later stage. Sometimes, on the other hand, you may need to validate attribute values even though you know that the structure of the document is not yet valid. Some checks may be more important for you than others, and new checks are likely to become necessary as your document evolves through various stages of its lifecycle.

2.2.1.2   Languages for setting rules

With a grammar-based language, it is difficult to extract part of a schema and use it independently of the rest. A grammar either matches a document in its entirety, or it does not match at all. This is where the second kind of schema languages may be more suitable: the *rule-based* languages, of which the best known is Schematron.[8]

Precision aiming. A Schematron schema consists of an arbitrary number of rules, each describing one aspect of document structure or data values. These rules do not have to cover the entire grammar; anything in the document for which no rule is found is assumed to be OK by a Schematron validator. Rules can be given in arbitrary order having nothing in common with the order of the corresponding structural units in the document.

Thus, it is easy to start a Schematron schema by defining rules for what you think are the most important — or the most likely to get botched by document authors — features of your document type. Even a one-rule schema is completely workable and may be useful.

---

8. www.ascc.net/xml/resource/schematron/schematron.html

Later, you can grow your schema "upward" by adding new rules to it as you see fit, either to reflect new structures in an evolving document type or to guard against further practical markup errors. Rules can be grouped into patterns, and patterns can be turned on or off during validation to implement different validation scenarios (such as checking attribute values without checking the structure of elements).

Schematron primer. A simple Schematron example illustrates the above points. Example 2.1 is a Schematron rule combining three checks. The context attribute specifies that these checks will be applied to each section element in the source document. The first two checks verify the presence of obligatory children elements (head and p). The last check uses the XPath function normalize-space() to ensure that the section element contains no child text nodes, that is, no "dangling" bits of textual data not enclosed into an appropriate element.

· ·

Example 2.1   A simple Schematron rule.

```
<rule context="section">
  <assert test="head">
    A 'section' must have a 'head'.
  </assert>
  <assert test="p">
    A 'section' must have at least one 'p' (paragraph).
  </assert>
  <assert test="normalize-space(text()) = ''">
    A 'section' cannot contain text. Use a 'p' element to include a
    paragraph of text.
  </assert>
</rule>
```

· ·

Of course, we could think up lots of other checks applicable to this simple structure. For instance, we could check that not more than one head element is a child of a section, or that a head comes before any p. However, those checks included in our example grew out of the everyday markup practice — they were added to prevent the most common errors in real documents. You can always add more checks (including those that are impossible with a grammar-based schema language) to respond to the changing requirements of XML authors.

As you can see, the only relatively tricky aspect of this example is the XPath expressions it uses. In fact, for those familiar with XPath, the learning curve of Schematron is nearly nonexistent. The reference implementation of Schematron (which we will use for our examples) is itself written in XSLT and translates a schema into an XSLT stylesheet (**5.1.2**). More complex Schematron schemas (Examples 3.3, 5.20) will be analyzed in the following chapters.

Growing rules into grammar. Ultimately, a set of rules in a Schematron schema may grow complete and thus become a grammar. Admittedly, because of the way it was developed, such a grammar may not be as prettily laid out and easy to read as an XSDL schema for the same document type (although it is likely to be more powerful). Of course, you can always organize it and clean it up if you feel like it, or you can even rewrite it completely in a grammar-based schema language. What's important is that your Schematron code has played its role: It allowed you to effectively validate your documents while they were being developed.

So, the rule-based approach makes Schematron an ideal "prototyping" schema language, useful at the early stages of any XML project. Moreover, the fact that Schematron is tightly coupled with XSLT and allows you to easily express rules on both document and super-document layers (**2.1.1**) makes it especially suitable for web site projects. If you use XSLT for transforming your XML and if you store the source in more than one document, Schematron is a natural choice.

Guided editing. One downside to a rule-based schema is that it cannot answer *arbitrary* questions about valid documents, such as "what attributes are permitted for this element type?" or "what type of element can come after this element?"

A rule-based schema is, in a sense, a collection of canned answers to questions that its developer deemed most important — so you cannot rely on it to contain the answer to your particular question. Conversely, a grammar-based schema is a complete description of a valid document, and you can use it to find out an answer to *any* question so long as it belongs to one of the types covered by this schema.

One practical consequence of this is that you need a grammar-based schema if you want your XML authoring tool to provide guided editing (**6.1.1.1**), that is, to suggest valid markup at any point in the document. In order to compile, for example, a list of element types that you can insert at some specific point, an XML editor must have a complete grammar of the document type, not a collection of disjointed checks from a rule-based schema.

Obviously, guided editing is a feature most useful for site editors, not developers. This gives you another reason to create a grammar of your source definition after it is developed and tested but before the bulk of the site's content is marked up with it.

Best of both worlds. With XSDL, you can embed modules written in other schema languages, including Schematron, into your grammar-based schemas. This approach is attractive because it combines the completeness and logical layout of XSDL with the power and precision of Schematron rules.

2.2.1.3 Modularity

Modularity is the best way to keep complex projects under control. Without breaking your work down to manageable and reusable pieces, further development and maintenance may soon become excessively difficult.

A web site's source definition is no exception. XML is intrinsically modular in that element types and attributes, declared once, can be reused arbitrarily many times. However, for practical purposes this is not sufficient. A schema must enforce some higher-level abstractions above element type and attribute declarations, so it can be split into modules that are sufficiently orthogonal (such that changing one module introduces little risk of breaking other modules), easy to maintain, and easy to reuse.

Different schema languages provide different high-level abstractions and therefore different methods of modularizing schemas. This is another important aspect that you should consider before selecting one of the languages. Try to choose the language whose way of dividing schemas into interconnected modules appears closest to the way *you* tend to think about your source definition.

Since all schema languages exist in the common XML universe, the pieces they consist of at the lowest level are the same: element type declarations, attribute declarations, and content models for specifying what elements, in what order, may occur within other elements. Also, most schema languages support the notion of a document type and allow modularizing schemas at this level. Beyond this, however, it becomes more interesting.

- **XSDL** emphasizes *data types* and provides an extensive set of tools that you can use to define, extend, restrict, inherit, and reuse data types. Therefore, one could say that XSDL is modular primarily at the data type level. A library of reusable components in XSDL is likely to consist mainly of type definitions that you can reuse in your schema's declarations.

- In **DTDs**, the modularization mechanism is *parameter entities* (see 2.2.1.4 for an example). An entity is similar to a text editor's macro in that it works at the character level and just replaces an identifier (called a *parameter entity reference*) with an associated fragment of text or external object. Any syntax checks are made only after all entity references are expanded.

  This approach is proven and powerful, but may lead to hard-to-track bugs. With DTDs, however, this paradigm is effective, as it allows you to create complex schemas that are pretty well modularized — even though sometimes hard to read.

  Unlike most other schema languages, DTDs do not support local element type declarations. This means that you cannot restrict an element type to certain contexts, such as within a certain parent element. Any element type you declare becomes global, and you cannot have two global element types with the same name. For example, if a book element can have an author child and so can a song element, a DTD will validate this only if these two `authors` have exactly the same children and attributes, or if `book` and `song` are in different document types. This is an important reason why DTDs are hard to modularize, although it provides consistency for the authors.

- **Schematron** is the only schema language that does not have explicit element type and attribute declarations as its basic building blocks. Instead, it allows you to specify arbitrary checks that a valid document must pass. Nothing prevents you, however, from arranging these checks into groups so that each group defines all aspects of one element type and is thus a functional equivalent of another schema language's element type declaration.

  On the other hand, you can group your checks in any way that makes sense for your application. Schematron offers several levels at which checks can be grouped (`rule`, `pattern`, `phase`), and you can switch different `phases` on or off for each validation pass. Finally, new rules can be defined to extend existing *abstract rules* when applied to specific contexts. This flexibility makes it possible to create Schematron schemas that are not only effective but modular and easy to extend.

2.2.1.4 Expressiveness

Fake integers in DTDs. A typical schema can *express* much more than it can *enforce*. For example, if you want to declare in your DTD an attribute that only takes integer values, you might think you're out of luck because an integer attribute type is not enforceable via a DTD. However, you can define an entity:

```
<!ENTITY % integer "CDATA">
```

(here `CDATA` means "any character data") and then use it whenever you want to define an integer-valued attribute. True, for an XML parser this trick is meaningless, as it still won't be able to tell that a value of `"xyz"` for such an attribute is wrong. But for a person looking up an element's attribute list in the DTD, a reference to such an entity

```
<!ATTLIST element
  attribute %integer; #IMPLIED
>
```

makes a lot more sense than just

```
<!ATTLIST element
  attribute CDATA #IMPLIED
>
```

to which it is formally equivalent.

Some might argue that this trickery is useless and can even be misleading, because it gives a DTD author a false feeling of security that is not based on any solid foundation. This may be true, but it is also true that readability is an important aspect of reliability. Other schema languages have other kinds of limitations where similar unenforceable hints might be necessary.

This is a complete sentence. Even though Schematron's XPath expressions are very powerful, you cannot use them to enforce rules that can't be formulated algorithmically, even though these rules may be very important for your source definition. For example, you may require that a heading is always a complete sentence (and not, say, a single word or a phrase). While you could output a warning if the number of words in a heading seems to be too small for a sentence, you cannot reliably catch this error using XPath.

You can, however, make your schema more expressive and more useful with regard to this rule in several ways:

- **Document the schema** (see also 2.2.3). This is the least obtrusive but the least efficient approach, as only those XML authors who bother to read the documentation will be aware of the restriction.

- **Provide validation-time diagnostics.** If you cannot check if an element satisfies a rule automatically, you can still *remind the user* to see to it whenever your schema runs across this element type. This is obviously a more obtrusive option, but it may be advisable if the element type in question does not occur too frequently or the requirement you're trying to enforce is very important.

- **Choose a "talking" name.** Even though it is the structural role that must be the basis for selecting the name for an element type (**2.3.4**), sometimes other factors can participate too. If there's an important but formally unenforceable requirement concerning some element type, you can reflect it right in its name — for example, by using `heading-sentence` instead of just `heading` if you want the heading to contain a complete sentence. This way, whoever is authoring the XML source will be reminded of the rule every time he or she inserts the corresponding element. Of course, longish and unwieldy names may become a major nuisance, so use this method only for *really* important aspects of your source definition.

Example 2.2 shows a fragment of a Schematron schema[9] that implements all three approaches listed above. The heading-is-a-complete-sentence rule is documented in the schema and is additionally reinforced by the choice of the element type name. An unconditional "reminder" is fired whenever a `heading-sentence` element is encountered, plus two additional checks ensure that the element's value contains at least one space between words and its last character is a letter.[10]

2.2.1.5 Strictness

The question of how strict your schema must be is equivalent to the question of how wide is the gray zone of XML structures which, from the viewpoint of the schema author, do not make much sense — but do no harm either and are therefore considered valid. There are two opposite approaches here: either "whatever is not permitted is forbidden" or "whatever is not forbidden is permitted."

Each of the schema languages naturally gravitates toward one of these two approaches. For example, if you don't explicitly permit a certain attribute on a certain element type in a DTD, using this attribute in

---

9. The function `matches()` in the test expressions is from XPath 2.0 (**4.2**).
10. Note that Schematron 1.5 does not allow `p` within `rule`, so I had to use XML comments to provide per-rule documentation.

Example 2.2 Checking `heading-sentence` with Schematron.

```
<pattern name="Heading checks">
  <p>This pattern's rules check the validity of
     various heading elements.</p>

  <rule context="heading-sentence">
    <!--This element must contain exactly one complete sentence (i.e., one
    with a subject and a predicate) but no punctuation at the end. -->
    <report test="true()">
      Check that this element contains a complete sentence.
    </report>
    <report test="matches(normalize-space(), '[^A-Za-z0-9]$')">
      The last character of this element's content is not a
      letter nor digit.
      Please check that there is no punctuation at the end
      of the heading sentence.
    </report>
    <report test="not(matches(normalize-space(), ' '))">
      This element's value has no spaces. You cannot write a
      complete sentence without at least one space between words.
    </report>
  </rule>
  <!-- more rules -->
</pattern>
```

an XML document is a validity error. On the other hand, if you say nothing about some element type in a Schematron schema, corresponding instance elements are always considered valid. Still, by using techniques such as wildcards you can to some extent emulate both approaches in any schema language.

Which approach is better? For database-like XML (1.2) produced and consumed by programs, something not explicitly prescribed in a schema is most likely an error. For documents written and read by human beings, the opposite is more often true. You cannot possibly foresee all the real-world circumstances that may force you to look for markup workarounds in your documents. Therefore, the "whatever is not forbidden is permitted" approach is usually more suitable for a web site source definition.

Once again, Schematron turns out to be designed for the task. A grammar-based schema, for example, would require you to explicitly list all allowed attributes in an element type declaration; with Schematron, you can prohibit or require certain attributes within certain elements (possibly depending on the context in which an element occurs) and pay no attention to all others. The Schematron motto is, "Don't bother defining it unless it causes you problems."

2.2.2   Schema creation scenarios

For those who prefer to get results fast, writing a formal source definition may look like a waste of time. XML is so intuitive that the temptation to jump straight into authoring (leaving the definition of the documents' structure for later) is very strong. And when the first sample pages are ready and tested (perhaps even with real content and a real stylesheet), the incentive to go back to a formal definition of what you've just created is even weaker. After all, the page templates are so self-explanatory, why bother describing them in yet another layer of complexity?

Indeed, the pedantic, make-a-plan-first-then-start-to-code approach may not be the best for everyone. Are there alternatives? This depends on the complexity of your project, your experience with XML, as well as the level of expertise of those who will be maintaining and supporting the site after it is launched. (In fact, it is likely that you'll get a strong motivation to formally define your markup once you see the incredible errors others are making in their documents.)

2.2.2.1   Working incrementally

If your site's source structure need not be too complex, and especially if you are reusing some bits from previous projects, you can work on the schema in parallel with the actual XML documents. This way, when you think you need a new structural unit, you add it both to the XML document you're writing and to the schema. Here, the actual documents are your drafting board — a schema is simply kept in sync so your documents will validate.

However, this approach will be pointless unless you take time to carefully review, clean up, modularize, and generalize your schema as soon as most of its components are in place.

Starting small. Especially convenient are schema languages that allow the schema to be incomplete but still workable, such as Schematron. For instance, you can quickly write a Schematron schema to check that a `heading` element has only `translation` children, each having a unique (within the `heading`) value of the `language` attribute (compare **2.3.5**). You need not specify any other restrictions or list any other element types or attributes for this schema to work; anything not mentioned in its single check will simply be ignored during validation.

As you continue to add new structural units to your XML, you can expand this schema to express more constraints. In principle, you can even declare the project finished with such an incomplete schema — if you are sure that it catches the most likely markup errors and that whoever authors new XML documents will not break anything "obvious" that the schema does not cover (this last assumption may sound more plausible if new documents are always created from templates, **2.2.3.3**, that already contain basic structural blocks). However, it is still advisable to fill in all the blanks and make the rule-based schema as complete as possible so that only fully compliant documents will pass validation in the daily maintenance of the site.

Ending big. Even if throughout the development cycle, you were working with a rule-based language such as Schematron, you may still need to provide a grammar-based schema (e.g., a DTD or an XSDL schema) when the source definition is complete. This may be a result of several factors.

First, you have to consider the limitations of your production setting. For example, if your web site is going to be part of a larger XML framework that supports only DTDs, you must provide DTDs for your document types. The same is true if you need to integrate the web site with existing schema libraries; for example, you may want to base your web page's data types on those defined in existing XSDL schemas.

Second, you should remember that a schema is more than just a filter that separates valid and invalid documents; it is also one of the principal parts of the system's documentation, the ultimate reference manual of your source definition. It must therefore reflect not only valid structures in your documents, but also the larger ideas and concepts behind these structures. The schema language ideally satisfying these documentation requirements will likely be different from the language that is most convenient for development and practical validation; obviously, complete grammars make better documentation than collections of disjointed validation checks.

Still another reason (already mentioned in **2.2.1.2**) to write a grammar for your source documents is to enable guided editing if your XML editor supports it.

2.2.2.2 Changing the rules

Don't worry if you don't get it right the first time and have to make changes to your source definition, either in the process of writing the stylesheet or even during after-launch site maintenance. Admittedly, such changes can be costly because they may necessitate modifying markup in a lot of documents (although in many cases, you can automate this by creating an XSLT stylesheet that will transform your documents from the old markup to the new one), but sometimes they are unavoidable. Here are some bits of advice:

- Accumulate many small changes into a few large "releases" that are put into effect simultaneously across the entire system. (Be careful, however, not to frighten your users by making these changes too sweeping.)

- Carefully document all changes (this, of course, implies that the original markup rules that you are changing were also well documented).

- Make sure that your schemas, transformation stylesheet, and other software are aware of both old and new versions of markup.

Provide corresponding checks and helpful error messages. Whenever possible, make the system backward-compatible, but warn the user that the old format, even if it still works, should be changed to the new one as soon as possible.

2.2.3 Documenting schemas

An ideal schema does not need documentation because it is documentation itself. Indeed, a complete human-readable specification of an XML vocabulary is also its "schema" in the sense that you can use it as the ultimate authority on whether or not an instance of that vocabulary is conformant. The only problem with such a "schema" is that you need a human to apply it to each document — which makes it costly, slow, and error-prone.

2.2.3.1 Documenting in different languages

It is only natural to try to combine formalized schemas that permit automatic validation with human-readable documentation. Schema languages provide embedded documentation tools that are as different as user requirements can be. Here are a few examples:

- With **DTDs**, you can add documentation to a schema by using `<!-- XML comments -->`. The comments can contain XML markup, except for other comments.

- **XSDL** offers a powerful mechanism whereby you can use element types from any vocabulary (e.g., HTML or DocBook) to provide any amount of documentation on the components of your schema. The documentation elements are distinguished from XSDL elements by their unique namespace. Because both the schema itself and its embedded documentation are in XML, it is possible to process schemas using an XSLT stylesheet (for example, to extract all documentation into a separate document).

- **Schematron** can also embed arbitrary XML elements in schemas.[11] However, Schematron's focus is different; its rules are typically much less structured than XSDL or DTD declarations, so trying to structure the documentation according to the layout of these rules may not be an optimal strategy. Instead, what Schematron excels in is on-demand *diagnostics* tied to specific markup contexts or triggered by specific errors.

  For many users, this "context-sensitive help" feature of Schematron can be even more useful than a narrative-style documentation, as it may help them learn practical markup much faster. Note also that Schematron diagnostics are delivered to the user directly and are not (unlike other languages) interspersed with markup declarations — for some users, this makes a lot of difference in terms of documentation usability.

2.2.3.2 Documentation components

What should be in the documentation of a source definition for it to be useful? Surely the idea of "well-written documentation" is quite subjective: Where one user would prefer a detailed narrative with examples and explanations, another would be perfectly happy with basic templates and a validator that provides minimal diagnostics for markup errors. Your best bet, therefore, is to discuss documentation requirements with the actual users of your source definition. In my experience, the components of successful documentation include, in order of decreasing usefulness, the following:

- **Any relevant rules that are not in the schema itself.** As we've seen, schema languages vary widely in how much of a complete source definition they can formally express. DTDs are particularly weak in this regard, but even with XPath-based Schematron rules, there may be certain conventions that you cannot check automatically. It's obviously a priority to supply such rules in

---

11. The Schematron 1.5 specification lists a number of element types permitted inside the p elements that are intended for documentation, but most implementations will allow you to use arbitrary markup there.

Example 2.3 An XSDL element declaration with embedded documentation containing markup examples.

```
<xsd:element name="block"
             xmlns:xsd="http://www.w3.org/2001/XMLSchema">
  <xsd:annotation xmlns="http://www.w3.org/1999/xhtml">
    <p>An example of a block:</p>
    <pre>
      <![CDATA[
        <block>
          <heading>A heading</heading> <!-- no full stop! -->
          <p>A paragraph of text.</p>
          <p>Possibly one more paragraph.</p>
        </block>
      ]]>
    </pre>
    <p>Note, however, that a block may be empty if it
    contains a reference to an external resource:</p>
    <pre>
      <![CDATA[
        <block idref="block-id"/>
      ]]>
    </pre>
  </xsd:annotation>
  ...
</xsd:element>
```

human-readable form so that XML authors can avoid bad practices or at least figure out what they've been doing wrong.

• **Markup examples.** As for documenting the rules that *are* in the schema, examples of conforming markup work best: An example is worth a thousand words. You should provide not only typical examples but also any special or borderline cases if they are likely to cause problems. If used in XML (as opposed to plain text or XML comments), use CDATA sections[12] for example code so it is not treated as part of the markup. Example 2.3 shows such a CDATA section embedded into HTML documentation in an XSDL schema.

---

12. www.w3.org/TR/REC-xml#sec-cdata-sect

Note how the examples alleviate the need for long descriptive documentation and allow the author to add a succinct note in an XML comment exactly where it is relevant. Note also that `CDATA` sections alone are not sufficient — they only protect special characters but are not elements themselves, so a `pre` element is added for each example.

- **Structural information**, such as descriptions of content models and attribute data types. In a grammar-based schema, this information is already formally expressed by the schema itself, but depending on users' familiarity with your particular schema notation, it may be beneficial to reword it in plain English (possibly adding some non-formalizable usage requirements or suggestions). For rule-based schemas such as Schematron, providing this information is even more of a necessity because such a schema may not contain any coherent formal description of document structure at all.

- **Metadata.** Finally, it is a good practice to document your schema's metadata, such as authorship and copyright information. For a schema that has already been in use, it is especially important to have a change log documenting all changes made to the current version since its first public release, including dates, authors, and details for each change (see also **2.2.2.2**). This information should be given prominently at the top of a schema document.

2.2.3.3   Page templates

An important part of a source definition is a set of document templates. A template is an example document with dummy (or no) data content, showing a typical layout of a valid XML document, usually with comments. Users can take the template as a starting point for creating a new document simply by filling in content between the template's supplied tags. You should provide a template for each sufficiently distinct type of source document.

Even if the users of your source definition (i.e., site editors and maintainers) have never worked with XML before, the concept of storing content units within matching pairs of tags should not be hard to grasp. It's actually a very natural way to think even for nontechnical people. However, starting a new document from scratch may be difficult even if you know what you want to get, and this is where page templates are invaluable.

A part of the difficulty is that, along with the meaningful content, an XML document may also contain a lot of metadata such as the XML declaration (`<?xml ... ?>`), a stylesheet processing instruction (`<?xml-stylesheet ... ?>`), a `DOCTYPE` declaration, or an internal DTD subset. To many "light" XML users, these constructs look (deservedly) much more frightening and indecipherable than the body of the document. So, providing a template with all this stuff already filled in (and making sure it doesn't need to change for each new document) is usually a good idea.

2.2.4 Using DTDs

As far as the document layer definitions are concerned, DTDs support basic constraints such as element type names, attribute lists, and content models. You cannot use DTDs to check the data type of an element's content,[13] express the dependence of an element's content model on the presence of an attribute, or perform complex syntactic checks of data values. As for the super-document layer, it's totally out of reach for DTDs.

On the other hand, the DTD notation stands apart from other schema languages in that it is defined right in the XML Recommendation.[14] Also, DTDs have been traditionally used for defining XML vocabularies (including W3C standards), and the DTD notation is still the default schema language in many existing XML tools and frameworks.

---

13. There exists a DTD extension for this purpose called *Datatypes for DTDs*; see `www.w3.org/TR/dt4dtd` for more information. Open source code is available at `www.XMLHandbook.com/DT4DTD`.

14. `www.w3.org/TR/REC-xml`

Another big advantage of this language is that a DTD validator is built into every validating XML parser, so you don't need any additional software for validation. Let's look at some of the issues related to using DTDs in a web site source definition.

2.2.4.1   DTDs and namespaces

DTDs are not namespace-aware, simply because namespaces were introduced to XML after the first version of the XML Recommendation, including the DTD syntax, was finalized. You can still use DTDs to declare and validate namespace-qualified names — but they must include a fixed namespace prefix and the ":" separator to be treated by a DTD validator as a whole.

For example, you *can* write a DTD declaration for an element type named `xsl:stylesheet` to specify its content model and attributes. However, from the DTD viewpoint, this element type will have nothing in common with `xsl:template` — and, more importantly, nothing in common with `my:stylesheet` even if the prefix `my` was declared for the same URI as `xsl`.

A partial workaround involves declaring names without prefixes in your DTD and always using the default (prefixless) namespace for them in your XML documents. By providing prefixless DTD declarations for your primary namespace and declarations with fixed prefixes as needed for foreign-namespace elements, you can to some extent reconcile the limitations of DTDs with the requirements of modern multi-namespace documents. (Although this approach is not likely to work if you freely mix elements from arbitrary namespaces in your documents, such documents would not be DTD-valid in any case, so the DTD would be irrelevant.)

2.2.4.2   Linking DTDs to documents

DTDs don't need a separate processor for validation. Any validating XML parser (possibly including the one that will read your documents to pass them on to the XSLT processor) will report DTD errors immediately. All you need to do is link each of your documents to its DTD, as follows:

```
<!DOCTYPE page SYSTEM "page.dtd">
<page>
  <!--...-->
</page>
```

Here, `page.dtd` is the name of the file containing your DTD (in this example, it is supposed to be in the same directory as your document file; if it is not, you can provide a relative path to the file or a URI instead). Note that the `DOCTYPE` declaration must also mention the name of the root element type of your document (`page`).

An XSLT processor with a validating parser will first read in the document and check it against the DTD. Only if it is valid will transformation begin. However, the same document without the `DOCTYPE` declaration will be transformed just as well, except that any DTD conformance errors will not be caught (only well-formedness errors, such as unclosed elements or missing quotes in attributes, will halt the parser). Therefore, you should use `DOCTYPE`-less documents if you have a schema other than a DTD and a corresponding processor for validation.

2.2.4.3   Mnemonic entity references

One feature of XML that you can't use without a DTD is *mnemonic entity references*, such as `&uuml;` for "ü".[15] For example, the HTML DTD defines many useful entities (for the Latin 1 character set and other special characters), but bare-bones XML has only a few entities for its own syntax characters (such as `&lt;` for "<" and `&amp;` for "&"). You can always access any Unicode character by a *numeric* character reference such as `&#x0410;`, but mnemonic references are easier to remember and use.

----

15. A new character encoding, called *UTF-8+names* (www.tbray.org/tag/utf-8+names.html), has been proposed to enable XML authors to use standard mnemonic character entities without having to declare them in a DTD.

An *internal DTD subset* is a part of an XML document's DTD stored within that document. It is not required to be a complete DTD, so you can conveniently use it to declare only the mnemonic entities you plan to use. For example, if you like HTML's ` ` for a no-break space better than its numeric reference, ` `, you can add the following at the beginning of your documents:

```
<!DOCTYPE root [
  <!ENTITY nbsp " ">
]>
```

where `root` must be replaced by the name of your root element type. Of course, if you want to declare not one but many entities and use them in many documents, it may be more convenient to put these declarations into an external DTD (referenced from your documents as described in **2.2.4.2**) rather than in the internal subset.

Note that you may need to insert a copy of the internal DTD subset with mnemonic entity declarations into the transformation stylesheet, as well as into your source files.

2.2.4.4   External entities

Similarly, an internal DTD subset can be used for declaring *external entities*. This is a native XML mechanism that allows you to reference externally stored components of your document by their URIs and include them just as if they were physically part of your document. References to such external XML fragments (called *parsed entities*) were discussed on page 53; references to non-XML entities (called *unparsed entities*) are quite different and are not covered here. Here's how you declare an external parsed entity:

```
<!DOCTYPE root [
  <!ENTITY ch3 SYSTEM "book/chapters/ch03.xml">
]>
```

and here's how you include it at a specific point in your document:

...will be discussed in the following chapter.</p>

&ch3;

<h1>Index</h1>

2.3 **The art of source definition**

Designing the markup to be used in your site's XML source may sound simple. In reality, however, it may well be the most challenging — and most interesting — part of the entire project. A simple static web site may make do with a dozen element types, but even those may not be easy to select. (In fact, defining one dozen element types may be more difficult than defining two dozen.) You need a solid knowledge of your site's subject area as well as good abstraction capabilities to develop a fully adequate, flexible yet compact source definition.

Below, we'll discuss some of the common errors and misconceptions pertaining to creating a new source definition from scratch. (When you look at the XML source of a finished site, such as our summary examples in **3.10**, it might seem obvious — but this simplicity may cost a lot of effort.) Only generic markup issues are covered here; no particular elements of a web page are examined, as this is the subject of Chapter 3.

2.3.1 Semantic analysis

Since our goal is to create a semantic XML vocabulary (**1.1.1**), the key concept is *semantic analysis*. Keep asking yourself questions like:

- What is it that this fragment of content is supposed to *mean*? What pertains to its meaning, as opposed to its visual presentation (style) or dynamic features (logic)?

- Where are the boundaries of this fragment from the semantic perspective — that is, what other material (adjacent or not) belongs to it?

- What material, even if it is rendered as part of this fragment, should be moved away in the source?

- What happens if I pull this fragment out of its context or move it to another context — how would this affect its meaning?

This way of thinking requires certain training. Learning to abstract out the meaningful core of a web page (which, at this stage, may only exist as a design draft with dummy content, or as a structureless pile of content with no design) is difficult to begin with. Even more difficult is figuring out where the abstracted meaning belongs; the fact that a fragment of content appears in a specific position on the final web page does not necessarily imply that its corresponding XML element must occupy the corresponding position in the source document. For example, if this fragment is copied over to more than one page, its proper place may not be in this source document at all.

2.3.2 Learn to think hierarchically

That XML is a formalism for serializing (i.e., representing sequentially) hierarchical data is usually well understood — in theory. In practice, however, authors often have trouble trying to think hierarchically. The resulting XML is then flatter than necessary, with a complex tree of variously scoped objects reduced to a long row of sibling elements. And when there is some depth to the tree, it is often a reflection of the two-dimensional layout of the rendered page, not of the intrinsic structure of the content.

There are cases when the choice between hierarchical and linear arrangements is not that obvious (for an example, see **2.3.7**). However, it is almost universally true that hierarchical structures are easier to navigate, which means the stylesheet processing a hierarchical XML document will be more straightforward to write and maintain.

In part, this is because with linear structures, XPath expressions will more likely include numeric indices (as in `/item[5]/label`). Such numeric pointers are almost meaningless to a stylesheet reader without seeing a document they apply to. What's worse, it is too easy to break them by modifying the document in such a way that the number of sibling elements in a sequence is changed.

2.3.3 Child elements vs. attributes

A puzzle that a great many XML authors run into is whether to represent a particular bit of information as an attribute of some element or as its child element. The three essential points of difference are these:

- **Attributes are not extensible:** You cannot have children or other attributes attached to an attribute (i.e., only character sequences can be stored in an attribute value), but you can always add children or attributes to an element.

- **Attributes are unique within their elements:** You cannot have two attributes with the same name under the same parent element, but elements pose no such restriction.

- **Attributes are unordered:** You cannot rely on the order of an element's attributes to be preserved during processing or transformation of any kind, but the order of child elements is always preserved.

There are several minor points as well:

- It is only possible to store one-line text fragments as attribute values. If necessary, a newline can be entered in an attribute value, but it is normalized to a space by the parser.

- For DTD users, it may be important that DTDs permit some basic data type checks on attributes, but not on data content within elements.

- Attributes cannot be commented separately: You cannot place an XML comment next to an attribute because comments must stay outside of tags. You can place comments inside or outside of an element as you see fit.

Other than that, it is mostly a matter of taste and semantic modeling accuracy. Attributes are commonly used to store metadata (data about data), while elements contain the data itself; although this distinction may in some cases be vague, it is still a useful rule of thumb to remember. For example, a unique identifier of an element is undoubtedly a piece of metadata, so it is always stored in an attribute (conventionally called `id`).

Another rule of thumb is that attributes tend to be used more often for numeric data and for various formal constructs such as URIs, whereas human-readable text (even if flat) is better stored in elements. The rationale behind this rule is that when stripped of any markup, XML is supposed to still make at least some sense to a human reader, which means that as much as possible of the document text must be in element content and not in attributes.

This means, by the way, that HTML's markup model by which an image description is stored in the `alt` attribute of an `img` element is not optimal. If you define a similar element type for your source markup, it is preferable to store the description text in the content of the element:

```
<image src="image.png">Company logo</image>
```

Note that the `object` element type, added to HTML later than `img`, uses this markup model.

2.3.4   The art of naming

Source definition means, among other things, thinking up names for your attributes and element types. It is of course a very subjective matter, but some recommendations may still be useful.

Spell out.   First of all, avoid abbreviations — use complete words (unless, of course, an abbreviation is more common or more familiar than its spelled-out form). XML is not supposed to be terse; it is supposed to be readable. Saving a few keystrokes now may cost you many lost seconds later as you'll be trying to remember how *exactly* you abbreviated that name.

Use case.   You can use all-uppercase names if you want your markup to really stand apart from the text. However, all-lowercase names look nicer and are easier to type and read. Initial capitals make no sense for single-word names and may be confusing for multiple-word names (such as SectionHeading) because they look somewhat like regular text with its mix of cases.[16] XML is case-sensitive, and mixed case ought to be considered harmful if only because it makes your markup a fertile ground for hard-to-catch case errors.

Hyphen-ate.   Unlike most programming languages, XML permits hyphens in names, and XSLT and many other XML vocabularies use them to separate parts of multiword names (e.g., apply-templates). In my opinion, this convention makes complex names easier to remember and more legible than using initial capitals. (It's also handy that, unlike the underscore sometimes used in other languages, a hyphen can be typed without pressing *Shift*.)

No matter what naming style you choose, be consistent and do not mix different styles within one application.

Readable markup.   Another consideration unique to XML is that some element type names will be used only in combination with the names of their required attributes. This allows you to use creative naming schemes that sound almost like English but are nevertheless strict and unambiguous. For example, if you need an element type to represent internal links with an obligatory attribute providing the link's address, then instead of

```
<internal-link address="address"/>
```

you could use

```
<internal link="address"/>
```

This "reversed grammar," with an adjective for the element type name and a noun for the attribute name, makes perfect sense for this construct and is easy to read and remember. You need to make sure, however, that the link attribute always comes before any other attributes of this element.

Similarly, if one element type is always a child of another, you can use the context of the parent to make the child's name shorter. For example, you don't need an author-name inside an author; just name will do. Do not worry if you have more than one name element type in your vocabulary; unless you use

---

16. Even more confusing is the so called "camel case" where all initials but the first are capped, e.g., camelCase.

DTDs for validation, you'll have no problems validating and processing different names differently depending on their context.

2.3.5 Structure vs. metadata

A common difficulty for beginner XML authors is separating *structure* of information from *metadata*. These two concepts do sometimes overlap. You can more easily differentiate between them, however, if you remember that structure tends to remain constant, while metadata is likely to change as the data itself is changed.

The inventory of your element types and attributes must describe the *structure* of your content, while metadata is information *about* that content that is stored *in* elements and attributes of a document.[17] In other words, your XML vocabulary must be able to store both your information and information about that information (metadata), but must not itself depend on any particular information it stores. It is normal to have to update your vocabulary as you see more instances of content, but every such update must make the vocabulary more flexible and general, not just patch it for a specific instance.

Example: translations.   Suppose you need to store two versions of a heading in different languages. Here, the language of each version is an example of metadata; if you mistake it for structure, this could result in markup like

```
<heading>
  <en>Customers</en>
  <de>Kunden</de>
</heading>
```

This will even work, so long as you only need these two languages. If you decide to add a third language, however, you will need to patch your schema to allow a new child element type (e.g., fr) under heading to store it. The obvious sign of a problem is that with this approach, you cannot make "one fix to end all fixes"; inevitably, each new language will require adding an element type of its own.

----

17. More precisely, metadata tends to go into attributes, while the content itself is more often in elements (**2.3.3**).

The correct solution is to use the *structural role* of the heading translation for the element type name and move the language metadata into an attribute:

```
<heading>
  <translation language="en">Customers</translation>
  <translation language="de">Kunden</translation>
</heading>
```

Admittedly, this approach is bulkier, but it is much more consistent and extensible.

2.3.6 Generalizing but not overgeneralizing

Creating XML markup for web site content requires abstracting out its meaningful core, leaving all the presentation details aside. This is so fundamental that, sometimes, XML authors tend to "overgeneralize" and treat pieces of content that are *structurally* different as metadata-differentiated variations of the same structural unit. For instance, for a heading and a paragraph of text, this could result in markup like

```
<block type="heading">Customers</block>
<block type="paragraph">Our customers are...</block>
```

Not only is this approach unnecessarily bulky and difficult to read, but it also makes validation more difficult because DTDs (as well as some other schema languages) cannot define content models that depend on an attribute's value. This means a DTD validator cannot enforce different rules for these two instances of block, nor can it check the proper order and/or nesting of block elements with different types. Better markup of course would be

```
<heading>Customers</heading>
<paragraph>Our customers are...</paragraph>
```

Troublesome heritage. It seems likely that the overgeneralization tendency is a result of HTML experience. With HTML, you have a very limited set of element types whose intended structural roles rarely match those you need for your content. So, the standard mindset of a hardcore HTML user defaults to searching among what is available and trying to adapt one of the existing element types whenever a new structural unit must be marked up, just as HTML's div and span are often used (with CSS properties) for all kinds of structures in HTML pages. It takes getting used to XML to be able to create vocabularies that are exactly as rich as the content they apply to.

2.3.7 Parallel vs. sequential

Web site content combines both parallel and sequential components. For example, in a site's master document (**2.1.2.1**) the order of many elements is not important; page sources, on the other hand, are sequential documents whose order of elements is supposed to be mostly preserved in the formatted web page. This distinction is intuitively clear and poses no problems until you have to combine parallel and sequential components within one element.

Anatomy of a menu item. Consider an `item` element that describes an item of a site's main menu. Let's say the item must provide several bits of data: the button label, the identifier of an image displayed alongside this menu item, and a list of links to appear on the item's drop-down submenu.

Here, the label and the image identifier are parallel pieces of data in that their order in the source file is not important. But the list of submenu items is sequential, because their order will translate into the visible submenu order and is therefore meaningful. It would be an error to treat all these elements as siblings:

```
<item>
  <label>Customers</label>
  <image src="customers_photo"/>
  <subitem href="references">References</subitem>
  <subitem href="clients">Clients</subitem>
  <subitem href="contact_us">Contact us</subitem>
</item>
```

How, then, should we separate the parallel and sequential data in this example? We could, of course, add two child elements to the `item` to group all sequential data in one child and all parallel data in the other, but that would be overkill. Indeed, the parallel data (the label and the image identifier) does not so much belong together as it belongs to its parent element, `item`. Adding an intermediate layer between the `item` and its parallel children is therefore counterintuitive. The sequential data, on the other hand, clearly represents a whole — a drop-down menu — that must be marked up as such:

```
<item>
  <label>Customers</label>
  <image src="customers_photo"/>
  <drop-down>
    <subitem href="references">References</subitem>
    <subitem href="clients">Clients</subitem>
    <subitem href="contact_us">Contact us</subitem>
  </drop-down>
</item>
```

Now, the first level of the tree under the `item` (the `label`, `image`, and `drop-down` elements) holds only parallel data, while the second level (the `subitem` elements within `drop-down`) is sequential. This conforms to the general rule: Never make siblings out of parallel and sequential data bits, but store them on different levels of your hierarchy.

2.3.8   Existing vocabularies

For specific kinds of documents or objects, many existing XML vocabularies have been created by various user groups and standards bodies. Examples include XLink[18] for link semantics, XForms[19] for interactive forms, and DocBook[20] for document markup. Should you reuse these vocabularies, in whole or in part, or should you develop your own markup? The answer to this question depends on three main factors.

- The **concepts** you need to express in your markup. Why was the existing XML vocabulary created in the first place? What are the concepts it formalizes and the abstractions it uses? Are these concepts and abstractions of any utility for your own goal of creating a simple, easy-to-remember semantic vocabulary that strikes the right balance between strictness and flexibility?

....

18. www.w3.org/TR/xlink
19. www.w3.org/MarkUp/Forms/
20. www.oasis-open.org/specs/docbook.shtml

The "stairway of abstractions" (**1.1.1**) is a useful analysis tool. For example, if you consider reusing (a part of) the XSL-FO[21] vocabulary for text formatting, you'll realize that it is focused on visual presentation, while your goal in the source is semantic markup. Therefore, for your purposes, XSL-FO is on a wrong step of the abstractions stairway no matter how rich or well thought out it is.

- The need for **interoperability**. Few sites exist in complete isolation. Most need to draw their content from outside sources, and some also need to provide their content to the world in a format different from that of the web pages (one example is an RSS[22] news feed). Quite naturally, the requirements of these inputs and outputs will affect your source definition and may, in some cases, justify reusing some of the existing XML vocabularies in your source markup.

  On the other hand, if your inputs or outputs are not XML, they are useless for your source definition, and if they are, it is often easier to use XSLT to translate between vocabularies than to try to prune and graft definitions from one vocabulary to another. Remember that the main goal of your XML source is to be a foundation of your unique web site, and no existing vocabulary can be quite suitable for that.

- The need for **completeness**. In those aspects of your source definition that might be covered by established standards, your choice must be based on the relative importance of those aspects for your content and the complexity of constructs they describe. A well-designed, widely accepted standard that went through several revisions and was tested in many projects is much better prepared for all the unexpected real-life problems. So, if some markup aspect is really important to your site and you reasonably expect that it will keep developing and becoming more complex, your

---

21. www.w3.org/TR/xsl
22. backend.userland.com/rss

best bet is to go with an appropriate existing standard even if at first glance it may seem like overkill.

In most cases, however, universality is a burden rather than an advantage. A minimalistic ad-hoc vocabulary is often much easier to use and maintain in the long run compared to an all-embracing multifarious standard that will bring its own bulky baggage if you incorporate it into your source definition. Remember that you can start simple (**2.2.2**) but keep adding new stuff to your vocabulary, provided you did not make any serious design mistakes in its core.

Chapter 3 mentions the most notable of the existing XML standards that could be used for some aspects of your source markup. It's up to you whether to borrow from these sources and to what extent.

2.3.9   Namespace strategies

As you are creating your own unique XML vocabulary, you need a unique namespace for your element type and attribute names. For it to be unique, it is natural to use the URL of your web site for the namespace URI. If you will be using mostly your own markup constructs while borrowing few, if any, constructs from existing vocabularies, then it is also natural to use the default namespace (without prefix) for your markup.

As for the stuff you borrow from existing vocabularies, two approaches are possible. You can treat your hired staff with due respect, fully preserving their identities (i.e., their namespaces). Or, you can be mean and basically enslave them by converting them into your own namespace.

In fact, those you convert to your namespace have no formal connection to their native land anymore. So it is not really elements or attributes that you borrow, but only their semantics and names;[23] what you do is just build your own house after someone else's designs. Still, what might be the advantages of the "namespaces' melting pot" strategy?

....

23. Local names, to be precise, for a namespace is a part of a fully qualified name.

- Unifying everything under your own namespace (and making that namespace the default) greatly simplifies things for those who will be authoring and maintaining your site, especially if they are novices in XML.

- Getting rid of the borrowed elements' original markup vocabulary means that you can also get rid of any limitations or inconsistencies in that vocabulary. Ever wished to add an `advertisement="{yes|no}"` attribute to HTML's `img` element? Now you can. Just copy everything from the original `img` into your own markup vocabulary, removing or adding stuff according to taste.

- Finally, severing the link to the original vocabulary from which you borrowed some bits of markup protects you from any future changes in that vocabulary. No need to worry if a future version of HTML deprecates, and the next one removes, your favorite element type that you heavily use in your markup.

These advantages have a flip side:

- Your changes to the borrowed markup constructs may run askew of the principles and structure of their original vocabulary.

- Partial borrowing or changing borrowed stuff may prevent you from reusing software or schemas written for the original vocabulary.

If any of these considerations are important in your situation, use the native namespace for borrowed stuff and keep everything as per the original specification.

3

Elements
of a web site

River and bridge and street and square
    Lay mine, as much at my beck and call,
Through the live translucent bath of air,
    As the sights in a magic crystal ball.

ROBERT BROWNING, *Old Pictures in Florence*

3

Elements of a web site

This chapter is a practical complement for Chapter 2, "The source definition." Having discussed the ins and outs of building a comprehensive and useful source definition, we'll now look at how these rules can be applied to real-world source XML documents of a typical web site.

I cannot claim to cover everything: Your web site may well contain unique elements that won't fit common schemes. Here, only the most general and frequently used constructs are covered, and the approaches described in this chapter may not be optimal for all situations. Many examples are given, but rather than copy them over, try to use the reasoning behind these examples to analyze your own constraints and requirements.

The first part of the chapter deals with markup constructs commonly used in page documents, including headings, paragraphs and paragraph-like elements, links, images and other non-XML objects, tables, and forms. Then we will analyze the master document (**3.9**) to find out what data it needs to store and what is the best XML representation for this data. The last section (**3.10**) presents complete summary examples of a page document, a master document, and a Schematron schema to validate them.

3.1 Page documents: top-level structures

In this and subsequent sections, we look at the informational core of a web page, stored in its own source document (*page document*). Peripheral components such as navigation, parameters of the site environment, and metadata are stored in the *master document*, the subject of **3.9**.

3.1.1 Page metadata

Every XML document has a root element, and since we're talking about page documents here, there's no reason not to call this element page. Its attributes and children are the natural place to store the page's *metadata*.

In addition to its primary content, each page document includes certain metadata. Some of it may end up as a visible part of the web page, some may be hidden in HTML metadata constructs (keywords and descriptions in meta elements), some may be used during transformation but not included in the resulting HTML code, and some may not be used at all except for reference or source annotation purposes. Common examples of metadata include page creation date, change log, author(s) and editor(s), copyright and licensing information, and the language of the page.

Note that only information specific to this particular page must be stored in it; if some metadata bits are shared by more than one page, their proper place is in the master document (**3.9**) and not in any of the page documents.

Page ID. The most important piece of metadata is the page's unique identifier used to resolve internal links (**3.5.3**). However, we cannot store this identifier in the page itself, or we'll have a catch-22 situation: We can get from the id to the page location, but to obtain the id we must access the page — that is, we must already know its location. Because of this, the proper place for the `ids` of all pages is in the site's master document.

Page coordinates. The same applies to the information on the position occupied by this page in the site's hierarchy. As we'll see later (**3.9.1.1**), the branch of the site's tree that this page is a leaf of is most naturally deduced from the site directory in the master document. Duplicating this information in the page document itself is unnecessary and prone to errors.

Everything else. Any other page metadata is normally stored in the page document. Simple values can be stored in attributes of the page's root element. More complex constructs that require their own elements can be placed either directly under the root or inside an umbrella parent element (e.g., `metadata`) that is a child of the root element.

Existing vocabularies. RDF (**1.1.5**), besides being the cornerstone of the Semantic Web, can be used as a powerful tool for representing metadata in the traditional Web. It allows you to use standardized descriptors for common values such as author and date, but you can just as well define your own semantics for your unique metadata.

3.1.2 Sections and blocks

You'll likely need some intermediate structural layers between the root element, `page`, and text markup constructs such as paragraphs and headings.

Sections or blocks? The traditional document hierarchy — sections, subsections, subsubsections, and so on — is not often seen on the Web. Instead, information is more commonly broken into relatively small *blocks* with few or no hierarchical relations between them. Different sites may call these blocks "stories," "blurbs," "columns," "modules," "writeups," and myriad other names.

Among these names, one which appears to be the most intuitive is the one you should use for your block construct's element type name. Contentwise, a block is a unit with mostly fixed structure that may include both obligatory (e.g., heading and body) and optional (e.g., icon, heading links, author byline) components in both parallel and sequential (**2.3.7**) arrangements. Here's an example:

```
<block id="unique" icon="block_icon" type="story">
  <head link="address">Block heading</head>
  <subhead>Optional block subheading</subhead>
  <p>And here goes a paragraph of text.</p>
  <p>Possibly one more paragraph.</p>
  <author>An optional author byline</author>
</block>
```

Block types.   It is likely that you will have more than one type of block construct — for example, front page news blocks, subpage body blocks, and ad blocks. In the simplest case, everything on the page can be treated as one big block, so the page's root element can be considered the root element of a block.

Different types of blocks will likely have many common structural features — in part because they all belong to one site with its common information architecture and visual design. Only if different types of blocks have clearly distinct structures can you use different element types for them; otherwise it is best to use the same generic element type (e.g., block) with different values of the type attribute. This provides two major benefits:

- Your validation code will be simpler to write and maintain.

- Management of orthogonal content (**2.1.2.2**) will be much easier to implement — for example, you may be able to reuse blocks from regular pages as orthogonals on other pages, or turn documents storing orthogonal content into regular pages.

In general, analogous but different structures should only differ by a minimum number of obvious features; avoid random, meaningless differences.

3.2 **Headings**

Brief highlighted text fragments that preface or summarize longer pieces of text are very common on web pages. A heading may apply to the entire page, a section within the page, or even a single sentence or link — but it must apply to something, for a heading only exists as a member of a "head and body" pair.

3.2.1 Element type names

Look up the number. HTML has long used the `h1` to `h6` element types for six levels of headings. You can borrow these names, or you can make them less cryptic by using `head1`, `head2`, and so on. In any case, this approach only works if you really need several levels of headings and if these levels are free of any additional semantics — that is, if you can more or less freely move a branch of your headings tree upward or downward in the hierarchy.

If this is not true — for example, if your third-level headings are reserved specifically for sidebars that cannot be promoted to second-level sections — then the number-based naming scheme is not a good idea at all. Imagine that one day you need to add sections *inside* a sidebar — this will look ugly if your sidebar headings are marked up, say, as `h4`, while sections are `h2`.

Ask my parent who I am. It is vastly more convenient to use some descriptive names, such as `chapter-head`, `section-head`, or `sidebar-head`. An even better approach is to take advantage of the "head and body" duality mentioned above. If you've defined different element types for the complete structural units (`section`, `sidebar`, etc.), then the single `head` element type can be used for headings at any level:

```
<section>
  <head>This is a section heading</head>
  ...
  <subsection>
    <head>And this is a subsection heading</head>
    ...
  </subsection>
</section>
```

This scheme is intuitive, easy to remember, and therefore easy to use. Even though there is only one heading element type, XSLT or Schematron will have no problem determining the role of each particular heading by checking its parent element. At the same time, implementing processing that is common to *all* headings is very straightforward with this approach.

XHTML 2.0[1] implements a similar scheme except that its element type for a heading, h, is always a child of a section (although sections can nest). This is understandable — XHTML cannot realistically cover all possible kinds of structural units that might require headings. On the other hand, this brings us back to an "anonymous" naming scheme that is only slightly better than the old h1...h6: Now you can easily move sections around with their headings, but still no useful semantics is attached to each heading. You can, however, use the CSS class attribute to designate exactly what kind of a heading or section this is.

3.2.2 Attributes

The next question is, what is the auxiliary information to be stored with your headings?[2] In most cases, the plain text of the heading itself is sufficient, but there are exceptions. For example, a heading usually has a unique (either within the page or, more usefully, within the entire site) id attribute used in cross-references or hyperlinks to this section from elsewhere.

---

1. www.w3.org/TR/2003/WD-xhtml2-20030131/
2. Formatting attributes such as font, color, or numbering style are out of the question — the whole point of semantic XML is that these must be abstracted away.

In fact, a typical reference is supposed to refer to the section (or other structural unit) to which the heading belongs, not to the heading itself. Still, most authors prefer to use headings for linking, partially due to the HTML inertia (there are no `sections` in today's HTML) and partially because this allows them to more easily reuse the text of the heading in the textual part of the link.

For example, if your heading is marked up as

```
<head id="attrib">Attributes</head>
```

and you have a reference to it from somewhere, written as

```
...see <link to="attrib"/> for more on this.
```

this can be easily transformed into

```
...see 2.1, "Attributes" for more on this.
```

in plain text, or to

```
...see <a href="#attrib">2.1, Attributes</a> for more on this.
```

in HTML (here, "2.1" comes from an automatic count of preceding and ancestor sections). On the other hand, given that XSLT can easily traverse from a heading element to its parent, there's no real reason to use headings for linking in XSLT-based projects. The same link rendering could just as well be obtained from

```
<section id="attrib">
  <head>Attributes</head>
  ...
</section>
```

which looks less tautological and better reflects the fact that both the `head` and the `id` are properties of the `section`.

If necessary for your site's design, you may need to store a reference to a graphic file for each heading (see **3.6** for a discussion of image references), but only if the correspondence between headings and images is not automatic. The image may be used, for example, as a background or an icon-like visual alongside the heading.

3.2.3 Children

The question of what children to allow within headings boils down to the question of how far beyond plain text you are willing to go. Would you need textual emphasis within headings? What about links? The laziest approach is to allow everything that is allowed within a paragraph of text — and it will work fine in most cases. Only if you think you may encounter problems with complex markup in headings and want to guard against them, might a different content model for headings be necessary.

Depending on your requirements, other children may be necessary for heading elements. For example, you may want to store the same heading in two or more languages, with the stylesheet selecting one of the languages for presentation depending on a global language parameter (see also **2.3.5**).

You may also want to keep both full and abridged versions of a heading. For example, newspapers often use a specific abbreviated English syntax for their headlines (as in *U.S. Patriot Act attacked as threat to freedom*), but for the purposes of automatic indexing and natural language processing, the fully grammatical version of the same heading might be required (*The U.S. Patriot Act was attacked as a threat to freedom*).

3.2.4 Web page title

A special kind of a heading specific to HTML documents is the `title` of a page, normally displayed in the title bar of a web browser window as well as in bookmarks or search results listing this page. Even though, as a general rule, your target vocabulary must not influence your semantic source vocabulary, you should plan ahead as to what source element(s) will be transformed into the web page title.

If each of your pages has a visible on-page heading that applies to the entire page, it is natural to duplicate it as a web page title. Otherwise, it is always a good idea to provide a heading for *any* sufficiently large information unit. Even if in your target rendition this heading will only be used for a peripheral element such as page title or not used at all, the very act of christening a piece of data disciplines your thinking and serves as an additional checkpoint to ensure the consistency of your source's information architecture. Besides, the title may turn out to be more important for other renditions of the same source document.

Multistage titles. A web page title is often used for orientation within the site. A sequence of parent sections' headings, culminating in the name of the entire site, may be appended or prepended to the current page's title (e.g., "Foobar Corporation — Products — Foobar Plus"). Such a hierarchical title may be informative and useful, especially with deep site trees (even if the same information is duplicated on the page itself). Of course, it is the stylesheet that builds such a compound title, while the XML source of each page only provides that page's unique part of the title.

3.3 Paragraphs

A paragraph is a sequence of sentences that traditionally represents a complete, single thought. Today, however, paragraphs are often used for structuring the text flow visually, rather than for organizing the flow of ideas within it. Online, paragraphs tend to be smaller than in print, and other means of text organization (such as blocks, **3.1.2**) may make traditional paragraphs less common.

Still, whenever you have a container for more than just a small bit of text, your schema should permit inserting one or more intermediate paragraph elements between this container and its text. In most cases, this intermediate level may be optional; for example, your block elements could be allowed to contain either direct text content (for short fragments less than a paragraph) or a sequence of paragraph elements (for longer pieces of text). This approach adds a degree of laxity to your schema but is very convenient in daily markup practice.

As for the element type name, there is no reason not to use HTML's p, although para would be more appropriate for users who might find p too cryptic.

3.3.1 Lists

Lists are a special construct that is closely related to paragraphs. Two common types of lists offered by HTML are unordered (bulleted) and ordered (numbered), differing in how the items in the list are adorned. For our XML markup, we could borrow HTML's model, with a parent element (e.g., `ordered-list`) enveloping the entire list and children elements (e.g., `item`) marking up individual items.

The only possible ambiguity with regard to list markup is how to correlate list items with paragraphs. Often, each list item is a paragraph, so you may be tempted to consider paragraph elements redundant and disallow them from list markup completely. However, as soon as you run into an item of two or more paragraphs, you may regret this decision. I recommend using the convention discussed in the last section: Allow *both* paragraphs and direct text content within list item elements.

In fact, this is what is implemented by HTML 4; its `li` element can contain both inline and block content (i.e., both text children and paragraph elements, among others).

3.3.2 Paragraphs as link targets

Most links refer to entire web pages, but sometimes you need to pinpoint a particular location within a page. In HTML, you can make a link target from as small a piece of text as you like, down to a single sentence or word (by enclosing it in an `a` element with the `name` attribute).[3] In most graphic browsers, however, the only visible result of jumping to an in-page link is the page being scrolled down so that the linked point is at the top edge of the window.

This means that — unless your linked sentence happens to start at the beginning of a screen line — the visible portion of the newly loaded page starts in mid-sentence. This result is quite confusing and

----

3. A linked element is often called an *anchor*, and HTML uses this term for both the source of the link (*source anchor*) and its destination (*destination anchor*); hence the use of the `a` element for both ends of a link.

makes it nearly impossible to guess what *exactly* the link referred to. For this reason alone, it is advisable to only allow anchoring links to block-level elements, including paragraphs.

With XML, it is easy to enforce that rule because you most likely won't have any target enveloping element (like a in HTML). What you need instead is an attribute, only applicable to block-level elements, that turns its element into a link target. It often makes sense to reuse the almost-standard id attribute for this purpose (in addition to its numerous other uses); it won't do any harm if some of the elements with ids will create HTML link targets but will never be linked to.

3.3.3 Displayed material

Sometimes, you'll need to present an object that breaks the paragraph flow, but doesn't necessarily start a new paragraph. Often, this is a mathematical formula or a programming code fragment that must start on a new line.

Such a piece of *displayed material* is a block-level element from an HTML perspective; semantically, however, it is often an inseparable part of an adjacent paragraph containing the introductory or explanatory text for this displayed item. Therefore, it makes sense to allow the displayed material elements to be used only as children of paragraph elements.

3.4 **Text markup**

The "HT" in HTML stands for *HyperText*, and the early historical Web was very much textual. Despite all the graphic and multimedia advances of recent years, this textual foundation has not eroded. The advance of XML has, if anything, only strengthened it.

Any text markup language must provide a sufficient inventory of markup constructs for in-flow text fragments that for some reason must be differentiated from their context. Examples of such fragments include emphasized words or phrases, names or identifiers, quotes, and foreign language citations.

Block and inline elements. HTML (as well as other presentation-oriented vocabularies, for instance XSL-FO) differentiates between *block-level* and *inline-level* objects. This distinction has to do mostly with visual formatting, as block-level elements are supposed to be stacked vertically, while inline elements are part of the horizontal flow of text.[4] Therefore, it is not really relevant for your semantic XML markup, which must reflect content structure, not formatting. Still, since HTML is your primary target format, the block/inline distinction may sometimes have repercussions for your source definition.

Thus, it may be difficult to handle situations where a source element that normally transforms into an inline-level target element has to apply to a larger fragment of a document (**3.4.3**). From the XSLT viewpoint (**4.5.1**), block-level elements are more often generated by pull-style trunk templates, while inline-level elements are the exclusive domain of push-style branch templates.

Existing vocabularies. DocBook[5] is an established standard dating from 1991 that is used mostly for technical books and documentation. It may well be the most widely used XML vocabulary after XHTML; when somebody tells you, "My documents are in XML," chances are it's actually DocBook. Software support for this vocabulary is also quite good.

DocBook is vast but not too deep, so it is simple to learn despite its large number of element types (epigraphs, bibliographies, programming code, glossaries, and so on). If you don't understand what a particular element type is supposed to do, probably you don't need it (yet). For those constructs you do need, however, DocBook may be a rich source of text markup and structuring wisdom.

TEI[6] (Text Encoding Initiative) is an older and bigger beast, developed for markup of all kinds of scientific and humanities texts. Compared to DocBook, it is focused more on low-level text markup than on high-level book structures. The TEI DTD offers many modules that cover everything from verse to graph theory, so it is highly

---

4. In Western writing systems, of course.
5. www.oasis-open.org/specs/docbook.shtml
6. www.tei-c.org

recommended if you need to mark up specialized texts. The *TEI Guidelines*[7] is a very comprehensive and detailed guidebook explaining the use of the TEI DTD as well as many finer points of marking up complex text constructs.

3.4.1   Mark up the meaning

Your source XML must be semantic; that is, it must reflect the meaning of text-level constructs, not their presentation. The em and i element types, both present in HTML, provide a canonic illustration of this principle. While an i element dictates using an italic face in visual media, an em only designates an *emphasis*, which is a semantic concept rendered differently in different media. For example, a fragment of text inside em can be set in italic in a graphic browser, but it can also be highlighted in a text-mode browser or read aloud emphatically by a speech browser.

Modern HTML deprecates i and other presentation-oriented element types; instead, you are supposed to use appropriate semantic element types such as em, possibly in combination with CSS. In your XML source, however, deprecating anything is not an option — you have to make sure that with your schema, no presentation-oriented markup is possible at all. Formatting hints (**3.6.2**) can only be used in your XML when absolutely unavoidable.

3.4.2   Rich markup

The same visible formatting may result from different source markup. For example, you may use the same italic font face for both emphasis and citations, but they must be marked up differently in your source. What only a human reader can distinguish in the formatted result should, ideally, be automatically distinguishable in the source.

In general, semantic markup in the source should be richer and more detailed than the resulting HTML markup after transformation. For example, it is often a good idea to use special element types to mark

----

7. `www.tei-c.org/P4X/`

up all dates, person names, or company names in your source, even though in the resulting web pages they are not formatted in any special way.

Why mark up what you don't need right here and now? Because your XML source is more than just an undeveloped (as in "undeveloped film") version of the web site. Rather, it is the start of a project that will keep growing and changing, sprouting new connections and renditions over time. For example, you may want to reuse your web site material in PDF brochures, interactive CDs, archival and search applications, and more.

This means that your XML source must be able to serve as the semantic foundation not only for your current site but also for everything it can potentially become. You may not need any extra markup right now, but it may come in very handy when you extend your site or reuse the source documents for anything beyond the web site pages.

Imagine that one day you need to convert all dates on your site from one format to another (e.g., from MM/DD/YY to DD/MM/YY). Dealing with dates scattered in the text is so much easier if all of them are marked up consistently — for example,

```
... which happened on
<date><month>09</month><day>04</day><year>2003</year></date>.
```

instead of simply

```
... which happened on 09/04/2003.
```

With rich markup, you can change dates' rendition (e.g., reorder date components or use a different separator character) without touching the source at all, simply by modifying the stylesheet.

On another occasion, you may decide to paint all company names (or only your own company's name) green on your web pages. Or, you may find it a good idea to automatically compile an index of all persons' names mentioned on your site. All of these tasks are only possible if your source XML has these elements consistently and unambiguously marked up.

The need for rich text markup obviously depends on the quality, value, and planned longevity of your material. You don't need rich markup for short-lived stuff, but if you want your material to remain useful in the long term, you should always try to think in terms of "what markup is perfect for this content" rather than "what markup is sufficient for the task at hand." Examples of long-lived or otherwise valuable content include standards, specifications, historical texts, etc.

Existing vocabularies. As an example (and a good source of ideas), consider NITF[8] (News Industry Text Format), which is a standard vocabulary for rich markup of news stories. Only a necessary minimum of NITF markup may be used in a story that goes directly to press; however, for exchange, syndication, or archival use, a complete enriched NITF markup is required. A properly prepared NITF news story uses rich markup to answer questions such as *who* the story is about, *when* and *where* the described event occurred, and even *why* it is considered newsworthy by the story author.

3.4.3 Transcending levels

The text elements we've discussed in this section would be termed *inline* in HTML, meaning they are only allowed within block elements such as paragraphs. However, this limitation does not always make sense. For example, a rich markup element such as emphasis may need to be applied to more than one complete paragraph.

Usually, this is an indication that these paragraphs constitute some logical entity, such as a quotation, which (rather than the emphasis itself) you need to mark up. However, there may be situations where no such element exists, but inline text markup still has to spread across one or more block elements. What are we to do in such cases?

Inserting a separate inline markup element within each paragraph is the least elegant solution:

---

8. www.nitf.org

```
<p><em>This is the first paragraph using emphasis throughout.</em></p>
<p><em>And this is the second emphasized paragraph.</em></p>
```

This leads to unnecessary duplication of markup, poor maintainability, and just plain ugliness. This is the only option, however, if your emphasis spans one paragraph *and a half*.

The simplest approach is to just do away with the inline/block distinction and allow any text markup to be applied at any level of the hierarchy, both below and above the paragraph level. This will allow you to enclose all affected paragraphs into a common parent element specifying emphasis:

```
<em>
<p>This is the first paragraph using emphasis throughout.</p>
<p>And this is the second emphasized paragraph. Note that we can use
<em>nested emphasis</em>.</p>
</em>
```

This might make sense, especially in contexts where you want to allow both paragraphs and short non-paragraph text fragments (**3.3**). The problem with this approach is that it blurs your hierarchy of element types, thereby making your documents harder to maintain and more prone to errors.

It might be argued, on the other hand, that the emphasis spanning one or more paragraphs is semantically different from the emphasis that spans one or more words. Therefore, they could use different element types:

```
<emphasis>
<p>This is the first paragraph using emphasis throughout.</p>
<p>And this is the second emphasized paragraph. Note that we can use
<em>nested emphasis</em>, but this time it is a different element
type for the inline level.</p>
</emphasis>
```

If the paragraph-level emphasis is semantically connected with the paragraph element, you can instead add an attribute to those paragraphs that fall within its scope:

```
<p type="emphasis">This is the first paragraph using emphasis
throughout.</p>
<p type="emphasis">And this is the second emphasized paragraph.
Again, <em>nested emphasis</em> is possible.</p>
```

Among these options, there is perhaps no single winner suitable for all situations. Your choice will depend on the semantics of the element in question, the frequency of its use at inline and block levels, and the possible connections between its semantics and that of the standard block-level element (paragraph).

3.4.4 Nested markup

Another issue with text markup is whether nesting elements of one type is to be allowed. Presentation-oriented markup never uses, for instance, i within i — but for semantic markup, a similar structure may be meaningful. Thus, emphasis within emphasis or a quote within a quote are both perfectly valid *semantically*, even though in an HTML rendition, nesting of the corresponding formatting elements may have no visible effect.

Therefore, to properly transform nested semantic markup, you must use different formatting depending on the nesting level of the semantic element. For example, if you use italic face for emphasis, nested emphasis can be rendered either as regular face ("toggle" approach, where you switch between regular and italic faces for each new nesting level) or as bold italic face ("additive" approach, in which the italic rendition of the parent is augmented by the bold formatting of the child).

3.5 **Links**

A hyperlink is a very rich concept, even though its implementation in HTML is rather primitive. Basically, an HTML link consists of two parts: the address that tells the browser where to go and the link element itself that (with its attributes and children) defines the link's presentation and behavior. However, in HTML, all possible address types are limited to a single syntax (URI), and all possible link types are served by one element type (a) with a limited set of attributes. Let's see how we can improve this scheme.

Note that this section only covers *inline links* that are part of the body of a page and thus need to be specified in the page's XML source. *Navigational links*, created by the stylesheet based on the master document data, are discussed in **3.9.1.1**.

3.5.1   Elements or attributes?

When deciding how to cast your linking semantics into XML constructs, it is natural to reuse the HTML approach with a link consisting of an element (signaling the link) and its attributes (providing the address and other link properties). For example, you might write

```
This was <link address="address">reviewed</link> elsewhere.
```

However, this only looks good when you're linking text fragments within a text flow. As soon as you have a separate element representing some object that may have a link property (among others), it is much more convenient to designate the link by an extra attribute of that element rather than a wrapper element. For example, it is easier to create a linked image like this:

```
<image src="button" link="address"/>
```

compared to the HTML-inspired approach:

```
<link address="address"><image src="button"/></link>
```

Not only the address but other properties of a link as well (such as its title, behavior, or classification) might similarly attach as attributes to an element that represents a nontextual link.

So, we see that it is natural to express linking semantics via a set of attributes that may apply to many different elements (or even to any element at all) instead of an element type with its own fixed attributes. This is because a link is most often an attribute of some object rather than an object in itself. This approach was implemented in W3C's

XLink standard,[9] and you may consider incorporating XLink into your source definition for link markup (however, please read the rest of **3.5** for other possible link properties, not all of which are supported by XLink).

For in-flow textual links, you still need a generic linking element type (such as `link` in the example above) that only serves as a markup container for the same set of linking attributes. Most schema languages have no problem defining a separate set of attributes that can be used in different element types.

3.5.2 Link types

Along with the `href` attribute with the link's URI, an `a` element in HTML may provide a `target` attribute for specifying the target window or frame for the linked resource. However, just as you can add attributes with JavaScript code to program various aspects of the link's behavior (e.g., actions performed when the link is activated), your source XML may also need to provide link properties other than the address.

This does not mean, of course, that you'll have to embed JavaScript into your XML source. As with any other data, what you need to do first is develop a *classification* of all possible types of link attributes or behaviors, without detailing their implementation. As soon as you have such a classification, it's easy to coin an appropriate attribute and define the vocabulary of allowed values for it.

Categorizing links. For example, analysis may reveal that your links fall into one of the following categories:

* *internal links* (links to other pages within the site);

* *external links* (links to other sites);

* *dictionary links* (links to a script on an online dictionary site providing definitions for linked words); and

....

9. `www.w3.org/TR/xlink/`

- *thumbnail links* (thumbnails linked to pop-up windows with larger versions of images or pages).

Both thumbnail links and dictionary links may be either internal or external. However, they need to be classified separately because of their special role on the pages, resulting in different formatting and behavior. On the other hand, you may not be planning any formatting or behavior differences between internal and external links, but separating them into different types is still a good idea because it is a natural classification and because this lets you make your address abbreviations (discussed in **3.5.3**) more logical.

Classifier attributes. To differentiate these link types, we could add a classifier attribute, e.g. `linktype`, specifying the type of the link:

```
...available on the <link linktype="external"
link="www.kirsanov.com/te/">original site</link> and
<link linktype="internal" link="mirror/te">mirrored here</link>.
```

This approach works both with standalone `link` elements and with any other elements that may need to use these linking attributes (e.g., `image`). Note that we used `linktype` rather than `type` and `link` rather than `address` for the attribute names so that the common prefix, `link`, will help you keep track of these attributes as a group without the risk of confusing them with their parent elements' native attributes. You can also separate all linking attributes into a namespace of their own, but this is not really necessary unless you plan to use them with different document vocabularies.

It's also advisable to make all linking attributes but the address (i.e., `link`) optional and provide sensible default values. For example, you can mandate that the missing `linktype` attribute in a linked element implies that the link is internal.

Classifier element types. For in-flow links, instead of (or, better, in addition to) the bulky classifier attribute, a separate element type for each link type is more convenient. As these element types will be used quite often, each should have a short but clear name:

...available on the `<ext link="www.kirsanov.com/tel/">`original
site`</ext>` and `<int link="mirror/te">`mirrored here`</int>`.

Separate element types have the additional advantage of being easier to validate with grammar-based schema languages like DTD or XML Schema.

Advanced link types. Other link types may have their own sets of required and optional attributes and may perform other functions, besides creating a link. For instance, dictionary links from the above classification are likely to be used only within text flow, so we can introduce a special element type for them and declare that whenever the address attribute is missing, the element's content is taken as the (abbreviated, **3.5.3**) address:

...was going to `<def>`disembogue`</def>` profusely.

...at which point it `<def word="disembogue">`disembogued`</def>` itself...

Here, two occurrences of the obscure word *disembogue* are linked to a dictionary site, so that a pop-up window or floating tooltip with the word's definition could be displayed when the link is activated in some way (e.g., clicked or hovered over). You don't need to specify the dictionary site to use, or the complete URL for accessing the dictionary script, or the JavaScript code to create the pop-up; all this is taken care of by the stylesheet. The only thing you may need in the source is the `word` attribute that optionally provides the base form of the linked word or phrase; if it is absent, the contents of the `def` element are used.

For generality, this special kind of link can also be given by a `link` element with `linktype="dictionary"` and the `link` attribute playing the role of `word`.

Similarly, a thumbnail link could be created by a `thumb` element with a single attribute (e.g., `image`). This attribute would provide the identifier of the corresponding image, with the stylesheet doing all the rest: inserting and formatting the thumbnail, creating a display page with the full-size version of the image, and linking it to the thumbnail. The stylesheet can even automatically create the thumbnail from a full-size image (**5.5.2.6**).

3.5.3 Abbreviating addresses

When creating a link, we usually want to specify a certain piece of *content* that the link will point to. What a URL allows us to specify, however, most often is a *file* that can be moved, renamed, or deleted even if the content we are interested in is still out there somewhere. Moreover, a URL includes a lot of technical information (protocol, file extension) that is not relevant for our purpose of establishing a content-level link.

All this invites the idea of using *abbreviated addresses* that would hide the underlying technical complexity of URLs and provide an abstraction layer protecting our semantic XML from URL changes. For each address, we will create an identifier to be used in the XML source; at transformation time, the stylesheet will resolve this identifier into the actual URL to be put into the corresponding HTML link element.

Example: RFC links. Suppose you often need to link to enumerated documents such as RFCs.[10] Such links could use a special value of the link classifier attribute and/or an element type of their own. However, to make them even more convenient, it is natural to use only the RFC number as an abbreviation for the complete URI:

```
...as per <rfc num="1489"/>.
```

Or, the same could be spelled out in a generic fashion:

```
...as per <link linktype="rfc" link="1489"/>.
```

This latter variant uses generic linking attributes that can be applied to different elements to make links out of the corresponding objects, whereas the `num` attribute is only recognized in an `rfc` element.

The XSLT stylesheet will have to recognize this type of link, possibly apply some special formatting to it, and most importantly resolve (*unabbreviate*) the abbreviated address. In this example, unabbreviation would supply the complete URL of the referenced document for the HTML link:

....

10. An RFC (*Request for Comments*) is one of the series of standards created by the Internet Engineering Task Force (IETF) and governing most of the underlying technical structure of the Internet.

...as per
`<a href="ftp://ftp.rfc-editor.org/in-notes/rfc1489.txt">`RFC 1489`</a>`.

You could also allow an `rfc` element to enclose character content:

...which was `<rfc num="1489">`defined`</rfc>` in 1993.

which would give the following in HTML:

...which was
`<a href="ftp://ftp.rfc-editor.org/in-notes/rfc1489.txt">`defined`</a>`
in 1993.

Mnemonic addressing. Abbreviated addresses in your source XML must be unique only within your site, as opposed to URLs that are globally unique. This means you can make them easier to remember and more meaningful (to you) than are URLs. The abbreviated addresses are also completely devoid of irrelevant technical details and can be arbitrarily long (i.e., detailed and readable) or arbitrarily short (i.e., quick to type and quick to read).

3.5.3.1   Multiple abbreviation schemes

You can use as many independent abbreviation schemes as necessary. Each more or less complete and logical group of addresses can be served by its own abbreviation algorithm (and the corresponding resolver in the stylesheet). For example, links to an online dictionary or search engine might be abbreviated to just the word you want to look up; links to W3C standards can be represented by their unique identifiers as used by the W3C site (e.g., `xslt20` for XSLT 2.0, which unabbreviates into `http://www.w3.org/TR/xslt20/`). Any address domain whose URLs can be "losslessly compressed" into a shorter or easier-to-remember form is ripe for abbreviation.

With multiple abbreviation schemes, the stylesheet must be able to know which one to use for each link. This is where link types (**3.5.2**) are useful, distinguished by a classifier attribute value (`<link linktype="rfc" ...>`) or the element type (`<rfc ...>`) used for each link. It is natural to define abbreviation schemes on a per-link-type basis, or even to define link types based on the abbreviation schemes they are using.

Along with resolving the address, your stylesheet can perform other processing tasks, such as retrieving the title of the referenced RFC to be displayed in the link's floating tooltip. A Schematron schema for your source definition, in addition to performing link syntax validation, can also check for broken links (**5.1.3.3**). Another important advantage is that you can easily change all your RFC links from one RFC repository to another simply by editing the stylesheet.

3.5.3.2   Unabbreviation algorithms

To expand the abbreviated addresses, your stylesheet may use any sources of information, such as local or remote database queries or even web search. It's easiest, however, to create simple algorithmic abbreviations that map to the corresponding URLs through some calculations or string manipulations.

Thus, for external links, the most obvious and perhaps the only sensible abbreviation is dropping the protocol specification (usually `http://`) from the URLs. Even this simple provision can make address input somewhat easier by allowing you to type `www.kirsanov.com` instead of `http://www.kirsanov.com`.

Note, however, that in this case the stylesheet must be able to recognize the protocol part of an address and only add `http://` if it is missing. Addresses that already contain a protocol specification (be it `http://`, `https://`, or `ftp://`) must not be modified in any way.

3.5.3.3   Multicomponent abbreviations

An address abbreviation may contain more than one component. This is often necessary to link to scripts (as opposed to static pages) that require a number of parameters in the request URI. Some of these parameters (e.g., the partner's ID or formatting options) are static and can therefore be filled in by the stylesheet, but the key information pointers (e.g., the date and the number of the article within that date) must be present in the source of the linking page. Here's an example of a link with a multicomponent abbreviated address:

As `<foonews`
     `date="02-12-2003"`
     `num="6490">reported</foonews>` by FooBarNews...

which could be expanded into the HTML link:

As `<a`
`href="http://foonews.com/news?date=02-12-2003&num=6490">reported</a>`
by FooBarNews...

3.5.3.4   Internal links

One highly recommended abbreviation scheme that makes sense for almost any site is using page identifiers, defined in the master document, instead of pathnames[11] for internal links. This will make your site's structure much more flexible because you will be able to rename a page or move it around without changing all the other pages that link to it.[12]

Linking a foobar.   For example, suppose you have a page on your site describing a product called Foobar Plus. You don't want to spell out the complete pathname each time you link to that page, as it may be quite long (e.g., `/products/personal/foobar_plus`). Much more convenient would be using that page's unique (within your site) and easy-to-remember identifier. Since you don't, in all probability, have another Foobar Plus on your web site, it is natural to use an abbreviated name of the product as the identifier:

Check out our new `<int link="fb+">`Foobar Plus`</int>`!

The correspondence between web pages and their identifiers is to be set in the master document (**3.9.1.2**, page 129). Now it doesn't matter if your Foobar Plus page is moved, say, from `/products/personal/` `foobar_plus` to `/products/corporate/foobarplus`. All you need to do is change the reference in the master document and retransform all site pages.

....

11. Strictly speaking, HTML links to URIs, not pathnames, but links within a site almost always use relative or absolute pathnames (without a server part) that are also valid URIs.

12. Unfortunately, this only works for your own site. Visitors coming from another site linking to yours will still get a 404 for a moved page.

Aliases. To make life even easier for site maintainers, you can allow them to use any of a number of *aliases* referring to the same page. For example, the Foobar Plus page might just as well be linked to as `fb+`, `foobar+`, or `foobar-plus`. All you need to do is register all such aliases in the master document (see Example 3.2 on page 143).

Linking translations.   In multilingual sites, a special kind of link that must be present on every page is the link(s) to the other language version(s) of the same page. The absolute minimum of information needed to construct such a link is, obviously, the identifier of the language we are linking to. Thus, if we write on the Foobar Plus page

```
<lang link="de">This page in German</lang>
```

then the stylesheet will use the current page's pathname to construct the proper HTML link — for example,

```
<a href="/products/personal/foobar_plus.de.html">This
page in German</a>
```

or

```
<a href="/products/personal/foobar_plus.html?lang=de">This
page in German</a>
```

or any other variant, depending on your web site setup. Once again, the correspondence between languages and link URIs is deduced from the master document's data.

3.6 Images and objects

The majority of static images, Java applets, and Flash animations on web pages are not independent objects. Most often, they are components of higher-level content constructs. An image may be a visual accompanying a section heading, a background of a table or the entire page, or a navigation button that is part of a larger navigation system.

In all these cases, your source XML will not contain any image references at all: It is the stylesheet's responsibility to know what images to use with what content structures, where to take these images, and how to format them. Much less frequently, usually within text flow, you might need to display an image for its own sake — such as a photo, a technical illustration, or a map. It's only these standalone objects that you'll have to specify explicitly in the semantic XML source of a page.

This section covers both static images and various embedded objects such as Java applets, ActiveX controls, and Flash animations. All of these are similar from the viewpoint of XML source markup; below we talk mostly about images, but you should keep in mind that the same applies to most non-HTML external objects used on web pages.

Element type names. The name of the element type for including standalone images in your documents may be either generic (e.g., `image`) or specific (e.g., `map` or `portrait`). If you're only planning to use a few well-defined types of images in a few well-defined situations, you can use narrow and descriptive names for each type. Otherwise (or if you do not yet have any specific plans for the use of images at all), a generic `image` element would be just fine.

Images as attributes. An image object may be quite complex, with additional components, such as a photo caption or credit, stored in attributes or child elements. However, quite often all you need to specify is a source location or an identifier for an image that is an attribute of some other object rather than a standalone object in its own right. For the image types that can be used this way, you can use an attribute of the same name as the standalone image's element type. For example, if your `sections` may feature a photo next to the section's heading, it is more convenient to write

```
<section image="location">
<head>Section heading</head>
...
</section>
```

than to write

```
<section>
<image src="location"/>
<head>Section heading</head>
...
</section>
```

even though your stylesheet may be programmed to create identical formatting for these two inputs.

3.6.1   Abbreviating location

Just as a link's main attribute is the destination address, an image element must, before all, specify the location of the image resource. And, just as we used abbreviated addresses in links, it is natural to use mnemonic identifiers instead of complete image locations. For example, by writing

```
<image src="nymap"/>
```

instead of

```
<image src="img/maps/nymap.png"/>
```

you make your XML source more readable, easier to edit manually, and less prone to errors.

In the simplest case, an abbreviated image reference can be made from its filename by removing the path and extension (which is supposed to remain constant for all images). In more complex cases, an abbreviation might be composed of several parts expressed as attributes, such as a date or a classifier. Finally, your master document could simply store a list of all image locations associated with arbitrary identifiers and possibly aliases (compare **3.9.1**); in this case, all image references in your source will be completely independent of the corresponding locations or other image properties.

Abbreviating aggressively.   Along with stripping directory and extension, filename-based abbreviations can be made even more convenient by programming the stylesheet to perform case folding (converting everything to lower- or uppercase) and to remove all whitespace and punctuation. With these provisions, to reference `img/maps/nymap.png` in the above example, we could use any of `nymap`, `ny map`, `N.Y. Map`, and so on.

The goal of using abbreviations is to have your image references named intuitively and consistently and to provide just enough information in XML for the stylesheet to be able to reconstruct the complete pathname or URI.

3.6.2 Formatting hints

Standalone images may be particularly difficult to separate into independent aspects of content and formatting. The idea of specifying an image identifier and possibly its role in the XML source and then letting the stylesheet figure out all the formatting parameters is attractive, but the reality may be not so neat. Sometimes, you'll have no choice but to add ugly formatting clues to the XML source to get the correct rendition.

An example is a layout where several images are placed on a page, interspersed with text, and aligned alternately against the left or right margin. It is natural to have the stylesheet do the alternating alignment so that only the image identifiers need to be supplied in the source. However, sometimes you may want to force a particular image to a particular margin in the middle of a page. Adding `align="right"` to your XML source is hardly semantic but may be unavoidable if, for example, a left-aligned image visually conflicts with a nearby left-aligned heading.

Think ahead. It is much easier to prevent a disease than to cure it. Thus, it is preferable to design your page layout in such a way that it can be created strictly automatically based on nothing but the semantic XML source. Avoid situations where only manual interaction can produce acceptable formatting.

For example, if you plan to use alternating alignment of images, you could either use centered headings (which will not conflict with either image alignment) or mandate that any image be at least one paragraph away from the nearest heading (this restriction is easy to enforce automatically using Schematron).

Separate namespaces. However, there are situations where adding manual formatting hints to your XML source cannot be avoided. This may happen not only with images, although they are a frequent source of problems. It is advisable to use a separate namespace for all hints that pertain to the same output format (e.g., HTML):

```
<page xmlns:forhtml="http://www.kirsanov.com/formatting-hints-html">
  <p forhtml:column-break="true">
    ...
    <image src="solid wood table" forhtml:align="right"/>
    ...
  </p>
</page>
```

Here, a hint is added to the p element specifying that this paragraph must start a new column in a multicolumn layout (assuming the stylesheet cannot figure this out automatically). Another hint floats an image within that paragraph to the right margin.

Now, if you want to render the same XML source into a different format, such as PDF, the new stylesheet will have no problems ignoring anything from the "for HTML" namespace. It is also very easy to strip all HTML formatting hints to produce a purely semantic version of the source. You can store several sets of formatting hints in the same source documents, each in its own namespace, and have the stylesheet select the set corresponding to the current output format (such as "HTML with columns," "HTML without columns," "printable HTML," "PDF," etc.).

HTML documents often use the height and width attributes in img elements as spatial hints to speed up rendering of the page in a browser. You don't need to supply these values in XML; a stylesheet can find out the dimensions of all referenced images itself (**5.5.1**).

3.6.3   Image metadata

Besides the location (full or abbreviated) and possibly formatting hints, an image element may contain various other information.

Textual descriptions. The XHTML specification requires that each image be provided with a piece of text describing what the image is. Traditionally, the alt attribute of an img element has been used for short descriptions, but in HTML 4.01 and XHTML the longdesc ("long description") attribute was added to complement alt. Normally, an image description should contain:

- nothing (empty string) for purely decorative images (such as components of frames, backgrounds, and separators);

- the text visible on the image for images that display text (thus, the `alt` of a graphic button must contain exactly the button's label and nothing else);

- a short description of the image's role or content for meaningful images (e.g., `John's photo`).

It's only in the last of the above cases that the image description may need to be supplied in the XML source, preferably in the content of an image element (**2.3.3**). However, if your abbreviated image identifiers are sufficiently readable most of the time, you can save some typing and just reuse these unresolved identifiers (such as `NY map`) for `alt` values.

Captions. Often, a standalone image must be accompanied by a visible descriptive piece of text (as opposed to `alt` descriptions that are normally not shown by graphic browsers). This may be a caption, a photo credit, a copyright notice, or anything else that semantically belongs to this image.

Since this content may need further inline markup, it is better to store it in children of your image element rather than in attributes (**2.3.3**, page 79). The formatting of a caption or caption-like element is determined by the type of the parent image element, which in turn is evident either from its element type name or from the value of a classifier attribute. For example, a photo could be marked up as follows:

```
<photo src="sight">
  <caption>A rare sight.</caption>
  <credit>Dmitry Kirsanov</credit>
</photo>
```

Upon encountering a `photo` element, the stylesheet would expect to format its `caption` child element as a photo caption and the `credit` child element, if present, as credit (e.g., separately from the caption, in a smaller font size, and with "Photo by" prepended to the credit text).

3.6.4 Imagemaps and interactive objects

A simple linked image can be created by adding linking attributes (**3.5.1**) to the image element. Sometimes, however, you may need to create an imagemap where different regions of the image are linked to different destination addresses.

The quick-and-dirty approach. It is natural to reuse the generic link element type for specifying multiple links inside an imagemap, by placing link elements in the image and adding coordinate attributes to define the linked area:

```
<image src="chart 3">
  <link link="address1" shape="rect" x1="0" y1="0" x2="100" y2="20"/>
  <link link="address2" shape="circle" x="50" y="50" radius="5"/>
</image>
```

In HTML, all coordinates for an imagemap area are cramped into one comma-separated attribute value string. You don't need to reproduce that in your XML — instead, you can specify one value per attribute and use descriptive attribute names. It's a good idea to use your schema to check that the set of coordinate attributes in each link element corresponds to the value of shape.

The thoroughly semantic approach. The syntax shown above may work for an occasional imagemap, but it is still not semantic enough and needs to be improved if you routinely use imagemaps (or other interactive objects). Namely, do the pixel values in the link attributes really belong in the source? Probably not, as they are closely bound to the image's "presentation" and tell us nothing about its "content." A better approach is to use each link element to associate the *identifier* of an image area with a link address — for example,

```
<image src="chart 3">
  <link link="address1" area="block1"/>
  <link link="address2" area="central-blob"/>
</image>
```

The correspondence between the area identifiers (block1 and central-blob in this example) and the actual pixel coordinates may be stored in the site's master document. If, however, you want an imagemap to be truly orthogonal to everything else on the site and easily portable to other sites, consider creating a separate XML document for each imagemap storing its active areas and their identifiers.

Accessibility. Interactive objects such as Java applets and Flash movies may also incorporate multiple links (one example is an animated Flash menu). Even though you don't have to specify these links in the HTML code embedding the object, it still makes sense to list them in the XML source of a page so that the stylesheet can construct an alternative access mechanism for those users who cannot (or don't want to) peruse this interactive object.

3.7 Tables

Tables are perhaps the most abused feature of HTML, with the vast majority of tables on web pages being used for layout purposes, not for presenting inherently tabular data. If (like most web designers) you are going to use HTML tables for web page layout, you cannot reflect that in the semantic XML source of a page in any way. It's only the stylesheet that needs to be concerned with layout table construction.

Sometimes, however, you may have some genuinely tabular data that you want to format into some sort of a table on a web page. Still, this does not mean that you have to think in terms of rows and columns when creating a semantic source for such a table.

If you have something you can name, do it. For example, consider a sales data table listing sales figures for several products across several years. The XML way of marking up this data would be to forget that you're working on a table and simply list all available data in an appropriately constructed element tree:

```
<sales-table>
  <product>
    <name>Foobar</name>
    <sold><year>1999</year><number>123</number></sold>
    <sold><year>2000</year><number>140</number></sold>
    <sold><year>2001</year><number>142</number></sold>
  </product>
  <product>
    <name>Barfoo</name>
    <sold><year>1998</year><number>89</number></sold>
    <sold><year>1999</year><number>14</number></sold>
  </product>
</sales-table>
```

This approach frees you from worrying about column alignment, sort order, or empty cells — just dump all your data and you're done. All the rest will be performed automatically by the stylesheet: It can filter out a subset of the provided data, group values in rows and columns, sort them, and fill in "N/A" for missing values. Thus, the above example might come out as follows:

	1998	1999	2000	2001
Barfoo	89	14	N/A	N/A
Foobar	N/A	123	140	142

Tables from triplets. In some cases, such a data-centric approach may also make your source significantly more compact than the table rendition. Thus, a sparse table with mostly empty cells can be represented in the source by *triplets* consisting of a row name, a column name, and the corresponding value at their intersection. Since such a source does not contain separate lists of all columns and rows, the stylesheet will compile them from the triplets.

Is it worth it? Granted, for an occasional table or two, this may be too much work: You'll have to program your stylesheet to recognize various element types and perform various operations (such as normalizing dates) that may be necessary for your tabular data. For simple isolated tables, you may be better off more or less directly reproducing in XML the structure of the target HTML table. However, if you have a lot of simple tables (or a few complex ones) with similar data, or if your tables are updated often, the benefits of the semantic data-centric approach may easily outweigh the simplicity of the straightforward HTML imitation.

Also, the tabular data on your web site is likely to be coming from some external source, such as a database or a spreadsheet. When you write the code to update your tables automatically, it is usually much easier to first transform the external data into a semantic XML tree and then let the stylesheet do table layout.

3.8 **Forms**

Interactive elements in HTML are grouped into *forms*. Simple forms such as site search or email newsletter subscription are often used on many pages of the site, and your XML does not need to detail the structure of these forms. Instead, in your source you can treat such a form as an indivisible entity — for example, as a special type of orthogonal block (**3.1.2**) that can be inserted wherever a normal block is allowed.

Sometimes, even this is not required. For example, if *all* pages on your site contain a search field in the page footer, you don't need to mention it in the XML source at all. Your stylesheet will simply add this form to every page it produces, just as it adds all other page components that remain the same from page to page.

What if you need to build something more complex, such as a shipping address input form or a survey form? In these cases you'll need to create an appropriate element type for each variety of the form's input controls (such as text fields, radio buttons, and drop-down lists) as well as for any higher level semantic constructs within the form. This work can be made much easier by reusing some of the existing form vocabularies.

Existing vocabularies. An obvious choice for the existing vocabulary from which you could borrow form-related markup is XHTML, especially if it is your target vocabulary. The Forms module,[13] available

------

13. www.w3.org/TR/xhtml-modularization/abstract_modules.html#s_forms

starting from XHTML 1.1, may be a good first approximation. It covers many widget types and allows for proper logical structuring of your form.

However, in many cases the XHTML form markup may be too presentation-oriented to be useful for your semantic XML — or simply too awkward. This is mostly due to the historic baggage of older HTML versions. Modern HTML and XHTML had to pile their logical markup provisions on top of the old — limited and inflexible — form components.

For instance, in XHTML you have to write

```
<label for="firstname">First name:</label>
<input type="text" id="firstname"/>
```

instead of the more natural

```
<textfield id="firstname">
  <label>First name:</label>
</textfield>
```

HTML 4.0 *had* to define a separate `label` element that is linked to its `input` by a `for` attribute simply because it had to stay compatible with older HTML versions that did not allow any children in an `input`.

In your source definition, you are free from these concerns and can therefore mark up your forms in a more logical and readable way. It is also important that your own markup may be better integrated with other parts of the system; for example, you could use an abbreviation (**3.5.3**) for the form submission address.

Another existing vocabulary worth looking at is XForms,[14] recently developed by the W3C (see **6.1.3.1** for an XForms example). This is a modern XML-based processing framework that defines not only forms markup but data submission and processing as well. Compared to XHTML forms, XForms markup is more logical and presentation-independent (for example, one form can be rendered both visually in

---

14. www.w3.org/MarkUp/Forms/

a graphical browser and aurally by a speech browser). Once again, your choice between borrowing XForms markup or developing your own should depend on the complexity of your forms and their relative importance in the project.

Formatting hints. Form presentation is a difficult task. Even with full manual control, it's not always easy to lay out a form so that it looks perfect and remains usable for any data that may be filled into it. Even more difficult is to automate form layout, enabling the stylesheet to consistently build good-looking form pages from the semantic description of the forms' structure. To add insult to injury, different browsers on different platforms often render form controls in wildly different ways.

The key is keeping the layout simple and flexible. Don't strive for precise placement or alignment of controls, as this is impossible to achieve given the vastly different font and screen sizes in browsers. (Also, do not tie the position of other parts of the page to the size or placement of a form — this often results in a broken page layout.) Take advantage of the form structure described in the source by separating groups of form controls into independent layout blocks.

All that said, adding formatting hints (**3.6.2**) to control form layout may turn out inevitable. The most common case is specifying the size of text input fields.[15] If you think you need something more elaborate than that, it is usually an indication that you should try instead to simplify your form's presentation (or your page design in general).

3.9 **Master document**

In the previous chapter (**2.1.2.1**, page 49), we found that any web site consisting of more than one page must have a master document providing shared content and a site directory. In this section, we'll look at some practical examples of constructs in a typical web site's master document.

---

15. It might be argued that the size of an input field is one of its essential semantic aspects and not a superficial formatting property.

You may find the sample master document described here (see Example 3.2, page 143, for a complete listing) somewhat eclectic. This eclecticism, however, stems from the real-world practice of XML web sites. In fact, the master document is more of a database than a document (**1.2**). The layout of components in this database is rarely important, as they are not processed sequentially but accessed in arbitrary order. For lots of ideas on how to access and use the master document content from the stylesheet, see Chapter 5.

A master document represents a new document type, with its root element type different from that of a page document, and most other element types usable only in a master document. However, if you don't use DTDs (**2.2.4**) or XSDL, this distinction has little practical value, and you can use one schema to validate all of your XML (both page documents and the master document). Such a schema written in Schematron is shown in Example 3.3, page 149 (see also **5.1.3** for advanced Schematron checks).

3.9.1 Site structure

The role of the master document is that of a hub that all other documents refer to when they need to figure out a wider context of the web site or establish mutual links. Whenever the stylesheet needs some information that is not supplied by the currently processed document, it will consult the master document to find either that information or a link to it.

Therefore, the most important part of a master document is the *site directory* — a collection of information about all pages of the site and their organization. This directory is used for building the site's navigation as well as for resolving abbreviated internal links (**3.5.3**).

Besides pages, other components of the site may also be mentioned in the master document, such as all Flash animations you have or all images of a specific kind used on the site. Units of orthogonal content must be listed in the master document as well (**3.9.1.3**) so that pages can reference and incorporate them. Finally, sources of dynamic content must be registered for the stylesheet to know what to insert into static page templates (**3.9.1.4**).

3.9.1.1   Menu structure

A flat list of all pages is not sufficient for building a usable site. We also need to represent the structure of the site's menu and the correspondence between menu items and pages.

A simple site's menu may be little more than a linear list of links to each of its pages. However, most sites require more complex menu structures. Common are hierarchical menus where some of the top-level items encompass multiple subpages and/or nested submenus. Such a structure is straightforward to express in XML.

Some sites may have more than one menu. For example, there may be a menu of *topics* (content sections) and another independent menu of *tools* (pages that help navigate the site, such as search and site map). Such orthogonal menu hierarchies can be stored in independent XML subtrees within the master document.

3.9.1.2   Menu items and pages

What do we need to store in the master document for each menu item? To build a clickable menu element, we must know at least its label (the visible text displayed in the menu) and the page that it is linked to. A label may contain inline markup and should therefore be stored in a child element. As for the link, it is natural to use the general linking attributes with abbreviated addresses that we've developed for in-flow links on site pages (**3.5.1**).

Items vs. pages.   A menu item is not the same as a page of the site. Some pages may not be available through the menu, while others may be linked from more than one menu item. Therefore, the page itself must be represented by a separate element that the menu item element will link to.

However, that does not mean that these page elements must be stored in a different part of the master document. You can still categorize all your pages under the branches of the menu tree: Even if a page is not *linked* from the menu, usually you can find a branch where it logically *belongs* (unless it is orthogonal content, **3.9.1.3**). The stylesheet will thus be able to read the menu structure both hierarchically (when looking for menu items) and sequentially (when looking for pages).

Here's a possible representation of a menu item:

```
<item link="products">
  <label>Products</label>
  <page id="products" title="Our products"
      src="products/"/>
  <page id="software" title="Our software"
      src="products/software/"/>
  <page id="hardware" title="Our hardware"
      src="products/hardware"/>
</item>
```

In addition to a `label` and one or more `page`s, an `item` may also contain other `item` children. A complete menu description would thus consist of a hierarchy of `item`s under one parent, e.g. `menu`. Note that in each `page` element, the `id` attribute provides a unique identifier of not only that element, but of the page itself. It is these identifiers that are used as abbreviated addresses (**3.5.3**) in internal links.

How unabbreviation works.   When resolving a link, the stylesheet translates the page identifier into the location of that page taken from the `src` attribute. However, that attribute's value is also somewhat "abbreviated" in that it omits irrelevant technical information such as the filename extension and the default filename (usually `index.html`) in a directory. These omitted parts are easy to restore by applying simple rules, so the three `page` elements in the above example would yield these page locations:

```
/products/index.html
/products/software/index.html
/products/hardware.html
```

Note that a location ending with a "/" is considered a directory and has "`index.html`" appended; other locations only receive the "`.html`" extension.

Accessing the source.   There is one more reason to store page pathnames without extensions. When locations are resolved for the purpose of accessing the source XML documents rather than creating an HTML link, the same `src` values are transformed into `*.xml` file locations (assuming the directory structure of the site source is similar to that of the transformed site, **3.9.3**). For stylesheet code examples to access this menu structure, see Chapter 5 (**5.1.1**, **5.7**).

Storing page metadata. Sometimes, a more complex layout for the `page` elements may be necessary. For example, if your bilingual site provides two language versions of each page, a `page` element could hold both metadata that is common to all language versions of the page (e.g., the page's identifier and source location) and language-specific metadata (e.g., title):

```
<page id="software" src="products/software/">
  <translation lang="en">Our software</translation>
  <translation lang="fr">Nos logiciels</translation>
</page>
```

Some of the metadata (**3.1.1**) may also be moved from page documents into the master document for convenient access. For example, if you want to control which pages of the site are to be seen by search engine spiders and which are hidden from them, you could add a corresponding value to each page's source document. However, since this information will be pulled from all pages of the site simultaneously, it is more convenient to add a spider control attribute to the `page` element in the master document. This way, the stylesheet will be able to produce a site-wide `robots.txt` file for external spiders and/or a configuration update for a local search engine spider without accessing all page documents.

3.9.1.3 Orthogonal content

Along with all pages, a master document should also list all the units of orthogonal content that your site will use (**2.1.2.2**, page 51). However, unlike pages, orthogonal content references cannot be categorized under the menu hierarchy (that is why this content is *orthogonal*, after all). You'll need to create a separate construct to associate orthogonal content identifiers with corresponding (abbreviated) source locations — for example,

```
<blocks>
  <block id="news" src="news/latest"/>
  <block id="subscribe" src="scripts/subscribe"/>
  <block id="donate" src="scripts/donate"/>
</blocks>
```

Now if the stylesheet processing a page document encounters a `block` that has no content of its own but references some orthogonal content unit — for example, by specifying `idref="news"` — the document at `news/latest.xml` will be retrieved and inserted into the current document, formatted as appropriate for an orthogonal content block.

It is important that the `id` and `src` attributes of a master document's `block` element have the same names and semantics as the attributes of `page` elements (**3.9.1.2**). We will use this when writing stylesheet code to unabbreviate links or search through all pages of the site (Chapter 5), since every page must be registered as either a `page` in the menu or a source of an orthogonal `block` (or both).

Extracting orthogonal content.   In the last example, each orthogonal block was stored in its own file — but this is not always the best approach. You may want to reuse parts of regular pages as orthogonal content.

For instance, the news page of a site is often a list of news items in reverse chronological order. You may want to automatically extract the most recent news item and display it in an orthogonal content block on other pages of the site. Another example is a "featured product" blurb extracted from that product's own page and reused on the front page of the site.

For these situations, what we need is a way to specify what part of the original page document is to be reused as orthogonal content on other pages. Since this part will most likely also be a `block`, we only need to indicate the `id` of the block we are interested in. Thus, if the most recent news `block` on the news page always has `id="last"`, we could write in the master document:

```
<block id="last-news" src="news/" select="last"/>
```

Now any page can place a copy of the latest news item by referencing the corresponding orthogonal block by its identifier, `last-news`. For example, your page document might contain

```
<block idref="last-news"/>
```

Likewise, the featured product blurb could be extracted from the `block` with `id="blurb"` on that product's page:

```
<block id="feature" src="products/foobar" select="blurb"/>
```

Here, the featured product is identified by the path to the corresponding document (`products/foobar.xml`). When you want to feature a different product, all you need to do is change this value so it points to another product's page (assuming each product page has exactly one `block` with `id="blurb"`; see also **5.1.3.7**). After that, all pages that use

```
<block idref="feature"/>
```

will (after you rerun the transformation) display the blurb for the new product.

Logically, without the `select` attribute, a master document's `block` will reference the entire content of the document pointed to by the `src` attribute. Your Schematron schema could also check that the referenced elements actually exist in the referenced documents (see **5.3.3.1**, page 224 for how to code this).

No perfection in this world. It would be even more natural to use XPath expressions for extracting orthogonal blocks. Then we could use not only the `id` attribute value but any XPath test for identifying the block we need. For instance, for the first `block` on the page, we would write

```
<block id="news" src="news/" xpath="//block[1]"/>
```

Selecting the last `block` that has a `section` inside would be as simple as

```
<block id="lastsection" src="dir/page"
    xpath="//block[section][last()]"/>
```

There's only one problem with this kind of selector: In XSLT, you can't take a string and treat it as an XPath expression — and what the master document (or any other document) stores in its attributes is always just strings from the XSLT processor viewpoint.

Saxon offers the `saxon:evaluate()` extension function (**4.4.2.1**) that might save the idea, but its implementation is quite limited, not to mention non-portable to other XSLT processors. Much better is the `dyn:evaluate()` function[16] from EXSLT (**4.4.1**) which is currently supported by several processors but not by Saxon.

3.9.1.4   Registering dynamic content

Recall our discussion of dynamic sites in **1.5**. We found that a dynamic web page is produced from two main parts — static templates and dynamic values — and that both can (and should) use XML markup. It's now time to see how these concepts fit into the source definition we are building.

One way of many.   There exist different ways to aggregate dynamic content and static templates. Some of them come before XSLT transformation, which is usually the last stage in a dynamic XML web site workflow; in these cases, you don't need any special source markup because your stylesheet will get complete seamless page source with both static and dynamic content. However, in some situations (notably offline XSLT processing, **1.4.1**) implementing dynamic content aggregation in XSLT is convenient. This section shows one approach to organizing such transformation-time incorporation of dynamic content.

Reusing blocks.   An orthogonal content block that the stylesheet extracts from another document may be considered a special case of a composite dynamic value. Therefore, it makes sense to extend our blocks' markup constructs so that they cover the "truly dynamic" content as well — content that is calculated or compiled by some external process and not just stored in a static document.

We can define a number of block conventions that will allow us to use blocks not only for enveloping independent bits of content but also as links to external sources of information. Once again, our guiding principle is: Let the page author use short mnemonic identifiers and hide all the gory details of accessing data in the master document and/or stylesheet.

---

16. `www.exslt.org/dyn/functions/evaluate`

Calling a process.   Suppose we want to build a site map page that automatically compiles a hierarchical list of all pages of the site. The first thing we need is the static part of that page — a document that stores all the static bits unique to the page, such as an introductory paragraph and heading(s). This is a normal page that is listed in the menu hierarchy in the master, just like any other page.

Wherever we want to insert our dynamic content into that static frame, we place a block reference, e.g.:

```
<block idref="sitemap"/>
```

In the master, however, we cannot associate the sitemap identifier with any source file, since no such file exists — the list of pages is generated dynamically.

Instead, we must associate our dynamic block identifier (sitemap) with an identifier of some abstract *process* that generates its data. You can think of a process as a kind of a script or application; it may accept some parameters that affect its output. Thus, if we write in the master document (within the same blocks envelope used for orthogonal blocks)

```
<block-process id="sitemap" process="sitemap" mode="text" depth="2"/>
```

then the stylesheet will know that a sitemap block needs to be filled in with data generated by the sitemap process with parameters mode="text" and depth="2". This process can be, for example, a callable template within the stylesheet (**4.5.1**) or an external program. With this approach, document authors don't need to know anything about processes or parameters; they use identifiers to refer to data sources, and the master document associates each source with a process and its set of parameters.

Watching a directory.   A stylesheet can access external files even if the list of these files is changing dynamically. For example, an external process (which may or may not be another stylesheet) might be dropping its output XML documents into a directory. Your stylesheet would then read the list of files in that directory (**5.3.2**) and do what it pleases with their content — such as dump all available content from all files into one page or perform some elaborate selection, filtering, or rotation.

If, for example, your stylesheet implements a `list-titles` process that takes a directory as a parameter and returns the list of `title` elements from all XML documents in the directory, then you could define a block to perform this operation on all (dynamically updated) documents in the `news` directory by writing in the master document

```
<block-process id="news-list" process="list-titles" dir="news/"/>
```

In a page document that wants to use this list, you would then write simply

```
<block idref="news-list"/>
```

XML, not HTML. Note that processes similar to `sitemap` or `list-titles` should only aggregate content, not format it. This means that the corresponding templates or functions in your stylesheet must produce valid XML data (nodesets), not HTML renditions. You would then feed these nodesets to the regular formatting templates in the same stylesheet (see **5.3.3.1** for ideas on how to chain templates together). If a process is implemented as an external program, it should return serialized XML data or plain text that the stylesheet will be able to convert to nodesets.

3.9.2 Common content and site metadata

On a typical web site, all pages contain bits of information that either remain the same or change predictably from page to page. Some of this repeating data, such as the company logo or tag line, actually belongs to the domain of presentation rather than content and therefore needs to be filled in by the stylesheet rather than stored in the source. Other components, such as webmaster email links, "designed by" signatures, copyright or legal notices, etc., are natural to store in the master document.

It is recommended that you envelop all such bits of content in one or more umbrella elements, each containing data with similar roles or positions on the pages. Here's a master document fragment defining the footer to be placed at the bottom of each page:

```
<page-footer>
  <designed-by>Site design: <ext link="www.kirsanov.com">Dmitry
  Kirsanov Studio</ext></designed-by>
  <legal linktype="internal" link="legal">Legal notices</legal>
  <contact linktype="internal" link="contact">Contact us</contact>
</page-footer>
```

Note that the elements inside `page-footer` may have mixed content with any of the text markup, linking, or other elements that were developed for page documents. In particular, we see internal and external links used in this example, each with its own address abbreviation scheme (**3.5.3**).

The `page-footer` parent element makes the stylesheet simpler and more bulletproof: Instead of providing templates for each of the individual footer elements, you can program the stylesheet to process all items within a `page-footer` in turn, and only provide separate templates for those that differ from others in formatting. With this approach, you'll be able to add a new element type for a new footer object even without changing the stylesheet.

Similarly, we can create an envelope for storing metadata that applies to the entire site. Examples of such metadata include site-wide keyword lists (which could be merged with page-specific keywords supplied by the page documents, **3.1.1**) and extended credits (which could be put in comments in the HTML code of the site's front page).

3.9.3 Processing parameters

Your stylesheet will need to know some parameters of the environment in which it is run as well as the environment where its HTML output will be placed. The most frequently required processing parameter is the base URI that the stylesheet will prepend to all the image and link pathnames. By changing this parameter, you can turn all internal link URIs from relative to absolute with an arbitrary base, which is useful for testing the site in different environments. Other parameters may provide the path to the source tree and the operating system under which the stylesheet is run (which, in turn, may affect the syntax of pathnames).

Grouping parameters into environments. It is important that the same set of source files may be processed on different computers — for example, on a developer's personal system, then in a temporary (staging) location on the server, and finally in the publicly accessible area on the target server. Each of these environments will require its own set of processing parameters. It is therefore convenient to define several groups of parameter values, one for each environment, and select only one of the groups by its identifier when running the transformation.

Where to store the environment groups? Obviously, the need to group parameters and assign a unique identifier to each group makes using XML very convenient — as opposed to, say, storing the values within scripts used to run the site build process (**6.5.1**). Note also that scripts are the most OS-dependent part of the site setup, so it is best to keep them as simple and therefore as portable as possible. And of all the XML documents of a web site, the two most likely choices are the XSLT stylesheet and the master document.

Your stylesheet is more likely to be shared (in whole or in part) among different projects, so it is not wise to use it for storing information that is too project-specific. Also, even though you can use XSLT variables for storing processing parameters, it is more convenient to use custom element hierarchies for structuring and accessing this data. For these reasons, the master document emerges as the most natural storage for processing parameters.

This does not mean that your master document will differ among environments. Instead, all identical copies of it will have information on all environments, and each environment will extract the relevant set of data by passing a parameter to the stylesheet.

Here's an example group of parameters that define the processing environment called `staging` (see **3.10.2** for the meanings of the elements):

```
<environment id="staging">
  <os>Linux</os>
  <src-path>/var/website/src/</src-path>
  <out-path>/var/website/out/</out-path>
  <target-path>/test/</target-path>
  <img-path>img</img-path>
</environment>
```

3.9.4 Site-wide content and formatting

Normally, formatting of web pages is created by the stylesheet. Sometimes, however, formatting is dependent on certain parameters that, being more content than style, belong in the site's source and not in the stylesheet. Also, sometimes the stylesheet may need to create objects that are used on many pages but do not belong to any one page in particular. In both these situations, the master document is a convenient place to store data.

Site-wide buttons.   An example of such an object is a pair of graphic buttons — "next" and "prev" — used on sequential pages (such as chapters in an online book). If your stylesheet generates other graphic buttons on the site (**5.5.2**), design consistency and maintainability will be much better if *all* buttons are done in the same way.

These buttons are not specific to any particular page; moreover, pages that use them don't even need to mention the buttons in the source because the stylesheet can automatically create the page sequence, including appropriate navigation. All we need is to store the button labels somewhere so the stylesheet can generate the buttons. It makes sense to use the master document for this.

You can store the button labels in a separate element in the master and program the stylesheet to regenerate the buttons when run with the corresponding parameter. For example,

```
<buttons>
  <button>prev</button>
  <button>next</button>
</buttons>
```

3.10 **Summary examples**

This section presents examples of complete documents that bring to-gether everything we've discussed in the last two chapters (and more). The content is fictitious, but the structure and markup are from real web site projects (somewhat abridged for readability).

3.10.1 Page document

Compared to the master document example (**3.10.2**), the page docu-ment in Example 3.1 is short and simple. This is, in fact, what you should strive for in your project. Page documents are the primary work area for those who will update and maintain the site, so the layout of a page document must be as simple and self-evident as possible. (For instance: Do we need indentation in page documents? Probably not, unless it is taken care of automatically.)

The main rule of thumb is: If you can move a bit of information away from a page document to the master or to the stylesheet, do that.

3.10.2 Master document

Example 3.2 shows a master document that compiles most of the data we discussed in **3.9** but adds a few new twists.

Languages. Our example site is bilingual (English and German), so all titles and labels are provided in two languages, and the languages themselves are listed in a `languages` element. We add an internal DTD subset with mnemonic entity references (**2.2.4.3**) for German characters.

Environments. For every installation where the site can be built, an `environment` element with a unique `id` supplies the following information:

- `src-path` is the base directory of the XML source documents tree.

. . . .

Example 3.1   `en/team/index.xml`: A page document.

```
<?xml version="1.0" encoding="us-ascii"?>
<page keywords="team, people, staff, competences, skills">

<title>Our team</title>

<!-- Main content block: -->
<block type="body">
<p>With backgrounds in technology and communications, FooBar's
experienced management team has - you guessed it -
<em>the right combination of skills for success</em>.</p>

<section image="mike">
<head>Mike M. Anager</head>
<subhead>CEO</subhead>
<p>CEO and Co-Founder, Mike leads FooBar towards bringing the vision
of "personal foobar" to reality. He previously served as Chief
Architect at <ext link="www.barfoo.com">BarFoo Corporation</ext>.</p>
</section>

<section image="ed">
<head>Ed N. Gineer</head>
<subhead>VP, Engineering</subhead>
<p>Ed has over 30 years of foobar design experience under his
belt. He has personally contributed to the most acclaimed of
our <int link="solutions">products</int>, including the famous
<int link="fbplus">Foobar Plus</int>.</p>
</section>

<section image="jack">
<head>Jack J. Anitor</head>
<subhead>Senior Janitor</subhead>
<p>Jack's expert janitorial skills and experience have been
critical in the success of FooBar.</p>
</section>
</block>

<!-- Orthogonal content blocks: -->
<block idref="subscribe"/>
<block idref="feature"/>

</page>
```

. . . .

- out-path is the directory where the output files will be placed (used in batch mode, **5.6**). It is also assumed that the images subdirectory (img-path) is under out-path.

- img-path is where all the images (both static and generated) are stored. This path is relative to out-path.

- target-path is the common part of all URIs used in the resulting HTML files to refer to images or other pages of the site. Thus, if you transform and view your pages locally at out-path, then target-path may be the same as out-path. If, however, you are going to upload the transformed site to a directory on a web server and access it at, say, http://www.example.org/test/, then target-path may be either /test/ (for absolute pathnames starting with /) or an empty string (for relative pathnames).

On Windows, all absolute paths must be given in the file:/ URL format.[17] This is the only standard and reliable way to represent an absolute pathname that includes a drive letter. In HTML, URLs with file:/ work for both links and image references in all browsers we tested. Other platforms may use absolute pathnames without the file:/.

Menu. The menu lists all the pages of the site. For each page, the src attribute contains the page's pathname (add .xml for source files or .html for output files) relative to the site's root directory.

Each page has an id attribute used to link to it. To make life easier, you can also provide a space-separated list of aliases in the alias attribute. In internal links to this page, you can use either its id or any of the aliases.

Each menu item has a label child storing the item's visible label. In the menu on a web page, each item is supposed to be linked to its first page child, so there's no need to specify a link in an item.

---

17. The single slash character in this URL means that the file is available locally and not on a network host.

It is assumed that the English and German versions of the source files are named the same but stored in different directory trees under the root directory. The corresponding directories are named after the language designations defined in `languages`. So, for instance, the complete path to the German `fbplus` source page in the `staging` environment would be constructed as follows:

`/home/d/web/de/solutions/foobar_plus.xml`

Blocks. The `blocks` element holds a list of orthogonal content blocks with their identifiers (`id`), source document locations (`src`), and block selectors (`select`, **3.9.1.3**). Note that the `subscribe` page is listed only once as an orthogonal source, while the `solutions/foobar_plus` page is both in the menu and in the `blocks` list. For this reason, a `block` must specify a complete location for the orthogonal content source and not just its `id`, as all other links do, because not all orthogonal documents are registered in the menu and assigned an `id`.

Misc. Finally, the master document lists the common part to be prepended to page titles (**3.2.4**) on all pages (`html-title`), page footer content (`page-footer`), and two labels for buttons that need to be created by the stylesheet (`buttons`).

Note that the `mailto` links used in `page-footer` represent a special link type (**3.5.2**, page 109) with an abbreviated address (the corresponding resolved URI will have `mailto:` prepended to the email address).

. . . .

Example 3.2   `_master.xml`: The master document.

```
<?xml version="1.0" encoding="utf-8"?>
<!DOCTYPE site [
  <!ENTITY auml "&#228;">
  <!ENTITY ouml "&#246;">
  <!ENTITY uuml "&#252;">
]>
```

```
<site>

  <!-- Environments: -->
  <environment id="local">
    <os>Windows</os>
    <src-path>file:/C:/Work/Website/XML/</src-path>
    <out-path>file:/C:/Work/Website/Out/</out-path>
    <target-path>file:/C:/Work/Website/Out/</target-path>
    <img-path>Images</img-path>
  </environment>
  <environment id="staging">
    <os>Linux</os>
    <src-path>/home/d/web/</src-path>
    <out-path>/home/d/web/out/</out-path>
    <target-path>/</target-path>
    <img-path>img</img-path>
  </environment>
  <environment id="final">
    <os>BSD</os>
    <src-path>/var/tomcat/webapps/cocoon/foobar/</src-path>
    <out-path>/var/tomcat/webapps/cocoon/foobar/</out-path>
    <target-path>/cocoon/foobar/</target-path>
    <img-path>img</img-path>
  </environment>

  <!-- Languages: -->
  <languages>
    <lang>en</lang>
    <lang>de</lang>
  </languages>

  <!-- Menu: -->
  <menu>
    <item>
      <label>
        <translation lang="en">Home</translation>
        <translation lang="de">Home</translation>
      </label>
      <page id="home" alias="index front fp frontpage" src="index"/>
    </item>
```

```
<item>
  <label>
    <translation lang="en">Solutions</translation>
    <translation lang="de">L&ouml;sungen</translation>
  </label>
  <page id="solutions" src="solutions/intro_solutions"/>
  <item>
    <label>
      <translation lang="en">Life</translation>
      <translation lang="de">Das Leben</translation>
    </label>
    <page id="life" src="solutions/life"/>
    <page id="fbplus" alias="foobar_plus fb+ foobar+"
        src="solutions/foobar_plus"/>
    <page id="fbminus" src="solutions/foobar_minus"/>
  </item>
  <page id="universe" src="solutions/universe"/>
  <page id="everything" src="solutions/everything"/>
</item>
<item>
  <label>
    <translation lang="en">Our team</translation>
    <translation lang="de">Unser Team</translation>
  </label>
  <page id="team" src="team/index"/>
  <page id="history" src="team/history"/>
  <page id="hire" src="team/hire"/>
</item>
<item>
  <label>
    <translation lang="en">Contact</translation>
    <translation lang="de">Kontakt</translation>
  </label>
  <page id="contact" src="contact/contact"/>
  <page id="map" src="contact/map"/>
</item>
</menu>
```

```
<!-- Orthogonal and dynamic blocks: -->
<blocks>
  <!-- Extract the 'summary' block from the product page: -->
  <block id="feature" src="solutions/foobar_plus"
     select="summary"/>
  <!-- Extract the 'last' block from the front page: -->
  <block id="news" src="index" select="last"/>
  <!-- Take the entire subscribe.xml: -->
  <block id="subscribe" src="subscribe"/>
  <!-- Run site map generation: -->
  <block-process id="sitemap" process="sitemap"
     mode="text" depth="2"/>
  <!-- Run list-titles on all files in news/: -->
  <block-process id="news-list" process="list-titles"
     dir="news/"/>
</blocks>

<!-- The common part of the page titles: -->
<html-title>
  <translation lang="en">Foobar Corporation AG</translation>
  <translation lang="de">Foobar Corporation AG</translation>
</html-title>

<!-- Page footer content: -->
<page-footer>
  <copyright>
    <translation lang="en">&#169; 2003 by Foobar Corporation AG.
      All rights reserved.</translation>
    <translation lang="de">&#169; 2003 by Foobar Corporation AG.
      All rights reserved.</translation>
  </copyright>

  <language-switch>
    <translation lang="en">
      <lang link="de">Diese Seite in deutsch</lang>
    </translation>
    <translation lang="de">
      <lang link="en">This page in English</lang>
    </translation>
  </language-switch>
```

```
<contact-webmaster>
  <translation lang="en">
    Problems using this site? Contact the
    <mailto link="webmaster@foobar.com">Webmaster</mailto>.
  </translation>
  <translation lang="de">
    Probleme mit dieser Web-Site? Kontaktieren Sie bitte unseren
    <mailto link="webmaster@foobar.com">Webmaster</mailto>.
  </translation>
</contact-webmaster>
</page-footer>

<!-- Sequence navigation buttons: -->
<buttons>
  <button id="prev">
    <translation lang="en">prev</translation>
    <translation lang="de">zur&uuml;ck</translation>
  </button>
  <button id="next">
    <translation lang="en">next</translation>
    <translation lang="de">vorw&auml;rts</translation>
  </button>
</buttons>

</site>
```

. . . .

3.10.3   Schematron schema

The schema in Example 3.3 is used to validate both the master document and page documents of our Foobar site. This makes sense because these document types have a lot in common. Still, for readability the schema is broken into three `patterns`: One tests the master document, another tests page documents, and the last one tests constructs that occur in both document types (this includes links, images, and text markup).

Languages.   The `lang-check` abstract rule checks that the element being checked contains exactly as many `translation` children as there are languages defined in the `languages` element. This rule can then be reused for any element that provides information in two languages. A separate rule with `context="translation"` additionally checks that the `lang` attributes correspond to the defined languages and that each language version is provided only once.

Element presence. In this schema, many element-presence checks are lumped together for simplicity (e.g., all children of an `environment` are checked in one `assert`). This does not have to be that way; if you want your schema to be really helpful, you can write a separate check with its own diagnostic message for each element type, explaining its role and the possible consequences of its being missing from the source.

Context-sensitive checks. Note that there are two different `page` element types: One is used in the master document, and the other is the root element type in a page document. The same applies to `blocks`. The schema, however, has no problems differentiating between these element types based on the context.

Reporting unknowns. One function of a schema is to check for unknown element type names (most often resulting from typos). In Schematron, this can be implemented by providing a dummy `rule` with no tests, listing all defined element types as possible contexts. Following that, a rule with `context="*"` signals error whenever the rule is activated. This technique is possible because each context will only match one rule per pattern; if an element was not matched by the dummy rule, it is caught by the next rule and reported as unrecognized.

It's only a beginning. This example schema demonstrates only the basic, most critical checks. Your own schema may be significantly larger and more detailed than this, although it will likely use mostly the same techniques. Consider this schema a phrasebook with common expressions for typical situations. Several advanced tricks for validating complex constraints are discussed in Chapter 5 (**5.1.3**).

. . . .

Example 3.3   `schema.sch`: A Schematron schema for validating page documents and the master document.

```
<schema xmlns="http://www.ascc.net/xml/schematron">

<!-- Checks for the master document: -->
<pattern name="master">

<rule context="site">
  <report test="count(//environment) = 1">
    Only one 'environment' found; you will need to create more if you
    want to build the site in a different environment.
  </report>
  <report test="count(//environment) = 0">
    No 'environment' elements found; the stylesheet will be unable to
    figure out pathnames.
  </report>
  <assert test="languages and menu and html-title and page-footer
                          and blocks">
    One of the required elements not found inside 'site'.
  </assert>
</rule>

<rule context="page-footer">
  <assert test="copyright and language-switch
                          and contact-webmaster">
    One of the required elements not found inside 'page-footer'.
  </assert>
</rule>

<rule context="environment">
  <assert test="src-path and out-path
                  and target-path and img-path and os">
    One of the required elements not found inside 'environment'.
  </assert>
  <assert test="@id">
    An 'environment' must have an 'id' attribute.
  </assert>
  <assert test="count(//environment/@id[. = current()/@id]) = 1">
    The 'id' attribute value of an 'environment' must be unique.
  </assert>
</rule>
```

```
<rule context="src-path | img-path | out-path | target-path">
  <report test="*">
    The '<name/>' element cannot have children.
  </report>
  <report test="(normalize-space(.) = ''
                 and not(name() = 'target-path')">
    The '<name/>' element cannot be empty.
  </report>
</rule>

<rule context="languages">
  <assert test="count(lang) = count (*)">
    The 'languages' element can only have 'lang' children.
  </assert>
  <assert test="count(lang) &gt; 0">
    The 'languages' element must have at least one 'lang' child.
  </assert>
</rule>

<rule context="languages/lang">
  <assert test="count(//languages/lang[. = current()]) = 1">
    Each language must be specified only once.
  </assert>
</rule>

<rule context="menu">
  <assert test="count(item) = count (*)">
    The 'menu' element cannot contain elements other than 'item'.
  </assert>
</rule>

<rule context="item">
  <assert test="label" diagnostics="label-element">
    A 'label' element is missing.
  </assert>
  <report test="count(label) &gt; 1" diagnostics="label-element">
    There is an extra 'label' element.
  </report>
  <assert test="page">
    At least one 'page' element should be specified within an 'item'.
  </assert>
</rule>
```

```
<rule context="menu//page">
  <assert test="@src">
    Each 'page' must have an 'src' attribute.
  </assert>
  <assert test="@id">
    Each 'page' must have a unique 'id' attribute.
  </assert>
  <assert test="count(//page/@id[. = current()/@id]) = 1">
    The 'id' attribute value of a 'page' must be unique.
  </assert>
</rule>

<!-- Abstract rule to check 'transformation' children: -->
<rule abstract="true" id="lang-check">
  <assert test="count(translation) = count(//languages/lang)">
    The number of 'translation' children in '<name/>' must correspond
    to the number of defined languages. If this element does not
    exist in one of the languages, use an empty 'translation' element.
  </assert>
  <assert test="count(translation) = count(*)">
    There must be no child elements here other than 'translation'.
  </assert>
</rule>

<!-- Applying the abstract rule to all bilingual elements: -->
<rule context="label | html-title | copyright
               | language-switch | contact-webmaster | button">
  <extends rule="lang-check"/>
</rule>

<rule context="translation">
  <assert test="@lang">
    Each 'translation' must have a 'lang' attribute.
  </assert>
  <assert test="@lang = //languages/lang/text()">
    The value of the 'lang' attribute must correspond to one of the
    defined languages.
  </assert>
  <report test="@lang = preceding-sibling::translation/@lang">
    There is another 'translation' element under this parent with the
    same value of the 'lang' attribute.
  </report>
</rule>
```

```
<rule context="blocks">
  <report test="*[not(self::block or self::block-process)]">
    A 'blocks' element must only contain one or more 'block' or
    'block-process' elements.
  </report>
</rule>

<rule context="blocks/block">
  <assert test="@id and @src">
    A 'block' defined in the master document must have both 'id' and
    'src' attributes.
  </assert>
  <assert test="count(//blocks/block/@id[. = current()/@id]) = 1">
    The 'id' attribute value of a 'block' must be unique.
  </assert>
</rule>

</pattern>

<!-- Checks for page documents: -->
<pattern name="page">

<rule context="/page">
  <assert test="@keywords">
    Please consider adding a list of keywords to the page. Use a
    'keywords' attribute for that.
  </assert>
  <assert test="title">
    Each 'page' must have a 'title'.
  </assert>
  <assert test="count(title) &lt; 2">
    A 'page' may have only one 'title'.
  </assert>
  <assert test="block">
    Each 'page' must have at least one 'block'.
  </assert>
</rule>

<rule context="page//block">
  <assert test="@idref or *">
    A block must have either an 'idref' attribute (referring to an
    orthogonal block) or children.
  </assert>
```

```
    <report test="@idref and *">
      A block cannot have both an 'idref' attribute and children.
    </report>
    <report test="count(p | section) &lt; count(*)">
      A block can only have 'p' or 'section' children.
    </report>
  </rule>

  <rule context="section">
    <assert test="head">
      A section must have a 'head'.
    </assert>
    <assert test="p">
      A section must have at least one 'p' (paragraph).
    </assert>
    <assert test="normalize-space(text()) = ''">
      A section cannot contain text. Use a 'p' element to include a
      paragraph of text.
    </assert>
  </rule>

</pattern>

<!-- Rules common for master and page documents: -->
<pattern name="common">

<rule context="int | link[@linktype='internal']">
  <assert test="@link">
    An internal link must use a 'link' attribute to specify the
    page being linked.
  </assert>
</rule>

<rule context="p">
  <report test="(normalize-space(text()) = '') and not(*)">
    A paragraph cannot be empty. If you want to increase vertical
    spacing here, modify the stylesheet.
  </report>
</rule>
```

```
<!-- Dummy rule listing all defined element types: -->
<rule context="
    block | block-process | blocks | button | buttons |
    contact-webmaster | copyright | environment | em | ext | head |
    html-title | img-path | int | item | label | lang |
    language-switch | languages | link | mailto | menu | os |
    out-path | p | page | page-footer | site | section | src-path |
    subhead | target-path | title | translation"/>

<!-- Report error if an element was not matched by the above: -->
<rule context="*">
  <report test="true()">
    Unrecognized element: '<name/>'.
  </report>
</rule>

</pattern>

<diagnostics>
  <diagnostic id="label-element">
    Every 'item' element must contain exactly one 'label' element
    specifying the corresponding top menu label.
  </diagnostic>
</diagnostics>

</schema>
```

An overview of XSLT

And yet, my primer suits me so
I would not choose a book to know
Than that, be sweeter wise;
Might some one else so learned be,
And leave me just my A B C,
Himself could have the skies.

EMILY DICKINSON, *The First Lesson*

4

An overview of XSLT

XSLT is a relatively simple but very powerful language. Its power comes not from a plethora of tools or hairy syntax, but from the data model it uses and the very convenient way to access the data. XSLT's data model is a tree of *nodes* corresponding to the tree of elements and character data in the source XML document, and XSLT's method of accessing this tree of nodes is called XPath.

I can't help singing an ode to XSLT — a wonderful, truly data-oriented (as opposed to algorithm-oriented) language where everything Just Works. You must have a good grasp of some basic concepts (admittedly, somewhat unusual from other languages' viewpoint), but after that, most of your code will likely work the first time you run it. XSLT and XPath are so high-level that you can actually think about *what* you want to do with your data, not *how*.

This book does not intend to be an XSLT tutorial; there are other excellent books that will help you learn this language in depth (see Bibliography, page 385). This chapter is just a refresher intended to bring you up to date with the latest XSLT developments and focus your attention on those features of the language that are important for building a web site transformation stylesheet.

Attention: Version bump ahead. Currently, most XSLT books and online guides cover XSLT 1.0. However, versions 2.0 of both XSLT and XPath represent a *huge* advance over 1.0. Processor support will need some time to catch up, but you may want to start poking into 2.0 now — if only because there's so much new ground to cover. A lot of really cool things are only possible with 2.0, and you'll discover very soon how limiting 1.0 is in comparison.

In fact, I started writing this book with the intention to stay within 1.0 territory, with only occasional forays into 2.0. However, as the book progressed (and as the 2.0 Working Drafts stabilized), I found that many examples could be rewritten in a more laconic and expressive way with 2.0 features, and still more very interesting examples are *only* possible with 2.0.

Accordingly, the chapter starts with a brief history of the language and an illustrated overview (**4.2**) of the most important new features in XSLT and XPath 2.0. After that, we'll look at some of the commonly used XSLT extensions (**4.4**) — XSLT 2.0 makes many of them obsolete, but not all.

4.1   XSLT history

For a technical standard, XSLT has had a surprisingly convoluted history. It was born as part of the Extended Stylesheet Language (XSL), envisioned as a comprehensive technology for presentation of XML documents. Like the DSSSL International Standard that inspired it, XSL divides the formatting process into two stages: First, the source XML tree is *transformed* into a target tree representing the formatted document, and second, the target tree is *rendered* for viewing.

XSLT was created as the transformation part of XSL. As it shared with the XPointer and XLink standards the need to specify arbitrary subsets of the source tree, its addressing language was separated into an independent specification called XPath. The XSLT 1.0 and XPath 1.0

specifications were published simultaneously in November 1999.[1] The XSL formatting vocabulary, unofficially called "XSL Formatting Objects (XSL-FO)," was published as XSL 1.0 in October 2001.

Originally, XSLT was intended to transform arbitrary XML into the XSL-FO vocabulary. Some experts say this fact proves that XSLT cannot be a universal XML transformation language.[2] Nevertheless, since no other technology offered the same compelling blend of XPath, template-based processing, and the endorsement of the W3C, XSLT quickly grew in popularity. Despite its limitations, XSLT is widely used nowadays for all kinds of XML-to-XML transformations.

Limitations? What limitations? Two things are usually considered to be the fundamental limitations of XSLT.

- One is inherent in the data model of XSLT. In order to provide arbitrary XPath access to the source tree, the entire source document must be parsed and loaded into memory before you can begin your transformation. For small documents it is not a problem, but as your documents grow, processing becomes not only slow but precipitously slow (as soon as swapping starts) or even impossible (when both RAM and swapping space on your system are exhausted). This limitation can sometimes be worked around by preceding the XSLT transformation in your toolchain with a script that breaks input documents into manageable chunks (this is more likely to work for database-like structures, 1.2).

- The second limitation is more like "a feature, not a bug." XSLT was designed as a *functional* programming language, and as such it has no variable assignment operator. You can create as many variables as you wish within any scope, but once a variable is defined, you cannot change its value within the same scope. This causes quite some trouble to beginner XSLT

---

1. www.w3.org/TR/xslt, www.w3.org/TR/xpath
2. Much like the experts who claimed that science proves bumblebees to be incapable of flight. In both cases, real-world experience suggests the contrary (see www.math.niu.edu/~rusin/known-math/98/bees).

programmers who have had previous experience with traditional (i.e., nonfunctional) programming languages such as C or Perl. However, as we'll see below (**4.3**), you *can* write efficient and elegant (or at the very least, efficient *or* elegant) stylesheets without any assignable variables.

Despite these limitations, for the task we're interested in — XML-to-HTML transformation — XSLT is nearly perfect. And where it's not, you can always plug in your own custom extensions (**4.4.3**).

XPath as a guest musician. The applicability domain of XPath is wider than that of XSLT. Libraries exist that allow one to use XPath to access XML data from other programming languages, such as Python or Perl. Moreover, XPath has inspired several minor but nifty scripting and shell languages, such as XPathScript[3] and xsh[4] (**6.3.2.3**). Some XML editors and IDEs offer built-in XPath engines for searching and navigating in documents (**6.1.1.1**).

Beyond 1.0. After cranking out versions 1.0 of XSLT and XPath, the W3C did not take a vacation. Processors based on the Working Drafts had already been actively used, and the work on the next version of the standard began immediately. Numbered 1.1, this new version included a handful of the features most obviously missing from 1.0 — in particular,

- the ability to create multiple output documents;

- the ability to define extension functions in arbitrary languages inside the stylesheet (using the `xsl:script` instruction, similar to the `script` element of HTML);

- several syntactic and semantic changes intended to make the language simpler and more consistent.

It was the second of these features that proved the most controversial. Some XSLT experts even claimed that XSLT was poised to go the way of HTML, as people would rush to create incompatible extensions in

---

3. `www.axkit.org`
4. `xsh.sf.net`

nonstandard languages and few stylesheets would be able to run on more than one processor. Partly because of this reaction and partly out of the realization that XSLT needed a much deeper overhaul, the 1.1 draft was abandoned and the work on 2.0 started instead.

4.2 A gentle introduction to 2.0

Many of the XSLT examples in this book use the latest XSLT 2.0 features. Some (but not all) of the examples can be rewritten in 1.0 without too much trouble. Otherwise, if your XSLT processor does not yet support 2.0, check if it can use an EXSLT element (**4.4.1**) or a proprietary extension with the same or similar semantics.

Compared to the canceled XSLT 1.1, the list of new features and incompatible changes is much longer in 2.0. Below are some highlights.

- The concept of *nodesets* is replaced by a more general concept of **sequences**. A nodeset, as the name implies, is a set of nodes, and each node must belong to one of the few types that directly follow from the structure of XML (element node, attribute node, etc.). Contrastingly, a sequence may combine arbitrary values and allows for automatic control over their types; for example, you can create a sequence of integer numbers and let the processor ensure type conformance for you.

  This change has had a profound impact on the entire language; all instructions that previously operated on nodesets now are generalized to sequences. Moreover, new attributes have been added to many instructions that make working with sequences (including nodesets) more convenient. For instance, to list the values of all child elements, separated by commas, in 1.0 you had to write

```
<xsl:for-each select="*">
  <xsl:value-of select="."/>
  <xsl:if test="position() != last()">
    <xsl:text>, </xsl:text>
  </xsl:if>
</xsl:for-each>
```

In 2.0, you can simply write

```
<xsl:value-of select="*" separator=", "/>
```

- XSLT 2.0 makes it possible to specify and check **data types** of variables, parameters, functions, and templates. To this end, it borrows a library of data types from XSDL (XML Schema). For example, here's how you declare an integer variable in 2.0:

```
<xsl:variable name="i" as="xs:integer" select="42"/>
```

And here is a variable that may contain a sequence of attribute nodes:

```
<xsl:variable name="a" as="attribute()*"/>
```

Note that the integer variable declaration above refers to an XSDL data type and therefore uses the xs: namespace prefix that must resolve to the namespace URI of http://www.w3.org/ 2001/XMLSchema. In the second example, attribute() is a node type native to XSLT, so no namespace prefix is necessary; the * at the end of the type specification makes this a sequence rather than a single attribute value.

- Another powerful concept is **grouping**. Although there's nothing really new here, as you could emulate this feature with the 1.0 facilities, the new syntax allows for very elegant constructs. You can group nodes (or other members of a sequence — remember, it is generalized!) by

  - the common value of an arbitrary XPath expression (e.g., group all nodes with the same child or attribute, or group sequence members that return equal values as arguments to some function); or

  - arbitrary properties of neighbors in the sequence (e.g., group all *adjacent* nodes sharing some property, or group all nodes starting from a heading node until the next heading).

This feature makes it possible to "deepen" an XML tree, adding hierarchy to a flat structure (see also **2.3.2**). The powerful new xsl:for-each-group instruction can be used, for example, to enclose into sections groups of elements that start with a heading:

```
<xsl:for-each-group select="*" group-starting-with="heading">
  <section>
    <xsl:copy-of select="."/>
  </section>
</xsl:for-each-group>
```

- The new **XPath 2.0** is chock full of goodies, especially in comparison to 1.0. Like XSLT 2.0, the new XPath supports schema-derived types and sequences. It also provides a lot of new — and sorely missing in 1.0 — functions that work with strings, numbers, dates, URIs, qualified names, nodes, and nodesets. Lowercasing a string, matching a regexp, resolving a relative URI, converting a date, finding the node with the highest numeric value in a nodeset — all of this is now possible without clumsy workarounds or nonportable extension functions.

  Moreover, XPath even encroaches on the domain of XSLT proper, offering its own variants of some XSLT constructs. These variants are not only less verbose but often look more natural from the "traditional programming languages" viewpoint. For example, instead of the old

  ```
  <xsl:attribute name="valign">
    <xsl:choose>
      <xsl:when test="$level &gt; 2">top</xsl:when>
      <xsl:otherwise>bottom</xsl:otherwise>
    </xsl:choose>
  </xsl:attribute>
  ```

  you can now write simply

  ```
  <xsl:attribute name="valign">
    <xsl:value-of select="
        if $level &gt; 2
          then 'top'
          else 'bottom'"/>
  </xsl:attribute>
  ```

Also, in XPath 2.0 you can explicitly check if *some* or *every* member of a sequence satisfies a condition (in 1.0 the *some* quantifier was always assumed).

- Despite the 1.1 setback, **extensibility** is in 2.0 too. There's no `xsl:script` anymore, but you can link up extension functions if your processor supports this (we'll use this feature a lot in Chapter 5). Perhaps more importantly, you can now define new functions written in XSLT[5] and use them in your XPath expressions (this feature will be used even more; Example 4.1 on page 167 is a simple illustration).

- The ability to create **multiple output documents** is also present, as it was in 1.1. The instruction that creates a new output document is called `xsl:result-document`. You can provide several `xsl:output` instructions, each storing a named collection of output parameters; different `xsl:result-document` instructions may refer to different `xsl:output` specifications, thus implementing a content/presentation separation of sorts: Now "presentation" (governed by `xsl:output` parameters) is removed from "content" (created by an `xsl:result-document`). This feature is used in **5.5.2** (page 238).

There is much more that is new in XSLT and XPath 2.0;[6] this section covers only what I think are the most important new features for a practical XSLT programmer. Minor nifty things include the `xsl:next-match` instruction, which allows firing more than one template rule for the same context in the same mode; the `function-available()` function to check whether your processor supports a particular function; the `unparsed-text()` function that reads an arbitrary text resource (file or URL) and returns it as a string without parsing (see **5.1.3.3** for a use case); and more.

....

5. Strange but true: A language intended to be *functional* did not support user-defined functions until version 2.0.

6. For a complete list of changes, see `www.w3.org/TR/xslt20/#changes`.

Fortunately, you don't have to learn all this at once. Most of your 1.0 stylesheets will work with a 2.0 processor without problems, and those that use 1.1 features or custom extensions (**4.4.3**) will likely require only minimal changes.

4.3 Taming a functional language

If you're coming from a different programming background, one feature of XSLT (all versions) may seem especially difficult to grasp. I'm not referring to the XML-based syntax; once you get a feel for it, it is surprisingly transparent (even if bulky). For many novices, much more puzzling is XSLT's lack of an assignment operator.[7]

Everything is possible by asking the right questions. XSLT was designed as a *functional* programming language. The functional programming paradigm dates from the 1980s[8] and has proved very useful, even if in a limited way. Other established functional languages include Haskell and Scheme.

A functional program, as the name implies, consists of functions. Unlike those in conventional programming languages, however, these functions are absolutely independent from each other. Each function has a set of arguments and returns a value, but it cannot produce — or be affected by — any *side effects*. In other words, if you pass the same set of arguments to a function, you will always get the same result, no matter at what point of program execution this happens or what other functions were called before it.

A conventional programming language encourages the *imperative* style of programming; in it, you give orders such as "take this, add to that, put the result there." Functional programming, on the other hand, is *expressive*; here you don't give orders, but write expressions that nest all the way up from built-in primitives to the final program output.

....

7. Note for C-literate readers: "=" in XPath always means comparison, never assignment.
8. Search the Web for *Why Functional Programming Matters*, a good historical article on functional programming.

You can think of it this way: The goal of each function is not to perform a task, but *to answer a question*. Naturally, if you ask the same question, you should always get the same answer — hence the ban on side effects.

Why is XSLT functional? This paradigm is naturally applicable to XSLT where a stylesheet consists of a number of largely independent templates (i.e., functions). It also enables an XSLT processor to perform efficient optimizations at runtime, for example by reordering or parallelizing the execution of templates.

The lack of variable assignment is thus a direct consequence of the functional programming paradigm. XSLT's variables are not in fact *variable*; being once assigned a value, they never change for the rest of their life. You can create any number of new variables within the scope of a template or function, but they are not changeable within this scope and are not accessible outside the scope.

Relearn, rethink, rewrite. Even with immutable variables, functional languages are Turing-complete, which means you can use them to implement any imaginable algorithm. Let's examine a few typical situations where the functional paradigm may appear especially limiting — and see how we can cope.

- **Local variables.** Sometimes, XSLT novices attempt to use global variables where local ones would suffice. If several templates of your stylesheet use a variable with the same meaning but unconnected values, you don't need to make this variable global. Each template may have its own *local* declaration and provide its own value for the same-named variable.

- **Passing parameters.** But what if you need to pass the value around, that is, to set the value in one template and use it in another? In accordance with the functional programming principles, you should make the second template callable (**4.5.1**) and *explicitly* pass the required value to it via a parameter. Thus, even though global variables are immutable, you can still exchange information among templates via parameters.

Quite often, however, the urge to share variables between templates is a sign of bad stylesheet design. See if you can rearrange your code into different template chunks, eliminating the need to communicate variable values among them. You may have to use template modes to let one source node trigger different templates (see Example 4.2, page 169).

- **Recursion.** You cannot change the value of a variable, but you can call a function or template with different values of parameters. This means that by *recursively* calling a function or template from itself, you can keep track of a counter or accumulator variable. Example 4.1 shows a definition for the function eg:fact() that calculates the factorial of its argument.

. . . .

Example 4.1   A function calculating factorial as an example of XSLT recursion.

```
<xsl:function name="eg:fact">
  <xsl:param name="n"/>
  <xsl:choose>
    <xsl:when test="$n = 1 or $n = 0">
      <xsl:value-of select="1"/>
    </xsl:when>
    <xsl:otherwise>
      <xsl:value-of select="$n * eg:fact($n - 1)"/>
    </xsl:otherwise>
  </xsl:choose>
</xsl:function>
```
. . . .

You can now use this function in your XPath expressions, for example:

```
<xsl:value-of select="eg:fact(12)"/> <!-- returns 479001600 -->
```

A downside to this approach is that in most processors, XSLT recursion is costly in terms of memory and may be very slow. If this is becoming a problem, read on for other suggestions.

- **XPath tools.** In some cases, algorithmic patterns that are difficult to express in a purely functional style become much more accessible if you take advantage of XPath functions and operators that work with sequences. For example, if you want to do something with each character of a string, in most programming languages you write a `while` loop with an index variable incremented on each iteration. With XSLT 2.0, you can use the `to` operator of XPath to create a sequence of integers and iterate over that sequence by an `xsl:for-each`:

```
<xsl:for-each select="1 to string-length($s)">
  The character at position <xsl:value-of select="."/>
  is '<xsl:value-of select="substring($s, ., 1)"/>'.
</xsl:for-each>
```

- You cannot change values of global variables, but you can store any values in **temporary XML documents** (with the `xsl:result-document` instruction) and read them back (with the `document()` function). The XSLT 2.0 specification forbids you from reading back the document you have just created *in the same stylesheet run*, but you can rely on it being there when you run that (or any other) stylesheet next time. Thus, temporary documents may be a complete functional substitute for assignable variables so long as you break your transformation algorithm into separate stylesheets so that no such "variable" is written and read in the same stylesheet run.

  This mechanism is especially useful when implementing complex multidocument transformations. For example, this is how the Index and the Table of Contents for this book were produced. When transforming each chapter (stored in a separate file), two auxiliary documents are created containing extracted index terms and section headings. Later, a separate stylesheet reads in these auxiliary documents from all chapters, merges them together, and processes the result to produce the Index and TOC.[9]

  With a wee bit of extension programming, you can even run one stylesheet from within another (**5.6**).

- **Chaining templates.** If you want to make some preliminary changes to the input document and then process this changed version, you don't even need two stylesheet runs for this. Just

....

9. Actually, this process is a bit more complex, since it also involves extracting the corresponding page numbers from formatted chapters.

assign a special `mode` attribute value, e.g. `first-pass`, to all the templates performing the preprocessing, save their output into a variable, and apply the second-pass templates to this variable instead of the input document. All of this could be done in a template matching `/`, as Example 4.2 demonstrates.

- -

Example 4.2   Processing input in two independent passes, storing the intermediate tree in a variable.

```
<xsl:template match="/">
  <!-- Store the output of the first pass: -->
  <xsl:variable name="intermediate">
    <xsl:apply-templates mode="first-pass" select="*"/>
  </xsl:variable>

  <!-- Dump results for debugging: -->
  <xsl:result-document href="intermediate.xml">
    <xsl:copy-of select="$intermediate"/>
  </xsl:result-document>

  <!-- Launch second pass: -->
  <xsl:apply-templates select="$intermediate/*"/>
</xsl:template>
```

- -

If you are adding a preprocessing pass to an existing stylesheet, no other changes are necessary. The templates of the second pass (those without any `mode` attribute) won't have the slightest suspicion that what they work with is not the genuine source document but its preprocessed version stored in a variable. This demonstrates that even though you cannot change global variable values within templates, you can still pass the value returned by one template *as input* to another using a third template's local variable.

- If none of the above methods work for you, you can write your own **extensions** in a nonfunctional programming language and link them up to your stylesheet. The language most frequently used for this purpose is Java, in part because some of the major

XSLT processors (**6.4.1**) are also written in Java and their extensibility mechanisms for this language are well defined.

The main advantage of this method is efficiency: Extension functions are usually faster than those written in XSLT. On the downside, with extension functions it may be difficult to pass and return complex values such as nodesets. Also, in an extension function you may have (depending on the processor) little or no access to the XPath engine or to the parsed tree of the source document. Because of this, extensions work best for simple but performance-critical tasks such as processing a document's data (**5.4.2**).

- As an absolutely last resort, Saxon offers the `saxon:assign` extension instruction; see **4.4.2.1** for a discussion.

4.4 **XSLT extensions**

Implementors of XSLT 1.0 soon discovered that the language, while being fairly complete for its stated goal, lacks many convenience functions that are common in practical programming languages. As a result, almost every XSLT processor included custom extensions. Typically, functions for dealing with nodesets, strings, and regular expressions, as well as common mathematical functions, were added. Some processors also implemented extension instructions or attributes.

4.4.1 EXSLT

EXSLT (Extended XSLT) emerged as a standard unifying common XSLT extensions to ensure interoperability between processors. A lot of EXSLT's goodies have become part of XSLT 2.0 and XPath 2.0.

The EXSLT web site[10] provides complete details on each extension and lists the processors implementing it natively. For some functions,

....

10. www.exslt.org

the site provides freely downloadable implementations in scripting languages (notably JavaScript).

EXSLT extensions include functions and instructions for:

- manipulating date and time values;

- dynamic (runtime) evaluation of strings containing XPath expressions;

- identifying and converting data types;

- mathematical calculations;

- matching and replacing with regular expressions;

- nodeset manipulation (difference, intersection, etc.);

- defining XSLT functions;

- creating multiple output documents.

4.4.2 Saxon extensions

Saxon[11] is a well-known, fast, and standards-compliant open source XSLT processor written by Michael Kay. Its author is also the editor of the W3C's XSLT specification.

Saxon is written in Java. Stable versions of Saxon (the 6.* series) implement XSLT 1.0; beta versions (the 7.* series) are a testbed implementation of XSLT 2.0. Saxon 7 was very robust and stable in my testing.

Among other things, Saxon is notable for its extensibility. You can write your own extension functions in Java and call them from your XSLT stylesheet. Saxon also offers a wide range of useful built-in extensions that are unique to this processor.

Using proprietary Saxon extensions is not recommended unless absolutely necessary. Not only are they nonportable to other processors, but in the beta

---

11. saxon.sf.net

7.* series they sometimes change or disappear between Saxon releases. Still, even if you never need any of these extensions, or if you use a different processor altogether, knowing what's available in a leading XSLT tool is entertaining and mind-widening.

4.4.2.1   The assignability dilemma

One of the most controversial extensions is the `saxon:assign`[12] instruction. It allows you to change the value of a variable that was declared with a `saxon:assignable="yes"` attribute in its `xsl:variable`.

This extension clearly violates the principles of functional programming, at the same time making the language easier to use for novice XSLT programmers by allowing all sorts of imperative constructs. However tempting `saxon:assign` may look to you, remember that it can make your stylesheet a nightmare to debug because of side effects.

You cannot count on `saxon:assign` always being available in Saxon nor on it ever becoming part of the XSLT standard. Quoth Michael Kay: "Using `saxon:assign` is cheating." The author of Saxon spends considerable effort improving its performance, and he has hinted that as soon as `saxon:assign` becomes an obstacle to these optimization efforts, it will be gone. So, beware of locking yourself into `saxon:assign`, as you may end up with an obsolete Saxon version without an upgrade path.

A related extension is the `saxon:while` instruction that lets you create a conventional "while" loop. About the only sensible way to use such a loop is in combination with `saxon:assignable` variables.

4.4.2.2   Optimization-related extensions

Besides being a fast processor by itself, Saxon also offers tools that you can use to speed up the execution of your stylesheet. These tools include:

- The `saxon:memo-function="yes"` attribute can be set on an `xsl:function` element if you want Saxon to cache the function's returned values. If the function is called again with the same arguments, the result is not calculated again but retrieved from the

....

12. In Saxon 7.*, the `saxon` prefix corresponds to the URI `http://saxon.sf.net/`.

cache. Obviously, this optimization may break if the function is affected by side effects, so it is incompatible with `saxon:assign`.

- The `saxon:expression(`*`string`*`)` function takes an XPath expression as a string, parses it, and returns an object representing this expression in a parsed and ready-to-run form. Then, you use the `saxon:eval(`*`expr`*`)` function to "call" this stored expression in the current context. If you just need to evaluate an expression stored in a string, use `saxon:evaluate(`*`string`*`)`. Unfortunately, both `eval()` and `evaluate()` functions are limited in that you cannot use your stylesheet's variables or functions within the evaluated expression.

  Why bother with turning an expression into an object? Because it is supposed to be faster than just using the same expression every time; whether it's actually faster is a subject for experimentation. More importantly, the ability to evaluate an expression stored in a string may make your source definition more powerful (**3.9.1.3**).

Before you jump into optimization, remember the old wisdom: "Premature optimization is the root of all evil."[13] Never spend a minute on optimization unless you are absolutely forced by performance constraints, and never optimize except where the real bottlenecks occur (see **6.4.4** for some XSLT profiling software).

4.4.2.3 Debugging extensions

Compared to other languages, debugging XSLT is made easier by the lack of side effects but more difficult by the fact that the processor may, for optimization, reorder templates during execution and skip unused variables (**4.5.3**), functions, or templates. Saxon's debugging tools are therefore very useful for a serious XSLT developer.

- The `saxon:path()` function returns the "canonical" XPath to the current node. It is an absolute path uniquely identifying the current node. For example, the template

---

13. Attributed to Donald Knuth.

```
<xsl:template match="p">
<xsl:message><xsl:value-of select="saxon:path()"/></xsl:message>
</xsl:template>
```

will output absolute XPaths for all p elements in the source (see also **6.3.2.1**):

```
/page[1]/block[1]/p[1]
/page[1]/block[1]/section[1]/p[1]
/page[1]/block[1]/section[1]/p[2]
...
```

- The saxon:line-number() function returns the line number corresponding to the context node in the source document. We'll use this function in our Schematron wrapper (**5.1.2**) in order to report the source line number for each validity error.

- The saxon:systemId() function returns the URI of the source document. It is useful not only for debugging; by parsing this string, you can get the absolute URI of the source document's directory, and this URI may be used for resolving all sorts of relative URIs or translating absolute URIs from one base directory to another. We will use this function in our stylesheet setup (**5.1.1**).

- The saxon:explain="yes" attribute can be set on any element, including literal result elements. This will cause Saxon, when compiling the stylesheet, to print the static type and internal representation of all XPath expressions in that element's attributes.

4.4.2.4 Miscellaneous goodies

Nodesets.   As mentioned in **4.2**, XPath 2.0 has a whole bunch of new functions for manipulating nodesets and sequences, as does EXSLT (**4.4.1**). Saxon adds a few more, such as the very useful saxon:has-same-nodes() function that tests if two nodesets have at least one node in common.

PIs, DTDs, entities. Saxon allows you to access or create those aspects of XML documents that are out of reach of standard XSLT. Thus, there's a function to access the pseudo-attributes of a processing instruction, a set of instructions for creating an internal DTD subset (**2.2.4.3**) in the output document, and an instruction to create an entity reference.

Output control. Saxon offers several additional `xsl:output` attributes to control how the output document is serialized. You can set the number of spaces to use for one level of indentation, control the entity representation of characters outside of the output character set, plug in a custom Java class as an alternative serializer (with optional well-formedness control), or pass the output to another stylesheet without serialization.

Parsing strings and serializing trees. A new function in XSLT 2.0, `unparsed-text()`, loads a text file into memory as a data string — that is, without XML parsing. Saxon offers two complementary and probably more useful functions: `saxon:parse()` parses a string representing a well-formed XML document and returns the root node of the resulting tree; `saxon:serialize()`, conversely, returns a string with a serialization of the node tree passed to it as an argument.

4.4.3 Custom extensions

Most XSLT processors let you write your own extensions in a programming language other than XSLT. Usually, you can add your custom functions to the set of built-in XPath functions, but some processors also let you add custom instructions (stylesheet element types).

The abandoned XSLT 1.1 draft (**4.1**) provided the `xsl:script` instruction that made it possible to place extension code right into your stylesheet. For good or for bad, this is now gone. To quote the 2.0 Working Draft, "This specification does not define any mechanism for creating or binding implementations of extension instructions or extension functions, and does not require that implementations support any such mechanism. Such mechanisms, if they exist, are implementation-defined."

For extension functions, you have to declare a namespace that will allow the processor to find the extension you created. For Java-based processors, this namespace's URI usually includes the complete class name of your extension function (e.g., `com.projectname.xslt.graph`). After that, functions whose names contain that namespace's prefix will be sought in the corresponding class. We'll see many examples of this in Chapter 5.

4.5 Overview of an XSLT stylesheet

This section attempts to describe and classify the main building blocks of a web site XSLT stylesheet. You may find it useful for exploring this book's stylesheet examples as well as for programming your own transformations.

4.5.1 Templates

The basic idea of XSLT is this: Run into a context, invoke the corresponding template. Templates usually constitute the bulk of a stylesheet's code. But are all templates created equal? There are several meaningful distinctions that you should keep in mind when building your template library.

- **Applicable vs. callable templates.** Most regular templates are of the *applicable* kind. Such a template has a `match` attribute and is activated automatically whenever the source context matches. You can also use an `xsl:apply-templates` instruction (hence the term *applicable*[14]) to specify a nodeset to feed through the built-in template-matching mechanism of XSLT.

  Callable templates, on the other hand, do not necessarily have a `match`, but they have a `name` attribute. To run such a named template, you use an `xsl:call-template` instruction (hence the

---

14. The XSLT specification calls applicable templates *template rules* because the `match` attribute is effectively a rule that governs when to apply the template. I'm trying to avoid the official term because *applicable template* seems to better describe a unit consisting of both the template itself and its applicability rule.

term *callable*[15]) supplying the template name and, optionally, parameters.

Formally, the dividing line between applicable and callable templates is rather blurry; you can use `xsl:call-template` to run an applicable template with `match` (if it also has a `name`), and both `xsl:call-template` and `xsl:apply-templates` can supply parameters to the templates they pass control to.

But architecturally, this is an important distinction. Use callable templates for chunks of code that you want to share between applicable templates. Moreover, use them for *any* sizable chunk of code that is sufficiently context-independent and represents a separate unit — even if it's only used once. Removing such independent units into aptly named callables will make your stylesheet more readable and easier to maintain.

One thing you should remember is that a callable template (even of the called-only-once kind) must really be context-independent. It cannot rely on the source context because it might be called from different contexts, but it may depend on parameters — which can therefore be used to add variability to the output of a callable template.

- **Push vs. pull templates.** The natural XSLT programming style whereby you let templates take care of their own execution is often called the push style. What you do with this approach is push your source into the stylesheet and let its many templates tear it into many pieces for processing. Push-oriented templates are relatively small and independent, with few, if any, control flow instructions.

  The opposite is of course the pull style, which is more like the approach of traditional programming languages. Here, you explicitly program your templates to pull information from the source by using XPath expressions and control flow code (such as

---

15. The XSLT specification uses the term *named templates*. Again, I consider the fact that a template can be called to be more important than the fact that it has a name.

for-each loops or conditional instructions). Pull-oriented templates are therefore bigger; they usually match top-level elements (like page or block) and are heavily linked to other templates by means of explicit xsl:call-template or xsl:apply-templates calls.

- **Trunk vs. branch templates.** The trunk and branches referred to in this distinction are, of course, those of the source document tree. Trunk templates are either callable, or they match absolute paths (e.g., / or /page) that are known to occur a fixed number of times in fixed contexts. Branch templates, conversely, handle "hanging" contexts (such as p or @id) that may occur almost anywhere.

The other distinctions we've talked about naturally parallel this one and are best understood in conjunction with it. Indeed, trunk templates more often pull than are pushed against. Their goal is to build the high-level structure of the HTML page, and this structure is usually quite different from the source structure. We cannot therefore sit and wait for the necessary bits to come our way; we must take control and pull what we need from the source. For the same reason, many trunk templates are callable rather than applicable; in some cases, only the root template (matching /) is applicable, and all other trunk templates are called from it.

This approach, however, only works down to a certain level. As we descend,[16] the source tree becomes wider and more varied. At some point, the pull style no longer works; we cannot foresee all possible combinations of elements that may happen at the lower levels of the source tree. This is where we switch to the branch templates that, conversely, are mostly push-oriented and applicable.

In terms of psychology, trunk templates are conscious plans, while branch templates are knee-jerk reactions. Both are necessary for survival.

. . . .

16. In computer science, trees grow downward, so you have to *descend* in order to go from a tree's trunk to its branches.

4.5.2   Layout code

That's the ancient curse of HTML . . . tables, transparent spacer images, `height` and `width` specifications, and tables again. CSS has alleviated the pain a lot, but you still have to fiddle with tables quite often, especially with complex multicolumn layouts. HTML design is beyond the topic of this book, so in the stylesheet examples, I'll skip or simplify most of this stuff; usually only comments will indicate the position and role of the main chunks of layout code.

It's not all static, of course; layout code may use XPath expressions for retrieving and/or calculating various values, such as width of a column that might depend on the number of items in it. Also, you may need to build, at transformation time, various paths or URIs used in HTML code — for example,

```
<img src="{$out-img}empty.gif" width="1" height="30" alt=""/>
```

4.5.3   Variables and functions

In XSLT, global variables are created by `xsl:variable` children of the `xsl:stylesheet`. For the value of a variable, you can put arbitrary XSLT code or literal result elements inside `xsl:variable`. Any kinds of values, including tree fragments, nodesets, and sequences, are valid for an XSLT variable (unless you limit its data type with an `as` attribute).

Don't force users to edit the stylesheet. In a web site transformation stylesheet, it may not even be a good idea to actually *store* values in stylesheet variables. Many values such as URIs, paths, text strings, and menu trees are best stored in the master document (**2.1.2.1**); use `xsl:variable`s to extract and prepare this data for the current stylesheet run. Only true constants that will never conceivably change during the lifetime of your web site can be stored right in the stylesheet.

Lazy evaluation. With a functional language such as XSLT, the only result of a variable declaration is that the variable now exists; no side effects are possible or allowed. This allows the XSLT processor to optimize stylesheet execution by declaring the variable only when — and if — necessary. This feature is called *lazy evaluation*, but not all XSLT processors behave that way; one of the "lazy" processors is Saxon.

Lazy evaluation means that if, for example, your `xsl:variable` declaration contains a debugging output (`xsl:message`) or a document creation instruction (`xsl:result-document`), neither will ever get control if its parent variable is not used. And the variable may remain unused simply because none of the templates that reference it are triggered by the current source document.[17]

Functions vs. templates. XSLT functions, introduced in 2.0, are similar to those in other programming languages in that they take zero or more arguments and return a value. However, the really nice thing about XSLT functions is that they can take and return not just atomic values, but sequences and nodesets too. In fact, the only essential difference between a callable template and a function is that callable templates by default attach their output to the result tree, while the output of a function is returned to whoever called it and can be used as a value in an XPath expression.

4.5.4 Control flow

In the push style, XSLT rarely needs any loops, conditional instructions, or function calls. The code inside push-oriented templates is usually linear, and the order of triggering these templates depends only on the structure of the source document. However, as we've just seen, pull-style XSLT occupies the top levels of template hierarchy, and this is where explicit passing of control is quite common.

The inventory of control flow instructions in XSLT is adequate for typical pull processing scenarios; moreover, some of these instructions have parallels in XPath. Thus, calling or applying templates (in XSLT) is similar to calling functions (in XPath). Often, you will use loops

---

17. In fact, about the only code that is *guaranteed* to run in a stylesheet is an `xsl:template match="/"` and whatever callable templates, variables, or functions it unconditionally uses.

(`xsl:for-each` in XSLT, `for` in XPath 2.0) and conditionals (`xsl:if`, `xsl:choose` in XSLT, `if` in XPath 2.0). On the other hand, the idea of a "goto" statement is apparently so far below and behind XSLT's level of abstraction that no XSLT tutorials I've seen even mention its nonexistence.

4.5.5 Debugging and documentation

Some of the debugging tools unique to Saxon were mentioned in **4.4.2.1**. Other than that, your debugging toolset is pretty much limited to issuing `xsl:messages` containing `xsl:value-ofs` to check the values of variables or expressions during execution. Do not underestimate this tool; it is perfectly suitable for anything except the most complex debugging tasks. Some software that may help you debug your stylesheets is reviewed in Chapter 6 (**6.4**).

As for documentation, XSLT allows you to use elements from arbitrary namespaces at the top level of the stylesheet. This means you can provide structured documentation by interspersing elements from an appropriate vocabulary (such as DocBook or HTML) with your templates, variables, functions, and so on. Since your stylesheet is a valid XML document that can be fed to another stylesheet, various "literate programming" techniques become possible, such as automatic annotation, extracting documentation, and indexing.

Unfortunately, this only works at the top level directly under `xsl:stylesheet`; in deeper contexts, foreign namespace elements are treated as literal result elements. This means that the only way to document the innards of a function or template is by using `<!-- XML comments -->`.

The XSLT stylesheet

There are two births; the one when light
First strikes the new awaken'd sense;
The other when two souls unite,
  And we must count our life from thence:
When you loved me and I loved you
Then both of us were born anew.

WILLIAM CARTWRIGHT, *To Chloe*

5

The XSLT stylesheet

This is the largest chapter of the book, and for a reason: We now come to the implementation of all the magic that was hinted at by our site's source definition. You have your source nicely marked up, but it is of little use if there's no software to understand this markup. This chapter (which could just as well be named after the entire book, *XSLT 2.0 Web Development*) shows you how to build such software with XSLT.

Compared to some other languages, XSLT is simple and logical, so if you have at least some programming experience, perhaps all you need to learn basic XSLT is examples. There are many of them in this chapter, and if you need more, look into the specification[1] (those green boxes are fascinating reading!).

I'll try to cover as many interesting and nontrivial XSLT bits as possible; it does not mean, of course, that your stylesheet will need all of them. Most examples are simple and rarely require deep knowledge of XSLT. What you *do* need to know before you are able to read this

---

1. www.w3.org/TR/xslt20/

chapter's examples is XPath. If you can parse the content of the numerous `select` attributes of a typical stylesheet, the rest of the code is in most cases self-explanatory thanks to the clear element type names and the nesting structure of XSLT instructions.

Focusing on what's important. For the sake of clarity, I have cut some material from the stylesheet examples. Literal result elements (which are mostly HTML layout constructs) are often dropped or replaced with comments, making the remaining XSLT code easier to understand. At first, we'll focus on the high-level structure of the stylesheet and the general principles of clean and modular XSLT processing; a complete working stylesheet example is given in the last section (**5.7**).

Not only XSLT. Even with all the glory of XSLT 2.0, some neat things are only possible if you write your own *extensions* in a different language. This is simpler than you may think. This chapter presents several extension functions written in Java for the Saxon XSLT processor. You can easily adapt them for other Java-based processors supporting custom extensions (**6.4.1**).

Does this mean you have to know Java? Not really. When you program in XSLT, the extension language you use, be it Java or something else, may well be a black box for you. If you need the functionality described in this chapter, you can copy-and-paste its Java examples[2] — they will work as advertised. If you want more, find a Java expert or search for free code on the Web — most likely, your needs will not exceed a couple of dozen lines of code.

5.1 Schematron validation

Before we start working on the main transformation stylesheet, let's discuss the implementation of a source validation subsystem. A basic Schematron schema was shown in Example 3.3 (page 149); here we'll see how to coordinate it with the stylesheet (**5.1.1**, **5.1.2**) and how to extend it with many advanced checks for the super-document layer of your source definition (**5.1.3**).

----

2. All code from this book is also available online at `www.kirsanov.com/xsltwd`.

Why coordinate? There are two reasons. First, you usually run your stylesheet after the source has been changed, so it is only natural to validate it just before transformation. Second, our schema language of choice, Schematron, is directly related to XSLT; we will use the reference implementation of Schematron written in XSLT. Therefore, for efficient validation, your schema must share some code with the stylesheet.

5.1.1   Shared XSLT library

What stylesheet code can we use during validation? An ideal schema must not only validate the document structure but also perform many types of content checks, such as checking for broken links. Recall the discussion of address abbreviations (**3.5.3**); a link-checking schema must be able to unabbreviate addresses in all types of links in your XML sources exactly as they are unabbreviated by the stylesheet during transformation. This means the unabbreviation functions must be shared between the schema and the stylesheet.

Before we can do any unabbreviation, we need to access the master document and retrieve the current processing parameters as well as any metadata it has for the current source document. This information must be checked against the reality and, if correct, stored in global variables that will be used later in many places. All of this is quite a chunk of code — and another candidate for sharing between the schema and the stylesheet.

Our first task, therefore, is to create a *shared XSLT library* that will be imported into both the schema and the stylesheet. A complete listing of such a library is given in Example 5.19 (page 256). Below, I highlight and discuss some of its more important parts.

5.1.1.1   Stylesheet parameters

First, the library declares the stylesheet parameters, $env and $images:

```
<xsl:param name="env" select="'final'"/>
<xsl:param name="images" select="'no'"/>
```

These are the values that the user may provide on each stylesheet execution (usually on the command line; see **5.1.2** and **5.7** for command-line examples). Keep the number of stylesheet parameters to a minimum and never use them to *supply* any information, only to *select* information stored somewhere else (usually in the master document).

Note the two pairs of quotes around the parameter values. The inner single quotes enclose string literals in XPath; the outer double quotes are obligatory for attribute values in XML.

You won't be running the library directly; instead, you'll import it at the very beginning of both the schema and the stylesheet. As a result, both will accept the same parameters, and both will use the same default values (in our example, `'final'` for $env and `'no'` for $images) if no parameters are supplied by the user.

5.1.1.2   Master document access

Before going any further, both the schema and the stylesheet need to access the master document. The $master variable solves this problem — it loads, parses, and stores the master document:

```
<xsl:variable name="master" select="document('_master.xml')"/>
```

Note that the filename (or, possibly, pathname or URI) of the master is hard-wired into the variable — simply because we have nowhere else to take it from at this point. This is the only bit of configuration that has to be stored in XSLT and therefore may not be easy to change by site maintainers (who might be unable to access the shared library and/or edit its XSLT code). Everything else, as we'll see below, grows out of this seed and is easy to modify by editing the master document.

Even the master document location can be made user-configurable if you add a stylesheet parameter supplying the pathname or URI of the master.

Who am I speaking to? Most of the time, the stylesheet will be run with a page document as input. However, for batch processing (**5.6**) we'll need to use the master document as input. Now, for convenience, let's find out if the current input document is the master (by checking the name of its root element type) and store this in a boolean variable:

```
<xsl:variable name="this-master" select="boolean(/*[name()='site'])"/>
```

5.1.1.3 Pathnames

Before we can do anything useful, we must figure out various pathnames specific to the current environment. To start, finding out
the root directory of the source tree, the output directory, and the
target directory is simple — they are stored in the children of the
corresponding environment element in the master:

```
<xsl:variable name="src-path"
    select="$master//environment[@id=$env]/src-path"/>
<xsl:variable name="out-path"
    select="$master//environment[@id=$env]/out-path"/>
<xsl:variable name="target-path"
    select="$master//environment[@id=$env]/target-path"/>
```

The images directory is assumed to be under the $out-path, and its
name is also stored in the environment:

```
<xsl:variable name="out-img">
  <xsl:value-of select="$out-path"/>
  <xsl:value-of select="$master//environment[@id=$env]/img-path"/>
  <xsl:text>/</xsl:text>
</xsl:variable>
```

The stylesheet assumes that the directory exists and all necessary image
files are already there (although it may add some generated images
itself, **5.5.2**).

For the img elements in the HTML pages we are creating, the image
directory must be prefixed by $target-path, not $out-path. We
therefore declare the $target-img variable that is identical to $out-img
except that it uses $target-path instead of $out-path:

```
<xsl:variable name="target-img">
  <xsl:value-of select="$target-path"/>
  <xsl:value-of select="$master//environment[@id=$env]/img-path"/>
  <xsl:text>/</xsl:text>
</xsl:variable>
```

We'll also frequently use filename extensions for source XML files and
output HTML files:

```
<xsl:variable name="src-ext">.xml</xsl:variable>
<xsl:variable name="out-ext">.html</xsl:variable>
```

Sometimes, you may want to use different output file extensions for different pages, site sections, or production environments. In this case, supply these extensions in the corresponding `menu` or `environment` branches in the master document instead of hard-wiring them into the stylesheet as we did here.

Where am I? For other parameters, the approach implemented below tries to guess as much as possible based on the source document's pathname (available via the `saxon:systemId()` function under Saxon), thus relieving the document author from the burden to specify that information in XML. This makes the system easier for daily mainte-nance and more error-proof.

Saxon's extension function `saxon:systemId()` returns the URL of the current source document, using the `file:` protocol prefix for local files (e.g., `file:/dir/page.xml`). Many other processors provide a similar extension function (for example, Xalan has an analogous function also called `systemId()`). If you don't have such a function available in your processor, you may need to rewrite this part of the shared library so that it relies on the page document's content (e.g., a `src` attribute of the page's root element) rather than its location. Another approach might use a stylesheet parameter set by some external processing framework that runs the XSLT transformation (compare **7.2.7**).

Language. Thus, in a multilingual site, instead of manually specifying the language of each page document (e.g., via an attribute of its root element), we assume that the site has several parallel directory trees, each under the subdirectory named after the language label. The `$lang` variable cuts out the part of the `saxon:systemId()` returned value that is between the `$src-path` and the first `/` character:

```
<xsl:variable name="lang">
  <xsl:choose>
    <xsl:when test="substring-after(saxon:systemId(), $src-path)=''">
      <xsl:message terminate="yes">
        Error: Source file path doesn't match $src-path
        $env = <xsl:value-of select="$env"/>
        systemId = <xsl:value-of select="saxon:systemId()"/>
      </xsl:message>
    </xsl:when>
```

```
<xsl:otherwise>
    <xsl:value-of select="
        substring-before(
          substring-after(saxon:systemId(), $src-path),
          '/')"/>
  </xsl:otherwise>
  </xsl:choose>
</xsl:variable>
```

If the string returned by `saxon:systemId()` does not start with `$src-path`, an error is reported. For example, a source document whose pathname starts with

```
{$src-path}de/
```

is assumed to be in German, and for it, the `$lang` variable will get the value `'de'`. Your directory layout may of course be different, but the code will likely be similar.

Abbreviated location. Next, we initialize the `$current` variable that is the pathname of the current source document after removing the `$src-path`, `$lang`, and the filename extension:

```
<xsl:variable name="current">
  <xsl:choose>
    <xsl:when test="
        not($master//languages/lang = $lang) and not($this-master)">
      <xsl:message terminate="yes">
        Error: Not in a valid language directory
        $lang = <xsl:value-of select="$lang"/>
      </xsl:message>
    </xsl:when>
    <xsl:otherwise>
      <xsl:value-of select="
          substring-before(
            substring-after(
              substring-after(saxon:systemId(), $src-path),
              concat($lang, '/')),
            $src-ext)"/>
    </xsl:otherwise>
  </xsl:choose>
</xsl:variable>
```

The idea is to be able to directly compare the value of `$current` to the `//page/@src` values in the master document. Thus, for

```
/var/www/xml/de/contact/contact.xml
```

the value of `$current` will be `contact/contact` (assuming `$src-path` for the current environment is `/var/www/xml/`).

No way. The variables `$lang` and `$current` complain if the source document path does not contain a valid language label or does not start with `$src-path`. These checks are done in the shared library and not in the schema because the stylesheet absolutely needs this information to be correct, or the transformation will fail. On the other hand, since our Schematron schema imports the shared library as well, these errors will be reported if you attempt to validate, not only transform, a wrongly placed document.

Finally, we create a boolean variable that checks if the current page is the site's front page (this might be useful, e.g., for creating a different layout on the home page of the site):

```
<xsl:variable name="frontpage" select="$current = 'index'"/>
```

Follow the right paths. All this fiddling with pathnames is an ugly but inevitable part of creating a web site. If you want to be able to run a transformation in more than one environment — and this cannot be avoided, because you don't want to do development or editing on a live site — the stylesheet setup described in this section can hardly be simplified.

I tried to make these examples as generic as possible, so you shouldn't have too many problems adapting them to your situation. Still, your production stylesheet may need to be even more complex. For example, you may have separate image directories for each language, or separate directories for downloadable content.

5.1.1.4 Unabbreviation functions

To finish our shared XSLT library, we implement a few simple unabbreviation functions. If you are new to user-defined functions in XSLT (it is a 2.0 feature), this is a good primer.

External links. Let's look at the external links unabbreviation first. The following function checks if the parameter string starts with a URL protocol part; if it does, the parameter is returned unchanged, otherwise it is concatenated with 'http://'. You can, of course, add tests for any other URL protocols in addition to http:// and ftp://.

```
<xsl:function name="eg:ext-link">
  <xsl:param name="abbr"/>
  <xsl:value-of select="
      if (starts-with($abbr, 'http://') or
          starts-with($abbr, 'ftp://'))
        then $abbr
        else concat('http://', $abbr)"/>
</xsl:function>
```

Every function must have a qualified name; the http://www.example.org/ namespace, with the prefix eg, is used in examples in this chapter for our XSLT functions.

Internal links. The internal links unabbreviation comes in two flavors, one for the source documents and the other for the transformed HTML pages.

• The page-src() function is often used for checking if the linked document is present (we need to look for the source because the corresponding HTML file may not be created yet) and for accessing its XML source (e.g., to extract the title from the linked page to use in the menu, or to pull out an orthogonal content block referenced on another page).

• The page-link() function is used for the actual href values in the links in HTML pages.

The first of these functions constructs the unabbreviated path from the base directory ($src-path), language subdirectory ($lang; you can, of course, drop that if your site is unilingual), the relative pathname of the page (the src attribute of the corresponding page or block element), and the source filename extension ($src-ext):

```
<xsl:function name="eg:page-src">
  <xsl:param name="abbr"/>
  <xsl:param name="lang"/>
  <xsl:value-of select="
      concat(
        $src-path,
        $lang, '/',
        $master//(page|block)[(@id, tokenize(@alias, '\s+')) = $abbr]
          /@src,
        $src-ext)"/>
</xsl:function>
```

The analogous function for HTML links differs only in the variables used to construct the complete pathname — $target-path instead of $src-path and $out-ext instead of $src-ext:

```
<xsl:function name="eg:page-link">
  <xsl:param name="abbr"/>
  <xsl:param name="lang"/>
  <xsl:value-of select="
      concat(
        $target-path,
        $lang, '/',
        $master//(page|block)[(@id, tokenize(@alias, '\s+')) = $abbr]
          /@src,
        $out-ext)"/>
</xsl:function>
```

These functions take two parameters:

- $abbr is the page id (i.e., the abbreviated address);

- $lang is the language of the target page.

A couple of points are worthy of note in these functions. First, the XPath expression that performs the actual lookup in the master document searches in both pages and blocks, hence (page|block) as a single location step; in XPath 1.0, only entire expressions and not steps within an expression could be arguments to the | operator.

Second, we can refer to a page not only by its id but also by its alias (**3.5.3.4**), and the alias attribute in the master can store several values separated by spaces (refer to Example 3.2, page 143). Thus, we tokenize() the page's alias and combine it with the id value into a single sequence using the comma operator. This sequence is then compared to $abbr; if any one of the sequence members passes the equality test, the = operator returns true.

Isn't XPath 2.0 wonderful?

Schematron wrapper for Saxon

If you're not interested in validation at this time, feel free to skip this and the next section; in **5.2** we'll finally start writing our main transformation stylesheet.

The reference implementation of Schematron, written in XSLT by Rick Jelliffe, consists of the "skeleton" library,[3] implementing the bulk of the Schematron functionality, and a set of wrappers (*metastylesheets*) that provide high-level interfaces to that functionality.

Custom wrapper. To run Schematron validation on Saxon, we will use the simplest wrapper, schematron-basic.xsl,[4] with these modifications:

- The Saxon-specific line-number() function is added to the error handler for reporting the source line number in each report. This makes the schema's output much easier to use for fixing errors.

- The shared XSLT library that we've just built (**5.1.1**) is imported.

- Several namespaces are declared in the output (using xsl:namespace) to access those of our extension functions that we'll need for super-document validation checks (**5.1.3**).

The complete listing of the schematron-saxon.xsl wrapper is shown in Example 5.1.

Deployment. The XSLT implementation of Schematron is actually a compiler that translates a Schematron schema into an XSLT stylesheet. This compiled schema is then applied to the document being checked. So, the two commands that you need to run in order

---

3. Latest version: www.ascc.net/xml/schematron/1.5/skeleton1-5.xsl
4. www.ascc.net/xml/schematron/1.5/basic1-5/schematron-basic.html

· ·

Example 5.1   Schematron wrapper for Saxon importing the _lib.xsl library (based on schematron-basic.xsl).

```xsl
<xsl:stylesheet
    xmlns:xsl="http://www.w3.org/1999/XSL/Transform" version="2.0"
    xmlns:axsl="http://www.w3.org/1999/XSL/TransformAlias"
    xmlns:saxon="http://saxon.sf.net/">
<xsl:import href="skeleton1-5.xsl"/>

<xsl:template name="process-prolog">
  <!-- Namespace node for our XSLT extension functions: -->
  <xsl:namespace name="eg">http://www.example.org/</xsl:namespace>
  <!-- Another namespace node for an extension class: -->
  <xsl:namespace name="f">com.projectname.xslt.files</xsl:namespace>
  <!-- Importing the shared library: -->
  <axsl:import href="_lib.xsl"/>
  <!-- We don't really need any output parameters: -->
  <axsl:output method="text"/>
</xsl:template>

<xsl:template name="process-root">
  <xsl:param name="title"/>
  <xsl:param name="contents"/>
  <xsl:value-of select="$title"/>
  <xsl:text>&#10;</xsl:text>
  <xsl:copy-of select="$contents"/>
</xsl:template>

<xsl:template name="process-message">
  <xsl:param name="pattern"/>
  <xsl:param name="role"/>
  <!-- Outputting the source line number: -->
  <xsl:text>Line </xsl:text>
    <axsl:value-of select="saxon:line-number()"/>
  <xsl:if test="$role">
    <xsl:text> (</xsl:text>
    <xsl:value-of select="$role"/>
    <xsl:text>)</xsl:text>
  </xsl:if>:
  <xsl:apply-templates mode="text"/>
  <xsl:text>&#10;</xsl:text>
</xsl:template>
</xsl:stylesheet>
```

· ·

to check the document `src.xml` against the schema `schema.sch` using our Saxon wrapper are these (you can create shell scripts or batch files to run them with different source files, or you can wait until **5.6** where we'll see how to run validation of all pages from within the transformation stylesheet):

```
saxon -o schema-compiled.xsl schema.sch schematron-saxon.xsl
```

> This command runs schema compilation by applying the wrapper stylesheet to the schema and producing a `schema-compiled.xsl` stylesheet. It is only necessary to rerun compilation if you have modified the schema. Replace `saxon` with (or make it an alias to) the command that runs the Saxon processor.[5]

```
saxon -l src.xml schema-compiled.xsl env=staging
```

> This second command does actual validation of a source document. Here you can supply parameters (such as `env`) exactly as you would do to a transformation stylesheet. This is the command that prints any schema diagnostics and reports errors. The `-l` switch forces Saxon to keep track of line numbers; without it, the `saxon:line-number()` function does not work.

Namespace aliasing. As with any stylesheet that produces another stylesheet, our wrapper needs to alias the XSLT namespace. The `axsl` prefix is declared as corresponding to a non-XSLT URI and thus prevents `axsl:*` elements from being executed as XSLT instructions when the wrapper is run. Later, Schematron's "skeleton" file does the substitution:

```
<xsl:namespace-alias stylesheet-prefix="axsl" result-prefix="xsl"/>
```

which results in all `axsl:*` elements being output as `xsl:*` into the compiled schema.

5.1.3 Advanced Schematron

Our basic Schematron schema (Example 3.3, page 149) already has many advantages over grammar-based (**2.2.1**) schemas. It sports custom, arbitrarily detailed diagnostics and complex algorithmic

---

5. On my system, it is `java net.sf.saxon.Transform`.

checks — for instance, verifying the correspondence between the number of defined languages and the number of `translation` children in an element.

However, that example is still a document layer schema (**2.1.1**) because it can only check one document at a time, be that a page document or the master document. As promised, we will now extend that schema so that it also covers the super-document layer by validating links and dependencies between page documents and the master document as well as among different page documents. Now that we've prepared a shared library (**5.1.1**) and the wrapper (**5.1.2**) for our Schematron set-up, we have all the tools we need for this.

You can add the new Schematron `rules` described in this section to the basic schema in Example 3.3. Alternatively, you can combine them into a separate schema and perform two-stage validation of your source — first checking the document layer with the basic schema, and then validating the super-document layer using the techniques of this section.

5.1.3.1   Document availability

Our first validation task is to make sure that all web site pages listed in the master are actually present as source XML documents and are readable by the XML parser (i.e., are well-formed). Moreover, in our multilingual site, we want to check for existence of all page documents in all defined languages. It is logical to only enable this check when we are validating the master document, because we don't want to scour the entire document tree every time we validate a single page.

Obviously, we need to get source paths for all page documents. However, we cannot simply look them up in the master. This is because our master document (Example 3.2) does not store a complete pathname for each language variant of each page; the subtree of pages and the subtree of languages are *separate*. If we were writing a stylesheet, we could run an `xsl:for-each` loop to find all combinations of children of these two subtrees. But the Schematron syntax is purely declarative and does not permit any loops. Or does it?

Recall (**4.2**) that XPath 2.0 makes it possible to emulate many of XSLT's processing constructs — including loops — right in an XPath expression. This means that if we run our schema on an XSLT 2.0-compliant processor, we can pack the entire loop into the `test` attribute of a `report` or `assert`. Here's how it might look:

```
<rule context="menu//page | blocks/block">
  <report test="
      (for $1 in $master//languages/lang
        return boolean(document(eg:page-src(@id, $1))))
      = false()">
    A source document not found for "<value-of select="@id"/>".
  </report>
</rule>
```

Here, the `for` loop in the XPath expression attempts to feed the built-in `document()` function with source paths of all language variants for the current `page` or `block` (remember that a page may be registered either as one of the orthogonal `blocks` or as a `page` in the `menu` hierarchy). We use our custom `page-src()` function from the shared library (**5.1.1.4**) to go from a page's `id` attribute and a language to the complete pathname of the corresponding source document.

By the way, the `page-src()` function itself accesses the master document and searches it for a `page` or `block` with the given `@id`. This might seem awkward — when the rule is fired, we are already in that element and only have to make one step to reach its `@src`. However, our approach has the advantage of being generic and therefore robust, while any attempts to "optimize" it would likely breed hard-to-catch bugs.

If one of these source documents fails to load, `document()` returns an empty nodeset that is converted to a boolean value of `false`. When we compare the sequence of boolean values returned by the `for` loop to a single `false()` value, the result is `true` if *at least one* of the values in the sequence is `false` — that is, if at least one of the documents failed to load.

With Saxon, an attempt to load a non-existent file with `document()` produces a Java error message (in addition to the Schematron diagnostics). This is implementation-dependent; other processors may handle this situation differently. If the file exists but is not well-formed XML, you'll get a parser error because `document()` attempts to parse the file it loads. If you only want to quickly check for the existence of an arbitrary file (e.g., an image), use a custom extension function, such as `files:exists()`, written in Java (**5.1.3.4**). It may have an additional advantage of more readable and customizable diagnostic messages for missing files.

5.1.3.2 Internal links

Now that we are sure that all documents mentioned in the master document are present and loadable, we can check the validity of internal links simply by looking them up in the master. Here's the `rule`:

```
<rule context="int | link[@linktype='internal']">
  <assert test="
    @link = (for $i in $master//(page|block)/(@id|@alias)
              return tokenize($i, '\s+'))">
  Broken internal link: no 'page' with
  @id="<value-of select="@link"/>" in the
  master document. Valid identifiers are:
  <value-of select="
    string-join((for $i in $master//(page|block)/(@id|@alias)
              return tokenize($i, '\s+')), ', ')"/>.
  </assert>
</rule>
```

Remember that links may use either an `id` or any of the defined `alias`es of a page. This means that here, just as in the unabbreviation functions (**5.1.1.4**), we have to go to some lengths in order to get a sequence of all valid page identifiers.

We start by creating a nodeset of all `@id` and `@alias` values of all `page`s and `block`s, and then apply the `tokenize()` function to each member of the nodeset. The second argument of `tokenize()` is a regular expression meaning "one or more whitespace characters." Therefore, for singleton `id` values, `tokenize()` does nothing; for space-separated `alias` lists, it breaks them into sequences. Everything returned by the function is then joined into one common sequence by `for` and compared to the current element's `link` attribute. The comparison yields `false` only if *none* of the sequence values matches.

The diagnostic message for this rule demonstrates how you can use Schematron's `value-of` element with an arbitrary XPath expression. This rule not only displays the `@link` value that is incorrect, but also lists all correct values from the master document (of course, this only makes sense if there aren't too many of them). For this, the same sequence-constructing expression as in the `test` attribute of `assert` is fed to the `string-join()` function that strings all sequence members together separated by `", "`.

5.1.3.3   External links

Now, the rule to check external links should seem easy:

```
<rule context="ext | link[@linktype='external']">
  <assert test="
      boolean(unparsed-text(eg:ext-link(@link), 'iso-8859-1'))">
    Broken external link: <value-of select="@link"/>.
  </assert>
</rule>
```

First of all, we unabbreviate the link by our `eg:ext-link()` function (**5.1.1.4**). Since we cannot expect all web pages that we link to to be valid XML, we use the `unparsed-text()` function to access the link URI because this function only retrieves the document without attempting to parse it. (Both `document()` and `unparsed-text()` can access URIs, not only local pathnames.) The boolean conversion returns `false` if the document is inaccessible (or empty).

A quest for a better probe. Unfortunately, the use of `unparsed-text()` has its share of problems:

- The XSLT specification[6] mandates that the URI for `unparsed-text()` must not contain a fragment identifier — that is, you cannot have a # in the URI you pass to the function. This means you'll have to add another wrapper function that would strip such fragment identifiers, if present, before handing the URIs over to `unparsed-text()`.

- The error that occurs when `unparsed-text()` cannot access its URI is defined as recoverable. However, currently (in version 7.5.1) Saxon does not recover and terminates processing on such an error. This means you can find at most one broken link per validation run, and if a valid URI is temporarily unavailable, your validation is halted. Hopefully, future

....

6. Unlike `document()`, `unparsed-text()` is an XSLT function, not an XPath function. This distinction may be confusing, but it rarely matters in practice.

versions of Saxon as well as other 2.0 processors will handle this error as recoverable.

- As the name implies, `unparsed-text()` retrieves text. Among other things, this means that all characters in the retrieved document must be valid for that document's encoding. As a result, this function will likely choke on most binary files that you make it swallow, so you can't safely use `unparsed-text()` to access image files or other non-text resources.

All these limitations suggest that it might be a better idea to write your own extension function to test external URIs for availability. Such a function could ignore fragment identifiers, perform several retries for addresses that fail to respond, and handle both textual and binary resources. Additionally, to save bandwidth, it could only query the remote host for the availability of a resource without actually transferring it.

5.1.3.4   Local images

Images used on web pages are usually stored locally, and we can use our `files:exists()` extension function written in Java (Example 5.6, page 221) to make sure they are available:

```
<rule context="section[@image]">
  <assert test="
      files:exists(eg:os-path(concat($out-img, @image, '.png')))">
    Image file missing:
    <value-of select="concat($out-img, @image, '.png')"/>.
  </assert>
</rule>
```

Here, only `section` elements with an `image` attribute are checked, for this is the only construct referring to an image in our sample site source (Example 3.1, page 141). You can, of course, write a similar rule for other image-referencing elements, such as a standalone `img` element.

I did not define, instead of the `concat()` expression, an `eg:image-link()` function that would take an image identifier and return the full pathname of the image file. Such a function can be written in XSLT if necessary.

Language links

A language link (**3.5.3.4**) uses a `lang` element, which should not be confused with a `lang` within `languages` in the master document (you can rename either of them, of course, if you perceive this as a problem):

```
<rule context="
    lang[not(ancestor::languages)] | link[@linktype='language']">
  <assert test="@link = $master//languages/lang">
    Broken language link:
    no "<value-of select="@link"/>" language.
  </assert>
</rule>
```

External blocks

Orthogonal block definitions. For orthogonal blocks, we must first verify that their definitions in the master document are valid. Remember that each such definition specifies a source document and the identifier of a block to be extracted from it (**3.9.1.3**). As for the presence of the source documents, this has already been tested (**5.1.3.1**). What remains is a check of the validity of the `@select` identifier, if it is present.

We can insert this check into the same `rule` context as the document availability check:

```
<rule context="menu//page | blocks/block">
  <!-- ... document availability check ... -->
  <assert test="
      every $i in
        (for $l in $master//languages/lang
          return (
            if (@select)
              then boolean(document(eg:page-src(@id, $l))
                              //block[@id=current()/@select])
              else true())))
        satisfies $i">
    A block with @id="<value-of select="@select"/>" that the
    "<value-of select="@id"/>" orthogonal block refers to is missing.
  </assert>
</rule>
```

Here, the test expression attempts to load documents with the current @id for all defined languages and searches each of them for a block whose @id matches our current @select. The *quantified expression* every ... in ... satisfies ... returns true only if all values in the sequence satisfy the test — in this case, if all pages or blocks with @select match existing blocks in the corresponding source documents in all languages.

Dynamic block definitions.   These checks only cover orthogonal blocks defined in the master document. Dynamic block definitions (**3.9.1.4**) can also be validated, but this validation will depend on the implementation of the creators of dynamic data. For example, if some of your dynamic processes are implemented as callable templates in the main transformation stylesheet, nothing prevents you from loading that stylesheet with document() and checking that it does in fact contain an xsl:template with the corresponding name and xsl:params.

Block references. Now, the rule for validating orthogonal or dynamic block references in page documents is very simple, as it only needs to look up a block with a given @id in the master:

```
<rule context="page//block[@idref]">
  <assert test="@idref = $master//blocks/block/@id">
    A block with @idref must match the @id of one of the 'block'
    elements in the master document.
  </assert>
</rule>
```

5.1.3.7   Uniqueness

IDs in DTDs.   XML has a limited mechanism for ensuring uniqueness of attribute values. If you declare an attribute of the type ID in your DTD, a validating parser will report an error if two or more elements in the same document share the same value of this attribute. It is easy to see three big problems with this approach:

* The uniqueness constraint applies only to a single document. There's no way to ensure cross-document (e.g., site-wide) uniqueness.

- The ID-typed attributes must be unique across *all* element types used in your document. For example, if you have `<foo id="xyz">`, not only the rest of `foo` elements but any other elements as well are prevented from having the same identifier value. In other words, you cannot specify one group of unique identifiers for paragraphs and another for sections; if these two groups overlap, this is a validity error.

- There is no way to check elements' content for uniqueness; the ID mechanism only applies to attribute values.

Along with these three big problems, there's a smaller one as well: To verify uniqueness, you must have a complete DTD and use a validating parser for your document. As we saw in Chapter 2 (**2.2.4**), you may prefer alternatives to DTDs, and introducing a DTD into your setup for the sole purpose of checking uniqueness is a major hassle.

The Schematron way. Suppose we want to be able to assign identifiers to our p and head elements and ensure that these ids are unique throughout the entire web site. On the other hand, if any other element (e.g., section) uses the same id, this is not an error.

Can our Schematron schema handle this? Easy:

```
<rule context="p[@id] | head[@id]">
  <assert test="
     count(
       for $src in distinct-values($master//(page|block)/@src)
       return
         document(concat($src-path, $lang, '/', $src, $src-ext))
           //(p|head)[@id=current()/@id]
     ) = 1">
  Non-unique @id in a 'p' or 'head':
  @id="<value-of select="current()/@id"/>" is used in:
```

```
<value-of select="
        string-join(
          $master
            //(page|block)
              [document(eg:page-src(@id, $lang))
                //(p|head)[@id=current()/@id]
              ]
              /@src,
            ', ')"/>
  </assert>
</rule>
```

The `test` expression is not as scary as it might seem at first. It simply searches across all registered page documents (`$master//(page|block)`) and finds all *distinct* values of their `@src` attributes. The `distinct-values()` call is necessary because some pages may be mentioned twice — for example, once in the menu and again as a source of an orthogonal block.

Then, `@src` values are unabbreviated into complete paths,[7] corresponding documents are opened, and all `p` and `heads` elements are taken. Of them, the expression selects those whose `@id` is the same as the current element's `@id`. If the number of such elements is exactly 1, we are fine. Otherwise, we have a problem.

Diagnostics. To report this problem, another XPath expression in `value-of` extracts the `@src` values (pathnames) of those source documents that contain the duplicate `id` attributes (at least one of them will correspond to the document you are validating). For example, you might get diagnostics like

```
Line 32:
  Non-unique @id in a 'p' or 'head':
  @id="foo" is used in:
  team/index, team/hire, subscribe.
```

Extensible uniqueness. The same mechanism may be used not only for identifiers and not only for attributes, but also for any other data

---

7. Note that here, we cannot use any of our unabbreviation functions because these functions take a page `@id` as input, but what we have is `@src`.

that must be unique. For example, you may want to ensure that each one from a set of images is referenced only once or that there are no two paragraphs with the same text across the site.

Stay tuned. I think the examples in this section are an impressive testament to the combined power of Schematron and XPath 2.0. Still, this is not the ultimate schema yet. At the end of the chapter, we'll enable the stylesheet to run batch validation of all source documents (**5.6**). Validating, transforming, and possibly even uploading the entire site by one simple command — now *that's* convenience!

5.2 Stylesheet: first steps

5.2.1 Setting up the environment

A typical transformation stylesheet is a much bigger piece of code than anything we've seen so far. You'll have to take care about a lot of things. In the rest of this chapter, we examine the principal parts of a stylesheet one by one, with the last section (**5.7**) presenting a complete, though bare-bones, stylesheet that can be used with our example XML sources from Chapter 3.

Preliminaries.   Let's take a look at the stylesheet's opening lines (Example 5.2). An internal DTD subset is added in case we want to use mnemonic character references (**2.2.4.3**, page 75) for special characters. The namespace declarations in xsl:stylesheet cover XSLT 2.0 (the xsl prefix), our custom XSLT functions (the eg prefix), and a number of extensions written in Java for this stylesheet (we will talk about them later). Most of the setup work is done in our _lib.xsl shared library (**5.1.1**); here we just import it.

Output settings.   There are three xsl:output declarations. The first one is unnamed; it sets the parameters of serializing the default output (i.e., the HTML pages we are creating). The second declaration will be used for plain text files we will be creating (e.g., the CSS style sheet), and the third one, for auxiliary XML documents (e.g., the SVG files for graphic generation, **5.5.2**).

. . . .

Example 5.2   Here our journey starts: The first lines of the main transformation stylesheet.

```
<?xml version="1.0" encoding="iso-8859-1"?>

<!DOCTYPE xsl:stylesheet [
  <!ENTITY copy  "&#169;">
  <!ENTITY nbsp  " ">
  <!ENTITY mdash "&#8212;">
]>

<xsl:stylesheet
    xmlns:xsl="http://www.w3.org/1999/XSL/Transform" version="2.0"
    xmlns:eg="http://www.example.org/"
    xmlns:files="com.projectname.xslt.files"
    xmlns:graph="com.projectname.xslt.graph"
    xmlns:text="com.projectname.xslt.text"
    extension-element-prefixes="eg files text graph">

<xsl:import href="_lib.xsl"/>

<xsl:output method="html" encoding="US-ASCII" indent="no"
    doctype-public="-//W3C//DTD HTML 4.0 Transitional//EN"/>
<xsl:output name="txt" method="text" encoding="iso-8859-1"
    omit-xml-declaration="yes"/>
<xsl:output name="xml" method="xml" encoding="iso-8859-1"
    indent="yes"/>
```

. . . .

5.2.2 Page skeleton

Usually, the first template in a stylesheet is the one that matches the source's root element and builds the skeleton of the output HTML page. It is a typical pull-oriented trunk template and the main processing hub of the stylesheet. Example 5.3 gives an outline.

This template intersperses the basic elements of a web page (head, body, and the top-level layout structures) with calls to templates that fill in the content. For those bits of content that are based on the XML source of the page, we launch applicable templates using xsl:apply-templates with appropriate select and sometimes mode attributes. For static content that does not depend on the XML source, we run callable templates using xsl:call-template instructions.

. . . .

Example 5.3 Stylesheet's first template matches /page and builds the skeleton of the output HTML page.

```
<xsl:template match="/page">
  <xsl:message>
    processing: <xsl:value-of select="$current"/>
  </xsl:message>
  <!-- Credits are in XML comments,
    so they can come before the root element: -->
  <xsl:call-template name="credits"/>
  <html>
    <head>
      <xsl:apply-templates select="@keywords | @description"
          mode="meta"/>
      <xsl:call-template name="title"/>
      <xsl:call-template name="css"/>
      <xsl:call-template name="javascript"/>
    </head>
    <body bgcolor="#ffffff" background="{$target-img}bg.gif">

      <!-- Main layout table starts here -->
      <table style="table-layout: fixed; width: 100%;"
        cellpadding="0" cellspacing="0" border="0">
        <xsl:choose>
          <xsl:when test="$frontpage">
            <!-- Static content (logo, etc.) specific to the front page -->
          </xsl:when>
          <xsl:otherwise>
            <!-- Static content specific to a subpage -->
          </xsl:otherwise>
        </xsl:choose>

        <!-- Layout code... -->

        <!-- Calling menu template: -->
        <xsl:call-template name="top-menu"/>

        <!-- More layout code... -->

        <!-- Processing content blocks: -->
        <xsl:apply-templates select="block[not(@idref)]"/>

        <!-- More layout code... -->
```

```
      <!-- Processing orthogonal blocks: -->
      <xsl:apply-templates select="block[@idref]"/>

      <!-- Inserting page footer: -->
      <xsl:call-template name="page-footer"/>

      <!-- Closing main layout table: -->
    </table>
  </body>
</html>

<!-- Creating another version of the page: -->
<xsl:result-document format="html"
    href="{$out-path}{$lang}{$current}-print{$out-ext}">
  <xsl:message>creating printer-friendly page</xsl:message>
  <html>
    <head>
      <xsl:call-template name="title"/>
      <xsl:call-template name="css-printable"/>
    </head>
    <body>
      <!-- Inserting a simple page header: -->
      <xsl:call-template name="printable-head"/>

      <!-- Processing content blocks: -->
      <xsl:apply-templates select="block[not(@idref)]"/>

      <!-- Inserting page footer: -->
      <xsl:call-template name="page-footer"/>
    </body>
  </html>
</xsl:result-document>

</xsl:template>
```
. . . .

Diagnostic output. Since this template will always run for any page
document — and it will be executed only once per stylesheet run —
it is a good place to output any runtime xsl:messages to the terminal
(see **4.5.3** for why you cannot put them into, e.g., global variable
declarations). Alongside credits or copyright notices, you might want

to display some important global variable values such as `$current`, `$lang`, or `$env`.

Page versions. This template is also where you can create versions of the page with the same or similar content but different formatting. For example, many sites provide a "printer-friendly" version of each page — no menu, no ads, no rigid table layout, just the body of content and a copyright notice. This is what the last part of Example 5.3 demonstrates: A second, much simpler HTML page skeleton wrapped into an `xsl:result-document` includes only direct (not orthogonal) blocks. Special templates are called to insert a printer-friendly CSS style sheet and a minimal header (containing, e.g., the site's logo and a link back to the full version of the page).

Other variants might include a paginated version of a document, where a single source XML document is transformed into a series of linked HTML pages. Under Cocoon (Chapter 7), it may be more convenient to remove the page version code into separate stylesheets run by different pipelines.

Layout tips. You can use any of the practical HTML methods of laying out a web page. Most commonly, it is a page-wide layout `table`, but you can also create a `frameset` or simply use CSS, perhaps with some floating or absolutely positioned blocks (the last option is the simplest to maintain and most standards-compliant).

Whatever your chosen layout method may be, make sure that each block's output fits nicely into the framework of the page layout. For example, if you have a `frameset`, make `block`s output properly nested `frame`s into separate documents.

With a table-based layout, avoid producing partial tables. It is a much more robust solution to let the main layout template produce a complete table with all `tr`s and `td`s in place. Subordinate templates will then spit out complete tables, too, to be embedded into the cells of the main layout table. An extra level of nested tables is an acceptable price for sane, readable templates and for avoiding the nightmare of debugging tables with fluctuating numbers of rows and columns.

5.2.3   Static templates

CSS.   Let's see what a static (i.e., generating the same content every time) callable template might look like. Example 5.4 shows a simple CSS template to be called from the page skeleton template.

. . . .

Example 5.4   The CSS template is static and callable.

```
<xsl:template name="css">
  <link rel="stylesheet" href="{$target-path}site.css"/>
  <xsl:message>creating: site.css</xsl:message>
  <xsl:result-document href="{$out-path}site.css" format="txt">
body      {font-family: serif; background-color: #ffffff;}
h1        {font-family: sans-serif; font-size: 120%;
            font-weight: normal;}
a         {text-decoration: none; border-bottom: 2px dotted;
            color: #003399;}
.footer   {font-size: 80%; margin-top: 1em; margin-left: 0.5em;}
.sideitem {text-align: middle; font-size: 70%; padding-top: 1em;
            margin: 0.5em; text-transform: uppercase;}
  </xsl:result-document>
</xsl:template>
```

. . . .

This template links up the external CSS style sheet (using HTML's link element) and immediately proceeds to creating this CSS file. This style sheet is shared by all pages of the site; if some pages need to override it, they can do so in their embedded style elements (although this is rarely needed).

Note that to access the CSS file in link, we prepend $target-path to its name. For *creating* the file, however, we use $out-path as the pathname prefix. See **5.1.1.3**, page 189 for a description of these variables.

The benefits of automation.   Why create CSS from XSLT and not just use a static CSS style sheet? Partly, this is the desire to have everything controlled from one place (the transformation stylesheet). There are other benefits as well: With complex CSS specifications, you may want to automate CSS generation using XSLT loops and master document variables for repeating or regularly changing values of colors, lengths, etc.

JavaScript. The JavaScript static template, if you need one, may be similar. Any JavaScript code used on more than one page can also be placed in an external script file to be imported with `<script src="URI">` into those HTML pages that need it.

5.2.4 Miscellaneous pieces, from title to footer

Title. Our next template, `title`, is not static — we need to write some XPath to build the value we want. This callable template composes the web page `title` from the common part stored in the master document (usually it is the company name) and the `title` of the current page document:

```
<xsl:template name="title">
  <title>
    <xsl:value-of select="
        $master//html-title/translation[@lang=$lang]/text()"/>
    <xsl:text>: </xsl:text>
    <xsl:value-of select="title/text()"/>
  </title>
</xsl:template>
```

Any other information can be just as easily added to the title. For example, you could program the template to extract the appropriate `translation` from the `label` of that page's parent in the master document `menu` (see Example 3.2, page 143). Sometimes, the `keywords` of a page are also added to the title to boost the page's rank in web searches on these keywords.

Metadata. The templates for the page's keywords and description are applicable, not callable:

```
<xsl:template match="page/@description" mode="meta">
  <meta name="description" content="{.}"/>
</xsl:template>

<xsl:template match="page/@keywords" mode="meta">
  <meta name="keywords" content="{.}"/>
</xsl:template>
```

All they do is convert the attributes of the `page` element into the corresponding HTML `meta` elements. The interesting point, however, is that you might want the same source data to trigger other processing as well. For example, you may want to insert the @description not only into the meta but also into the body of the page.

Such collisions are resolved by using template modes. XSLT allows you to create any number of templates with the same match but different values of the mode attribute. Then, you can call the necessary template with its mode supplied in the apply-templates instruction.

Bottom stuff.   The last example in this section illustrates how applicable templates can be applied not only to the current source document but to any other — in this case, to the master document. Itself, the page-footer template is callable, but it takes whatever elements are inside the page-footer element in the master and pushes them into our stylesheet.

Then, an applicable template with an appropriate match (e.g., match="page-footer/*") grabs these pushed elements and processes them, unaware of where they come from. Below, such an applicable template selects the relevant translation and outputs a separator (a | character surrounded by two no-break spaces) after every item except the last.

```
<xsl:template name="page-footer">
  <p class="bottom">
    <xsl:apply-templates select="$master//page-footer/*"/>
  </p>
</xsl:template>

<xsl:template match="page-footer/*">
  <xsl:apply-templates select="translation[@lang=$lang]"/>
  <xsl:if test="following-sibling::*"> | </xsl:if>
</xsl:template>
```

Alternatively, we could combine these two templates into one and use an xsl:for-each loop in the page-footer callable template to iterate over all page-footer children. But why fiddle with manual loops when we can get the same result from XSLT's built-in template-matching mechanism for free?

5.3 **Top-level structures**

The basic layout of the web page has already been built by the skeleton template (**5.2.2**). In this section, we look at the other generic top-level constructs, in particular navigation menus and blocks. All of them are usually created by pull-oriented trunk templates (**4.5.1**).

5.3.1 Menu

Our next task is creating a menu for our web page. The code in Example 5.5 builds the site's main menu reflecting the top level of the site hierarchy (there are four top-level items in the menu in our sample master document, so the menu will have four buttons).

....

Example 5.5   Menu templates and related functions.

```
<xsl:template name="top-menu">
  <!-- Menu layout code... -->
  <xsl:apply-templates select="$master//menu/item"/>
  <!-- Menu layout code... -->
</xsl:template>

<xsl:template match="menu/item">
  <xsl:variable name="src" select="page[1]/@src"/>
  <xsl:variable name="label" select="
      label/translation[@lang=$lang]"/>

  <!-- Composing filename for the graphic menu button: -->
  <xsl:variable name="filename" select="
      concat(
        string(1 + count(preceding-sibling::*)),
        eg:letters-only($label))"/>

  <!-- Generating the menu button image: -->
  <xsl:if test="$images='yes'">
    <xsl:call-template name="create-image">
      <xsl:with-param name="label" select="$label"/>
      <xsl:with-param name="filename" select="
          concat($out-img, $filename)"/>
    </xsl:call-template>
  </xsl:if>
```

```
<!-- Menu item layout code... -->
<xsl:choose>
  <xsl:when test="$src = $current">
    <!-- Current page is the root of this branch
    (no link, branch active): -->
    <span class="active">
      <img src="{$target-img}{$filename}.png" alt="{$label}"/>
    </span>
  </xsl:when>

  <xsl:when test="($src != $current) and (page/@src = $current)">
    <!-- Current page is one of the pages (not root) of this branch
    (link, branch active): -->
    <a href="{$target-path}{$lang}/{$src}{$out-ext}"
      class="active">
      <img src="{$target-img}{$filename}.png" alt="{$label}"/>
    </a>
  </xsl:when>

  <xsl:when test="$src != $current">
    <!-- Current page does not belong to this branch
    (link, branch inactive): -->
    <a href="{$target-path}{$lang}/{$src}{$out-ext}"
      class="inactive">
      <img src="{$target-img}{$filename}.png" alt="{$label}"/>
    </a>
  </xsl:when>
</xsl:choose>
<!-- Menu item layout code... -->
</xsl:template>

<xsl:function name="eg:letters-only">
  <xsl:param name="s"/>
  <xsl:value-of select="
      lower-case(replace($s, '\ |,|\.|!|\?', ''))"/>
</xsl:function>
```

As with `page-footer`, there are two templates here. The first one is callable; it encloses the entire menu into appropriate layout constructions and iterates through the top-level items. The second template is applicable; it creates one menu item on each invocation.

Items as images. Implementation-wise, the menu can be textual, graphic, Flash, and so on. To illustrate one of the most common practical scenarios, Example 5.5 builds a menu out of static .png images (one per menu item), which are generated by the stylesheet itself (**5.5.2**). Layout code is not shown; add according to taste.

For each item, three variables are declared:

- $src is the pathname (taken from the src attribute) of the item's first page child;

- $label is the item's label in the current language; and

- $filename is the name for the generated image file, made out of the item's number in the sequence of siblings and its label (with spaces and punctuation removed). Using the label ensures that different language versions of the menu will have different button filenames (even though, in our implementation, they are all stored in a common directory).

Then, the create-image template is called; it creates the button image taking the $label and $filename as parameters. For an implementation of this callable template, see Example 5.16 (page 247).

Item states. The core of the menu item template is a choice among several possible relationships between the currently processed menu item and the current page document. Our example differentiates between:

- the root page of the menu branch headed by the current item: Button image is not linked (you cannot link a page to itself) and has class="active";

- a page that belongs to the current branch but is not its root: Image is linked (so you can ascend to the root of the branch) and has class="active";

- a page that is outside of the current menu branch: Image is linked and has class="inactive".

The CSS classes `active` and `inactive` provide the formatting for the current and non-current menu items. For example, you can use a different background color or margins for the current item.

The complexity range. Of course, you can use totally different formatting options for your menu items (such as DHTML or JavaScript effects), or you can recognize different logical states of an item. For instance, the simplest possible non-hierarchical menu might line up all its items and link them without any correlation with the current page. A slightly more complex setup could skip the current page's item or leave it unlinked.

On the other end of the scale, the three-state distinction in Example 5.5 might be further complicated by an orthogonal set of pages that do not belong in the menu hierarchy and therefore do not affect the formatting or behavior of the menu (but do display the menus themselves), or by the site's front page that may have a completely different presentation of the menu compared to all other pages of the site.

Submenu organization.   Lower levels of the menu hierarchy, if present, may be formatted in a variety of ways. Common options include

- **static submenus**: subitems are listed statically under their parent top-level items;

- **orthogonal menus**: a subspecies of static submenus, with only one (current) submenu displayed on each page, usually without a visible connection to the main menu (e.g., the main menu may run horizontally across the top of page, and the submenu, vertically in the left margin — hence "orthogonal");

- **interactive submenus**: same as static, but the lists of subitems are shown and hidden interactively using JavaScript or Dynamic HTML code snippets, for example, on a click or mouseover;

- **collapsing trees**: similar to interactive submenus in that subitem branches are shown and hidden interactively, but are more suitable for deeply nested content hierarchies, as you can collapse or expand the tree to arbitrary depth.

We don't need to discuss specific stylesheet templates for any of these options. Once you understand how the main menu template works, there's nothing new in a submenu. For the sake of completeness, however, our summary example (Example 5.21, page 267) contains a simple orthogonal submenu template.

Recursive menu.   One interesting possibility is a single *recursive* menu template that alone builds all levels of the menu hierarchy by calling itself for each submenu level. Such a template would not, however, be too useful unless all of your menu levels use similar formatting (which might be the case, for example, for a collapsing tree menu).

5.3.2   Dynamic menus

One type of menu that we did not cover when discussing source markup in Chapter 3 was the *dynamic* menu. The reason we missed it was that a dynamic menu is built by the stylesheet not from an XML document but from another data source, such as a database or a list of files in a directory. In other words, there's nothing in any static XML document that would correspond to the final list of items on the page (although your master document may store a reference to the place from which this list will be retrieved by the stylesheet).

Suppose you need to build a dynamic menu that reflects the current list of files in a directory. You want this menu to be built totally automatically, so that you can simply drop or remove files in the "watched" directory, rerun the transformation, and have the menu updated to reflect the changes. How do we go about it?

5.3.2.1   Reading a directory with Java

As mentioned before (**4.4.3**), many XSLT processors let you write your own functions in some programming language and call these functions from your XPath expressions. For example, Saxon, itself written in Java, allows you to link up any Java classes and call their methods.[8]

String or nodeset? Thus, to watch a directory, all we need to do is write a Java method that takes a directory path as an argument and returns its list of files. This list of files can be returned simply as a string — and XSLT 2.0 with its spiffy new regexp functions will have no problems parsing it. More elegant, of course, would be a method returning a nodeset looking something like this (serialized):

```
<file>file1.xml</file>
<file>file3.xml</file>
<file>oddfile.xml</file>
```

Then, we could run a simple `xsl:for-each` loop over the result returned by such a method. Unfortunately, constructing a nodeset in an extension function is more trouble than it's worth. With some processors, you may have to use DOM classes to create nodes, while with Saxon, you can only return nodes conforming to Saxon's own (optimized and nonportable) tree implementation.

So, we'll go the simple route and write a class with a method returning the list of files in a string, separated by newlines:

```
file1.xml
file3.xml
oddfile.xml
```

The `dir()` method in the `files` class (Example 5.6) does just that. This class also provides the `exists()` method that checks for existence of a file (we'll need this later).

While we are at it, you might want to extend the `files` class with other useful methods, such as moving or deleting files, querying the operating system name and version, etc. These methods may be used in the batch processing code in the stylesheet (**5.6**).

Filtering files. If you want the `dir()` method to list only some of the files (e.g., only `*.xml` files), you may write another class implementing the `FilenameFilter` interface[9] and give an instance of that class as an argument

---

8. *Methods* is Java-speak for what most other languages call functions.
9. java.sun.com/j2se/1.4.2/docs/api/java/io/FilenameFilter.html

Example 5.6 A Java class whose `dir()` method returns, as a `StringBuffer`, a newline-separated list of filenames in a given directory.

```java
package com.projectname.xslt;

import java.io.*;
import java.util.*;

public class files {

  private static File[] flist;

  public static boolean exists (String fileName) {
    File file = new File (fileName);
    return file.exists ();
  }

  public static StringBuffer dir (String dirName) {
    StringBuffer sb = new StringBuffer ();
    File fdir = new File (dirName);
    flist = fdir.listFiles ();
    for (int i = 0; i < flist.length; i ++) {
      sb.append (flist[i].getAbsolutePath () + "\n");
    }
    return sb;
  }
}
```

to `fdir.listFiles`. A less cumbersome solution is to filter the returned list in XSLT using `ends-with()` with the filename extension you are interested in.

5.3.2.2 Setting up Java extensions

As this is our first extension class (more are used later in this chapter), let's see how to install it into a Java environment and link to the stylesheet.

Installing a class. Store your `files` class in a file with the same name and `.java` extension (`files.java`) and compile it (`javac files.java`). Java expects the resulting `.class` file to be located in a subdirectory tree that corresponds to the full package name as declared in the class source. Thus, for the `com.projectname.xslt` package in our example, do this:

- create a `classes` directory in any convenient place;

- create a chain of subdirectories `classes/com/projectname/xslt`;

- place `files.class` into `xslt`;

- add the full path to `classes` to your CLASSPATH environment variable by typing

  ```
  set CLASSPATH=%CLASSPATH%;full/path/to/classes/
  ```

  on Windows (note the semicolon) or

  ```
  export CLASSPATH=$CLASSPATH:full/path/to/classes/
  ```

  on Unix (note the colon).

Plugging it in. In your XSLT stylesheet, you need to declare the new extension class before you can use it. This is done via a namespace declaration, with the class path being the namespace URI. The arbitrary prefix you associate with that URI will be prepended to the function name in XPath expressions. We already did this in the opening `xsl:stylesheet` tag in Example 5.2 (page 208): The URI `com.projectname.xslt.files` identifies the `files` class we've just created.

Other Java-based processors use similar methods of linking up external classes. If your processor is not written in Java, you may have to rewrite the extensions in another language, but the principle remains the same: You use a namespace declaration to identify the source of an external module and then call that module's functions with the corresponding namespace prefix.

5.3.2.3   Example: linking files

Now, to build a menu linking all files in a directory, all you need to do is this (assuming each file in `$dir` is well-formed XML and has a `/title` element for the text of the link):

```
<xsl:for-each select="tokenize(string(files:dir($dir)), '\n')">
  <xsl:if test=".">
    <a href="{replace(., $src-ext, $out-ext)}">
      <xsl:value-of select="document(.)/title"/>
    </a>
  </xsl:if>
</xsl:for-each>
```

Of note:

- Unlike 1.0, XSLT 2.0 is a strongly typed language, so we have to explicitly convert the value returned by `files:dir()` to a string.

- We need to test for the filename being non-empty (`<xsl:if test=".">`) because the Java method will return a string with a newline at the end, which the `tokenize()` function will convert into an empty item.

- The `href` attribute contains the returned filename with `$src-ext` replaced by `$out-ext`. We therefore assume that all source XML files in `$dir` will get transformed to web pages that we can link. In fact, as we'll see in **5.6**, we can use a similar mechanism to perform such batch transformation from within the stylesheet.

5.3.3 Blocks

Just as there may be many different types of blocks (recall our discussion in **3.1.2**, page 93), you may need to create many different block templates. The key concept is *modularity*; make sure that each block template's output properly fits into the corresponding slot in your page skeleton (**5.2.2**) or any other places it may need to fit into (for example, some blocks may nest into each other).

What block templates mostly consist of is layout code. You will want to set the block apart from its surroundings by a background, frame, or other means. You'll also need to create standard block accessories, such as heading, icon, author name, and of course the body text. Creative possibilities are endless; you can vary formatting of your blocks depending on how many other blocks are there before or after this block on the page, on the name of the author, on the age of the information, or on anything else.

Just as in the top-level skeleton template, you can use either callable or (more commonly) applicable templates to insert bits of data into their layout slots. Do not use `xsl:value-of` for this purpose unless you are absolutely sure the element you refer to will always contain flat text with no markup.

The inner core of a block template is usually an `xsl:apply-templates` *without* a `select` attribute. It passes control further into the applicable templates that take care of low-level text markup. So, finally, here's the point where the trunk templates are finished and branch processing starts (**5.4**). The pull is over — let's start pushing!

5.3.3.1   Orthogonal blocks

With blocks, the only nontrivial bit is processing the orthogonal content (**2.1.2.2**, page 51). In our examples in Chapter 3, orthogonal blocks were supposed to be extracted from arbitrary pages of the site. The correspondence between an orthogonal block `id`, its source document, and the `id` of the block to be extracted from that source is given in the master document. In page documents, each `block` either has its own content or provides an `idref` attribute referring to an orthogonal block declared in the master.

A template with multiple inputs.   With regard to formatting, however, there may be no big difference between native and orthogonal blocks. Therefore, it is convenient to have one template handle all blocks with similar formatting, no matter where they come from. Can this be done in XSLT? You bet.

In the `block`-matching template, we first declare the `$from` variable storing the nodeset that we will be working on. In Example 5.7, this nodeset may be either an orthogonal block fetched from its original location or the source document's current `block` node. It may also be a nodeset generated by some dynamic process (**3.9.1.4**). Then, we construct our block as usual, but prepend `$from` to all `select`

....

Example 5.7 A block template handling both native and orthogonal blocks.

```
<xsl:template match="block">
  <xsl:variable name="from" select="
      if (@idref != '')
        then
          document(eg:page-src(@idref, $lang))
            //block[@id=current()/@idref]
        else . "/>

  <!-- Block layout code... -->
  <!-- Creating block heading: -->
  <xsl:apply-templates select="$from/heading"/>
  <!-- Processing paragraphs: -->
  <xsl:apply-templates select="$from/p"/>
  <!-- Block layout code... -->
</xsl:template>
```

....

values in `xsl:apply-templates` instructions that fill in the content of the block.

Unabbreviation of orthogonal sources. Note that to get the full pathname of the orthogonal block's source document, we use the `eg:page-src()` unabbreviation function defined in the shared XSLT library (**5.1.1**). This is possible because that function searches both `pages` and `blocks` in the master document to find out the `@src` corresponding to a given `@id`.

5.4 Bottom-level structures

The pull-oriented trunk templates in the previous sections had one thing in common: They were rather big, mostly due to a lot of HTML layout code they had to provide. However, as we descend the stylesheet hierarchy, templates become much more lightweight and transparent.

One-to-one mapping. A typical push-oriented branch template `matches` one source element type and converts it into one corresponding HTML element type — no complex layout, no `if`s or `for-each`es, no callable templates. For example, paragraphs are converted to `p` elements, emphasis to `em`, and so on.

Be careful with shadows. Inside a branch template, there's usually an `xsl:apply-templates` without a `select` attribute working as a catch-all for the children of the current element. Use specific patterns in a `select` only if you are sure that no other elements may legally occur in that position — otherwise you run the risk of losing data. For example, if you only have `<xsl:apply-templates select="p"/>` inside a `section` template, any non-p children of a `section` will be ignored even if you have templates for them. In this situation, anything except p is said to be "shadowed" under a `section`.

5.4.1 Processing links

The interesting thing about link templates is unabbreviating link addresses (**3.5.3**, page 112): It is much more convenient to write links using an abbreviated notation in the source, but we need to construct full URIs for the resulting HTML links.

Our shared XSLT library (**5.1.1**) contains a few simple unabbreviation functions. In a real stylesheet, you will likely need more such functions, one for each link type (**3.5.2**, page 109). The link templates calling these functions don't need to be complex, as shown in Example 5.8.

In the stylesheet, we don't need to check for the existence of the `link` attribute or for the validity of the resulting link; these checks have already been made by the Schematron schema run before the transformation (**5.1.3.2**, **5.1.3.3**). However, if you do not use Schematron, you may want to add certain link checks and corresponding diagnostics to the stylesheet templates.

5.4.2 Text processing

Most branch templates transform low-level text markup. Is there anything interesting at still lower levels of the source hierarchy?

Now that we've descended to the level of character data, you may think that our work is over. This is not quite true. Even for plain text, HTML presentation may differ from that of the source XML, and a conversion should therefore be taken care of by the stylesheet.

Example 5.8 Link templates for various link types.

```
<xsl:template match="link[@type='internal'] | int">
  <a href="{eg:page-link(@link, $lang)}"><xsl:apply-templates/></a>
</xsl:template>

<xsl:template match="link[@type='external'] | ext">
  <a href="{eg:ext-link(@link)}"><xsl:apply-templates/></a>
</xsl:template>

<xsl:template match="link[@type='rfc']">
  <a href="{eg:rfc-link(@link)}"
     target="_new"><xsl:apply-templates/></a>
</xsl:template>
```

A common source of problems is the presentation of special characters, i.e., those outside of the ASCII range.[10] Common examples in English texts are the em-dash (—), single and double curly quotes ('', ""), and the apostrophe (same as the closing single curly quote). The problem is that there are many ways in which these characters may be encoded, and the way they are represented in your source XML is not necessarily the best for the HTML output.

5.4.2.1 Charset conversions

You probably don't need to worry about it if all you require is a conversion from one standard character encoding into another. On the Web, it is advisable to represent characters outside of the ASCII range by either mnemonic or numeric character references (**2.2.4.3**) to protect them against miscommunication of the page's charset that may happen between the server and the client browser.[11] Character references refer to Unicode code points and are therefore immune to any reencodings of the source document. These character references

---

10. In English; other languages may have different notions of what characters are special and what are not. The ASCII range, though, is considered unspecial pretty much all over the world.

11. Unless your language uses *mostly* non-ASCII characters, in which case following this advice will result in too much overhead.

should work in all modern browsers — provided the browser can, in principle, display the corresponding character (i.e., has an appropriate font).

Fortunately, you don't have to do anything special to obtain proper character references in the output. All you have to do is this:

- Make sure all the source documents correctly indicate their encoding in the XML declaration. The most commonly used encoding is ISO 8859–1, for which the declaration should read

  ```
  <?xml version="1.0" encoding="iso-8859-1"?>
  ```

- Make sure you specify ASCII as the output encoding in your stylesheet — for example,

  ```
  <xsl:output method="html" encoding="US-ASCII"
      doctype-public="-//W3C//DTD HTML 4.0 Transitional//EN"/>
  ```

If both these requirements are met (and your XSLT processor is standards-compliant), any non-ASCII characters in the input will be converted to numeric character references in the output. For example,

She said, "Mr Filkë is — and always was — my respected teacher."

becomes[12]

```
She said, &#8220;Mr Filk&#235; is &#8212; and always was &#8212;
my respected teacher.&#8221;
```

in HTML — which, in turn, will again render the nice curly quotes, accented characters, and em-dashes in the browser window.

5.4.2.2   Search and replace

It's not always that easy, though; not all content authors use correct ISO 8859–1 characters to start with. This very much depends on what kind of tool they use for XML authoring (**6.1**), but chances are that the XML you get from the authors will have no fancy characters at all, but only plain ASCII quotes (", ') instead of curly quotes and

---

12. Depending on setup, your XSLT processor may output equivalent hexadecimal numeric character references instead of decimal.

hyphens (-) instead of dashes. Rather than bug the author, you might want to replace these ASCII approximations by proper character references automatically.

The brute force approach. Perhaps the first idea to come to your mind will be writing a simple AWK or Perl script to handle these search-and-replace tasks. However, you'll quickly realize that you don't want to replace *all* of your quotes and hyphens because a lot of them are part of markup (e.g., quotes around attribute values) and not character data. Moreover, even some parts of character data (such as examples of programming code or XML markup) must be protected from any replacements. To reliably distinguish between those parts of the input stream that are to be processed and those that are not, you basically have to implement a complete XML parser — which makes the entire idea look hardly feasible.

The XSLT 1.0 approach. It's clear, therefore, that the character replacement job can only be handled by an XPath-enabled language. And while we're writing an XSLT stylesheet, why not assign it this task — along with all the other tasks it has to perform?

Unfortunately, XSLT 1.0 is badly suited for this kind of job. Matching regexps and replacing parts of a text string cannot be done except via extensions; in pure XSLT, you can only use recursion to parse the string into a sequence of character tokens to be processed in a `for-each` loop. Which is possible but, believe me, way too awkward and agonizingly slow.

The XSLT 2.0 approach. XSLT 2.0 and XPath 2.0 are much better equipped for text processing, since the new XPath provides functions for regexp matching and replacing. For example, the `eg:letters-only()` function from Example 5.5 (page 215) uses these new tools to build a filename from a text string by lowercasing it and removing spaces and punctuation. Thus, it will transform the heading

```
What, Where, and When?
```

into

```
whatwhereandwhen
```

The combined approach. For more complex processing, we have to write an extension function and link it to our stylesheet. Let's see how this could be done in Java with Saxon. To process all regular text of a web page, we can write in the stylesheet

```
<xsl:template match="p//text() | head//text()">
  <xsl:value-of select="text:typography(.)"/>
</xsl:template>
```

This template matches all text() nodes under p and head, passes each node to the typography() method, and outputs the returned string value. The text namespace prefix, as always, points to the class containing this method. The Java source for that class is shown in Example 5.9.

Alternating quotes. The interesting bit is that ASCII has only one symbol for double quote (") while proper typography requires that open and closing quote characters (" ") be used. To work around this, our class stores an internal flag variable, quoteFlag, set alternatively to 0 or 1 on each quote replacement. If quoteFlag == 0, we replace the next ASCII quote with an opening quote; otherwise, a closing quote.

It is worth noting that the quoteFlag variable belongs to the class, not to the method itself, and is therefore persistent between method calls. As a result, this simple mechanism gives correct results even when a single text unit is broken into several text nodes. For instance, if your text contains a fragment within quotes enclosed in an inline element, such as

```
She said, "<name>Mr Filk&#235;</name> is - and always was - my
respected teacher."
```

this will be correctly translated into what renders as

She said, "Mr Filkë is — and always was — my respected teacher."

Example 5.9 The text class provides the typography() method that replaces some ASCII characters with their improved typographic lookalikes.

```java
package com.projectname.xslt;

public class text {
  static int quoteFlag = 0;

  public static String typography (String s) {
    int i;

    // replace space followed by hyphen
    // by no-break space followed by em-dash
    i = 0;
    while ((i = s.indexOf (" -", i + 1)) != -1) {
      s = s.substring (0, i)
          + "\u00a0" + "\u2014"
          + s.substring (i + 2);
    }

    // use right single curly quote instead of '
    s = s.replace ('\'', '\u2019');

    // replace " by alternating left and right double curly quotes
    while ((i = s.indexOf ("\"")) != -1) {
      if (quoteFlag == 0) {
        s = s.substring (0, i) + "\u201c" + s.substring (i + 1);
        quoteFlag = 1;
      }
      else if (quoteFlag == 1) {
        s = s.substring (0, i) + "\u201d" + s.substring (i + 1);
        quoteFlag = 0;
      }
    }
    return s;
  }
}
```

(with, if necessary, additional formatting for the `name`) even though this sentence is broken into three text nodes and therefore triggers three calls to `text:typography()`.

Note, however, that this approach is risky and can only be used after testing with a specific processor. This is because XSLT does not require that the document order be preserved when the `text()` nodes (or any other nodes) are matched against the corresponding templates, and an XSLT processor may therefore freely reorder the `text:typography()` method calls.

Punctuation as style, not content. If some element type, such as `quote`, *always* requires quotation marks, you should program your stylesheet to insert them automatically for `quote` elements and free the author of the burden to supply both markup and punctuation that duplicate each other.

5.4.2.3 Text preparation guidelines

If you decide that you do need search-and-replace text processing similar to what we've just discussed, the `text` class in Example 5.9 is only a starting point. Your authors may have their own idiosyncrasies regarding ASCII punctuation. For example, some prefer to use double hyphens (`--`) to represent em-dashes; others may use ASCII backquotes (`` ` ``) and straight quotes (`'`) for opening and closing quotation marks.

Typographic conventions in output may also vary considerably. For instance, you may or may not have spaces around em-dashes; besides em-dashes, you may need en-dashes (between digits) and longish quotation dashes; the different approaches to the use of single and double quotes, as well as adjacent punctuation characters, is a topic unto itself. Finally, other languages may impose their own typographic rules, which you must respect even if all you need is a short foreign-language citation.

Standardize. You should make painfully clear to anyone involved in writing or editing web site content what is the accepted standard source representation for any nontrivial characters. Try to keep your guidelines simple and logical, but always be more flexible in your stylesheet code than you are in the guidelines (i.e., try to accommodate as much nonstandard input as possible, so long as it is unambiguous).

If your site is going to contain any significant amount of text and/or be massively updated, take time to develop and publicize your very own *Web Site Style Guide* (preferably in collaboration with the site's editor and graphic designer). Find a good typographical reference whose recommendations you trust *and* like. Learn from existing web sites whose typography is above average. Unicode charts[13] will not only help you find the codes for the characters you want but will also provide hints on their usage. Don't expect your guide to be ready at the web site launch; the best style guides grow from everyday practice. Last but not least, always test your web typography on all major platforms and browsers.

Reuse. If you are not new to web design, you have probably accumulated a library of text-processing scripts that you often use for preparing web pages. When migrating to XSLT, you don't have to abandon those scripts just because they may be difficult to reimplement in a functional language. You can still use them as extensions, getting the best of both worlds — the power of XPath in the stylesheet and the efficiency of traditional text-processing algorithms in extensions.

Do not abuse this possibility, however. Try to use XML markup for any *semantic* aspects of your source, and only resort to extensions when your algorithms are too complex for XSLT or when you don't want to place unreasonable markup requirements on your authors.

5.4.2.4 Adding structure

One common text-processing task is adding markup where no markup exists in the source — that is, marking up fragments of a source document's text based on some patterns or regular expressions. With XSLT 2.0, this task is achievable even without extensions.

For example, suppose we want to uppercase the first two words of every paragraph. The `eg:upcase2()` function in Example 5.10 achieves

---

13. www.unicode.org/charts/

. . . .

Example 5.10   Uppercasing the first two words of each p (more precisely, of the first text node within each p).

```
<xsl:template match="p/text()[1]">
  <xsl:copy-of select="eg:upcase2(.)"/>
</xsl:template>

<xsl:function name="eg:upcase2" as="item()*">
  <xsl:param name="str"/>
  <xsl:variable name="seq" select="tokenize($str, '\s+')"/>
  <xsl:sequence>
    <span style="text-transform: uppercase;">
      <xsl:for-each select="1 to 2">
        <xsl:value-of select="item-at($seq, .)"/>
        <xsl:text> </xsl:text>
      </xsl:for-each>
    </span>
    <xsl:for-each select="3 to count($seq)">
      <xsl:value-of select="item-at($seq, .)"/>
      <xsl:text> </xsl:text>
    </xsl:for-each>
  </xsl:sequence>
</xsl:function>
```

. . . .

this by breaking its argument into a sequence of words and then reassembling it, adding a span with an appropriate CSS property around the first two words.

Note that we apply this function to p/text()[1] and not just p/text() because a p may have several child text nodes, and we only want to process the first one. Therefore, this trick won't work if there is any source markup around the first and/or second word of a p.

5.5 Dealing with non-XML objects

So far, we were concerned with our stylesheet's HTML output. But a typical web page is more than just HTML. Web sites invariably contain images; some of them embed Flash animations or Java applets; many sites also present some of their content in PDF. This section will show you how to use XSLT to generate such objects automatically from the site's XML source.

5.5.1 Accessing images

No matter how powerful XSLT is, not all external objects *need* to be generated by the stylesheet. Those that are static — i.e., those that do not change when the content of the site changes (1.3.4) — are produced once and for all by the site's graphic designer. However, the stylesheet can still benefit from a method to *access* such static objects. Why? There are two reasons.

Checking existence. First, the stylesheet must be able to check if these objects actually exist. This kind of validation cannot be done by a schema simply because schemas check source XML, and source XML has no knowledge of the static images or other objects used for web page layout or decoration. It is the stylesheet actually building the site that stores references to all such objects — and can verify that they really are there and the site will therefore not give any nasty formatting surprises.

Retrieving objects' properties. Second, to properly embed external objects (both static and dynamic), the stylesheet must be able to extract some information from them. For images, you'll want to know their dimensions so you can put them in the `height` and `width` attributes of the corresponding `img` element (this speeds up loading the page, especially a complex one). For static images, you can simply hardcode these values into the stylesheet, but this is tedious manual work, inefficient and prone to errors. Let's see if there is a way to do this automagically.

Getting dimensions. XSLT itself is not quite up to the challenge. Once again, we need to write a couple of extension functions — they would take an image pathname or URI and return its dimensions. Example 5.11 shows a Java class implementing this. (Not exactly the most elegant piece of code, but it does its job.)

....

Example 5.11 The `graph` class provides methods that return width and height of an image (works with the PNG, GIF, and JPEG formats).

```java
package com.projectname.xslt;

import java.awt.*;
import java.awt.image.ImageObserver;

public class graph {

  static ImageObserver observer;
  static Image img;

  private static void init (String name) {
    Toolkit tk = Toolkit.getDefaultToolkit ();
    img = tk.getImage (name);
    observer = new ImageObserver () {
      public boolean imageUpdate (Image img, int flags,
                                  int x, int y, int w, int h) {
        return (flags & (ALLBITS | ABORT)) == 0;
      }
    };
    try {
      MediaTracker imageTracker = new MediaTracker (new Frame ());
      imageTracker.addImage (img, 0);
      imageTracker.waitForID (0);
    }
    catch (Exception e) {
      System.err.println (e.getMessage ());
    }
  }

  public static int geth (String name) {
    init (name);
    return img.getHeight (observer);
  }

  public static int getw (String name) {
    init (name);
    return img.getWidth (observer);
  }
}
```

....

Image insertion template. Now in XSLT, all we need to do is declare a namespace prefix (e.g., `graph`) for `com.project-name.xslt.graph` so we can use its methods. As for file existence checks, we already have the `files:exists()` method (Example 5.6, page 221).

Example 5.12 shows a callable template for inserting static images. You call this template with an image filename (e.g., `img/logo.png`) and its description (e.g., `Company logo`) as parameters; the template will check if the image file exists, retrieve its dimensions, and create the corresponding `img` element.

. . . .

Example 5.12   The `image` template checks if an image exists and inserts it into HTML.

```
<xsl:template name="image">
  <xsl:param name="filename"/>
  <xsl:param name="alt"/>
  <xsl:variable name="path" select="concat($im-path, $filename)"/>
  <xsl:if test="not(files:exists($path))">
    <xsl:message terminate="yes">
      Error: Image <xsl:value-of select="$path"/> not found
    </xsl:message>
  </xsl:if>
  <img
      src="{$path}"
      width="{graph:getw($path)}"
      height="{graph:geth($path)}"
      alt="{$alt}" border="0"/>
</xsl:template>
```

. . . .

Building an image gallery.   Example 5.13 combines the methods of the `graph` class with the `dir()` method from the `files` class (**5.3.2.1**) to present all images in the `$dir` directory in an automated gallery.

The `graph:geth()` and `graph:getw()` functions will be especially useful for generated images (discussed in the next section) whose dimensions cannot be known in advance.

Example 5.13   This loop uses extension functions to access and link all images from `$dir`.

```
<xsl:for-each select="tokenize(string(files:dir($dir)), '\n')">
  <xsl:if test="
      . and (
        ends-with(., '.png') or
        ends-with(., '.gif') or
        ends-with(., '.jpg')
      )">
    <img
      src="{.}" alt="{.}"
      width="{graph:getw(.)}"
      height="{graph:geth(.)}"/>
  </xsl:if>
</xsl:for-each>
```

5.5.2   Creating images

XSLT was created as an XML-to-XML transformation tool, but in practice, only the input to an XSLT stylesheet has to be well-formed XML. The output of a transformation can be in any textual format. So, for example, it is easy to write a stylesheet to transform an XML spreadsheet into a comma-separated text file. But what if we need binary files, such as images or Flash?

Two-stage conversion. An obvious approach is to program the stylesheet to output an intermediate textual (or, better yet, XML) format that has at least a one-way mapping to the required binary format. Then, we can call an external conversion utility to create a binary file from that intermediate format. This is the general idea that we'll explore in more detail below in reference to bitmap images. Other binary formats used on the Web are briefly discussed in **5.5.3**.

What is the best intermediate format for images? Remember that we are not interested in *all* images that can be displayed on a site; our focus is on those that (may) need to be updated when the site's source is updated. This means that in a great majority of cases, we'll be creating images consisting primarily of text, perhaps combined with some static backgrounds or overlays.

Why put text into images? Isn't it bad web design? Often it is; a piece of text petrified in a static bitmap suffers from bad accessibility in text-only user agents, not to mention that it is annoyingly unscalable in most graphic browsers. On the other hand, accessibility can be improved by proper metadata markup (use an `alt` attribute with the same text as in the image), whereas from the designer's viewpoint, it is sometimes critical to ensure the pixel-precise rendition of a textual element such as a menu label or a heading.

Corporate sites care a lot about design consistency which improves branding and recognizability, and font consistency is an important aspect of it. With the current HTML state of the art, the simplest and most reliable way to typeset some textual element using a specific font face is to cast it into a bitmap. Besides, a lot of web surfers still do not have fully antialiased text display, so if you want a bit of text to stand out quality-wise, a properly rasterized bitmap is the way to go.

Finally, sometimes you may need to work from an existing image — for example, overlay a text string on top of an ad banner. This means we must be prepared to include textual images in our XML/XSLT ecosystem should such a need arise.

5.5.2.1   Choosing format

There's really no shortage of text-based formats that can be converted into images. TeX, XSL-FO, PostScript — all of them can be used for producing a bitmap image with text in it. But if we narrow our search by excluding non-XML formats as well as those requiring complex renderer setup, the best open format for our task appears to be SVG.[14]

SVG (Scalable Vector Graphics) is an XML-based vector graphics format designed by the W3C to be used on the Web and to fit well with other W3C standards. SVG is not really suitable for complex typography; for example, you cannot flow a long text string into a paragraph with automatic line breaks. However, for things like buttons or headings on a web site, it fits the bill perfectly.

....

14. Latest version as of this writing: www.w3.org/TR/SVG11/.

Strictly speaking, SVG is intended to be supported directly by the browsers, but you cannot count on that support just yet.[15] This does not mean, however, that we cannot successfully use SVG for automatically generating traditional bitmap images — for example in PNG format — to be served from the web site.

I have already hinted at the possibility by including a call to the `create-image` template in the menu template (Example 5.5). Now let's see what this `create-image` looks like.

5.5.2.2   Choosing a rasterizer

There are several SVG rasterizers available, including both commercial and open source products. In this book, we use the **Batik** suite developed by the Apache XML Project.[16] Batik claims complete support of the static features of SVG (i.e., excluding animation); it is written in Java and includes a rasterizer (program converting SVG to a bitmap) as well as a font conversion utility that makes it possible to use TrueType fonts in SVG. Install the latest version of Batik to run the examples in this section.

Another free SVG renderer is a part of the **Imagemagick** suite of graphic tools.[17] You are supposed to be able to run

```
convert image.svg image.png
```

(where `convert` is the image conversion utility in Imagemagick) to rasterize an SVG document. However, Imagemagick's SVG support is less robust and uses nonstandard font handling, so we'll stick with Batik for our rasterizing needs. You may still need Imagemagick to postprocess your bitmap files (**5.5.2.6**), and it is generally a good piece of software to have around, so install it too.[18]

----

15. Browser plugins for viewing SVG exist.

16. `xml.apache.org/batik/`. Batik will run on any Java-enabled system (JDK 1.4 or better required).

17. `www.imagemagick.org`

18. If you don't have it installed already — Imagemagick is included in most Linux distributions. On the Imagemagick web site, you'll find binaries for Windows, Linux, Mac OS X, and other platforms.

5.5.2.3 Preparing fonts

To create an image containing text, we start by choosing and preparing the font(s) to be used by that text. SVG uses its own scalable font format; fortunately, Batik includes a font conversion utility for TrueType fonts. If you have a font file called `pushkin.ttf`, run this command:

```
java org.apache.batik.svggen.font.SVGFont pushkin.ttf -id font_id \
                                          > pushkin.svg
```

(Make sure all Batik's `.jars` are in the Java `CLASSPATH` before issuing this command.) This will create the file `pushkin.svg`, which is our font converted to SVG format. The `-id` command-line option sets the internal identifier of the new font that we'll use later to refer to it from our SVG files.

A good font editor capable of working directly with SVG fonts (as well as TrueType, OpenType, and PostScript Type 1 fonts) is **PfaEdit**.[19] It can be used for font conversions as well as for editing character outlines, adjusting kern pairs, reencoding fonts, and so on.

5.5.2.4 Creating SVG

Now that we have the tools and the font, let's write a sample SVG file to test our setup. We will use the free cursive Pushkin font[20] to render the string "Scalable Vector Graphics." After we test rasterizing of a manually created SVG file, we'll look into how to enable our XSLT stylesheet to do the same automatically.

Another language to learn? SVG is a complex format; what is shown in Example 5.14 is only a "Hello World." Fortunately, you don't need to learn all the details of the SVG specification. If what you have in mind is a complex graphic composition, you can use any SVG-capable vector editor,[21] save the result into SVG, and use it as a

---

19. `pfaedit.sf.net`
20. Created by Paratype based on the handwriting of Alexander Pushkin, see `www.fonts.ru/news/pushkin.html`.
21. Adobe Illustrator can import and export SVG. A small but promising native-SVG editor is Inkscape, `www.inkscape.org`.

template for your stylesheet-generated images. The only thing you need to know for this is how to deal with fonts and basic text layout, and this is what Example 5.14 illustrates.

....

Example 5.14   A sample SVG file.

```
<?xml version="1.0" encoding="iso-8859-1"?>
<svg
    width="500px" height="100px"
    xmlns="http://www.w3.org/2000/svg"
    xmlns:xlink="http://www.w3.org/1999/xlink">
  <defs>
    <font-face font-family="Pushkin">
      <font-face-src>
        <font-face-uri xlink:href="pushkin.svg#font_id"/>
      </font-face-src>
    </font-face>
  </defs>

  <text style="
      fill: #000000;
      font-family: Pushkin;
      font-size: 25pt;"
      x="10px" y="50px">Scalable Vector Graphics</text>
</svg>
```

....

Defining the canvas.   The root element, svg, sets the size of the canvas that we'll be painting on. Since you cannot know in advance how much space will be taken by your text string, make sure you have ample room even for the longest label or heading you will need to create. This element also declares the SVG and XLink namespaces, the latter necessary for linking up the font file.

Linking the font.   The defs element, generally used for all sorts of document setup and definitions, here contains only a reference to the font stored in a separate SVG file. Make sure the xlink:href attribute contains the correct relative URI of the pushkin.svg file we created previously. The selector part after # in that URI must match the -id value that we specified when converting the font into SVG.

Creating the text. As you can see from the `text` element, SVG uses CSS for specifying text properties. This is good news, since you'll be able to leverage your CSS experience. The two non-CSS attributes in the `text` element, `x` and `y`, specify the position of the text string in pixels relative to the coordinate origin (in SVG, it is in the top left corner).

5.5.2.5 Running conversion

Save Example 5.14 into a file, say `test.svg`, and type this command:

```
java org.apache.batik.apps.rasterizer.Main test.svg
```

For this to work, the `batik-rasterizer.jar` file from the Batik distribution must be in your Java CLASSPATH. Note that the Batik documentation suggests running the rasterizer by launching its `.jar` file:

```
java -jar /full/path/to/batik-rasterizer.jar test.svg
```

However, our variant specifying the Java path to the rasterizer's `Main` class works just as well and has the big advantage of not having to worry about the `.jar` file pathname that might be different across environments.

When the command is finished, you have a brand new `test.png` file in the same directory (Figure 5.1).

Wow! Antialiasing is flawless, kerning pairs are correctly kerned, and overall, the text looks just right. Even if you reduce the font size to a barely readable minimum, letters still look even and smooth. Since we didn't specify any background color, the background is transparent, and the antialiased contour pixels are actually half-black, half-transparent (instead of half-black, half-white). This is only possible in PNG with its alpha channel transparency, and the end result is that the image will look smoothly antialiased over *any* background, be it solid color or pattern.

Designers beware. Yes, it *does* looks smoothly antialiased, but only in a standards-compliant browser, such as Mozilla. Microsoft's Internet Explorer, unfortunately, does not support alpha transparency in PNG. To create a page that would be correctly displayed in all modern browsers, you need to explicitly add to your SVG a nontransparent background rectangle whose color is the same as that of the web page background. And if you want a complex

Figure 5.1   The Batik-rasterized version of Example 5.14. The image is magnified to demonstrate anti-aliasing; the actual size is approximately 400 by 60 pixels.

patterned background under your image, you're out of luck — without alpha transparency, you can't have both antialiasing and a fancy background at the same time.

5.5.2.6   Postprocessing

The image may not require any postprocessing; it is quite usable as is (bar the PNG transparency problem in MSIE). Sometimes, however, you may want to fiddle with it some more. For example, it may be necessary to trim the margins of the image down to the bounding rectangle of the text string. With Imagemagick, this is done by

```
mogrify -trim test.png
```

After that operation, the dimensions of the image are unpredictable, so you'll need to use the `graph:getw()` and `graph:geth()` extension functions (**5.5.1**) if you want the corresponding `img` element in your HTML to specify exact `width` and `height`.

You can also scale the image, reduce the number of colors, convert it to other formats, and so on. The complete list of capabilities available via Imagemagick's command-line tools is quite impressive. For example, the following commands add a nice drop shadow to our image (Figure 5.2):

```
convert -blur 7x7 test.png test-shadow.png
composite -geometry +2+4 test-shadow.png test.png test.png
```

Scalable Vector Graphics

Figure 5.2 Drop shadow added to Figure 5.1 by Imagemagick.

5.5.2.7 Once more, with XSLT

Java as a launchpad. To automate the process we just ran manually, the first thing we need is a way to run external applications from within the stylesheet. Once again, Java comes to our rescue. Add the `run()` method shown in Example 5.15 to the `files` class in Example 5.6 (page 221). This method takes a command line as an argument, executes it, and returns the same argument string.

Why so much code for such a simple task? It turns out that Java's `Runtime.exec()` method shuts off the executed program's console output, so we must explicitly grab its output (both `stdout` and `stderr`) and print it if we want to read what the program has to say. Unfortunately, `stdout` and `stderr` are grabbed and reprinted separately, which may sometimes lead to weird ordering of output lines. No output will be lost, though.

Image generation template. All the components of the `create-image` implementation should be obvious by now. Still, an outline (with most of the static SVG code dropped for readability) is given in Example 5.16. The template first creates the SVG file, then runs Batik to rasterize it and Imagemagick's `mogrify` to trim edges.

The `files:run()` function is called from within an `xsl:value-of` which, in turn, is inside `xsl:message`. Since `files:run()` returns the command line it received as argument, you will see the actual command line being executed in your terminal as a useful debugging hint.

You can write a similar template (or extend this one by adding more parameters to control its SVG output) for generating other images on your site. Examples might include headings, sequence navigation buttons (**3.9.4**), or even a graphic copyright notice with your logo (e.g., to be added as a semitransparent watermark to the photos you publish on your site).

. . . .

Example 5.15 A Java method to run a command (add to the `files` class).

```java
public static String run (String s) {
  try {
    String str;
    Process p = Runtime.getRuntime ().exec (s);
    BufferedReader is =
      new BufferedReader (new InputStreamReader
                                  (p.getInputStream ()));
    BufferedReader es =
      new BufferedReader (new InputStreamReader
                                  (p.getErrorStream ()));
    try {
      while ((str = is.readLine ()) != null) {
        System.out.println (str);
      }
      while ((str = es.readLine ()) != null) {
        System.out.println (str);
      }
    } catch (IOException e) {
      System.exit (0);
    }
  } catch (IOException e1) {
    System.err.println (e1);
    System.exit (1);
  }
  return (s+'\n');
}
```

. . . .

Not exactly fly. The only problem with Batik's SVG rasterization is that it is not very fast and therefore may not be suitable for on-the-fly image generation on the server (especially if you need to create more than one image at once). This is why in our menu template (Example 5.5), `create-image` is only called if the `$images` stylesheet parameter is set to `yes`, since regenerating all menu buttons on each page update may be quite time-consuming.

5.5.3 Creating other binary formats

Now that you've got an idea of how a bitmap image can be generated from an XML source, I don't need to go into much detail on creating

Example 5.16   A callable template creating an image via SVG.

```
<xsl:template name="create-image">
  <xsl:param name="label"/>
  <xsl:param name="filename"/>

  <xsl:variable name="svg" select="concat($filename, '.svg')"/>
  <xsl:variable name="png" select="concat($filename, '.png')"/>

  <xsl:result-document href="{$svg}" format="xml">
    <svg ...>
      <!-- SVG preamble... -->
      <text ...><xsl:value-of select="$label"/></text>
    </svg>
  </xsl:result-document>

  <xsl:message>
    <xsl:value-of select="
        files:run(concat(
          'java org.apache.batik.apps.rasterizer.Main ',
          $svg))"/>
  </xsl:message>
  <xsl:message>
    <xsl:value-of select="
        files:run(concat('mogrify -trim ', $png))"/>
  </xsl:message>

</xsl:template>
```

other objects. The only problem you can run into is choosing an appropriate intermediate format and a fast and reliable renderer for it.

5.5.3.1   Flash

Macromedia Flash, sometimes called ShockWave Flash (SWF), is an open format[22] for animated vector graphics, widely used on the Web. In most cases, Flash objects include textual elements that you might want to update from time to time, ideally by linking to an external

---

22. www.openswf.org

data source. Such objects would benefit from becoming part of an XML-based web design workflow.

Macromedia's own Flash creation software[23] includes (in "professional" versions) functionality to update animation objects, such as text or links, using data from XML documents or dynamic XML sources. However, you might be using some other Flash authoring software (there is plenty of it on different platforms). Moreover, you might want to generate simple animations in a completely automatic fashion from the stylesheet, as we did for images. A search for a comprehensive text-based "Flash source" format reveals two candidates that may make this possible.

One is **SWFML** (SWF Markup Language), developed by Saxess.[24] This language is XML-based and the renderer offered by Saxess, called X-Wave, is written in Java. This is a commercial product (a preview edition is available). SWFML's coverage of SWF features, both static and animated, is probably sufficient for the majority of applications.[25]

Another textual equivalent of Flash is an open source **Ming** library[26] whose functions can be used from several languages including PHP, Python, and Perl. None of these languages is XML, of course, but this should not stop you: If *you* can write a script to generate the Flash animation you need, so can your XSLT stylesheet. On the upside, Ming is faster than X-Wave and, via PHP, can be easily incorporated into a web site setup to generate Flash bits on the fly. SWF features covered by Ming include all of the essentials: shapes, text, links, bitmaps, and audio.

A disadvantage of both SWFML and Ming is that they cannot reuse existing Flash content. That is, you cannot draw a nice animation in a GUI Flash editor, export it into a textual format, use it as a template

---

23. www.macromedia.com/software/flash

24. www.saxess.com

25. The animated Flash menu on www.kirsanov.com was implemented via SWFML. You can download the complete source code of that XML-based site at www.kirsanov.com/dk-site.zip.

26. ming.sf.net

to fill in your content by the stylesheet, and then reassemble it back into binary SWF. You can, however, embed a stylesheet-generated movie into another movie, thereby combining a manually drawn "template" and automatically generated "content" into a seamless animated object.

PDF

Adobe's PDF (Portable Document Format) is a stripped-down and compressed version of PostScript, which is a textual page description language. You don't want to write PostScript code manually, however, as it is a really low-level machine-oriented language.

What then are your options if you want to generate nice-looking PDF documents from XML sources? The two major high-level page description languages worth considering are XSL-FO and TEX. Yes, I do mean TEX; although a marriage between TEX and XML may seem strange, it is feasible and may have its advantages.

In fact, the choice between TEX and XSL-FO can be tricky. **TEX**[27] is much faster (compared to the existing Java-based XSL-FO formatters such as FOP[28] or XEP[29]), but XSL-FO is XML. TEX offers better control over typography and page layout, but XSL-FO has much more straightforward i18n support (again, because it is based on XML).

Choose TEX if any of the following is true:

- you've already had (positive) experience with it;

- you are satisfied by the standard LATEX document styles and don't want to tweak anything; or

- (on the contrary) your typographic requirements are very high and you're not afraid to spend some time instructing TEX to do exactly what you want.

....

27. www.tug.org
28. xml.apache.org/fop
29. www.renderx.com. This book was produced using XEP.

Otherwise, **XSL-FO**[30] may be a better choice for you. It doesn't offer such a huge library of free styles, packages, and add-ons as does TEX, but creating a simple new style from scratch is actually doable in XSL-FO (in reasonable time) even without any previous experience. Another advantage of XSL-FO is its better integration with XSLT; for example, Saxon 6 can pass its transformation result directly to FOP without serialization.

5.6 Batch processing

Just one more coding session, and we'll make our stylesheet at least an order of magnitude more convenient to use.

Statement of the problem. No matter what XSLT processor you use, to run a stylesheet on a page document you normally have to specify full pathnames of the input and output files. These pathnames may be relative — for example,

```
saxon -o out/de/index.html de/index.xml style.xsl env=staging
```

— but only if you are running this command from the correct base directory.

And therein lies a problem. Our `$src-path` and `$out-path` are stored in and retrieved from the master document — and now we have to spell them out once again in the command line! All sorts of unpleasant surprises are bound to happen if our command line does not correspond to the environment parameters stored in the master document.

This is indeed a problem, and we are going to deal with it immediately. Instead of applying the stylesheet manually to each page document, we can relatively easily implement *batch processing* — that is, transforming many pages at once. (And while we're at it, why not validate all those pages before transformation?) The idea is to run the stylesheet on one source file — the master document — and let it figure out

---

30. www.w3.org/Style/XSL

automatically the input/output paths of all page documents registered in the master.

The importance of being functional. In principle, we could use XSLT's ability to handle multiple input and multiple output documents to open, transform, and write out all site pages registered in the master during one stylesheet run. For example, a template matching a page element in the master and transforming the corresponding page document might be as simple as[31]

```
<xsl:template match="site//page">
  <xsl:result-document href="eg:page-out(@id, $lang)" format="html">
    <xsl:apply-templates
        select="document(eg:page-src(@id, $lang))"/>
  </xsl:result-document>
</xsl:template>
```

There's a serious problem with this approach, however: It only works if we have no global variables, or if our global variable values are equally applicable to all page documents. This is not the case with our stylesheet. Recall (**5.1.1**) that many of the global variables defined in our stylesheet store the path, language, and other parameters directly related to the currently processed page document. And XSLT won't allow us to change the values of these variables when we're finished with one page and move on to the next one.

This is an interesting situation illustrating how the principles of functional programming (**4.3**) affect the design of an XSLT stylesheet. In this case, the entire stylesheet is a function whose input is one XML page document and whose output is one HTML web page. If we want to process several documents, we are supposed to simply *call* this function several times, not try to cram all processing into one call.

----

31. The page-out() function in this example is similar to page-link() (**5.1.1.4**) but uses $out-path instead of $target-path. It is only necessary for meta-functionality such as batch processing where the stylesheet needs to access the files it creates.

5.6.1   Launcher templates

But can we really call our stylesheet as a function from within itself? Remember that we have the `files:run()` extension function (**5.5.2.7**) — and we're not afraid to use it to run as many copies of the XSLT processor as necessary to validate and transform all pages of the site.

Launching transformation.   Example 5.17 is a template that runs transformation on all language versions of one `page`. Note the `mode` value of `transform`; we want this template to activate only when specifically called with this `mode`. Within the `xsl:for-each` loop that iterates over all defined languages, an `xsl:message` first reports the pathname of the file being transformed. Then, the complete command line is constructed and fed to the `files:run()` function.

....

Example 5.17   The transformation template uses the `files:run()` function to launch one instance of the XSLT processor per page document.

```
<xsl:template match="page" mode="transform">
  <xsl:variable name="id" select="@id"/>
  <xsl:for-each select="$master//languages/lang">
    <xsl:message>
      Transforming <xsl:value-of select="eg:page-src($id, .)"/>
    </xsl:message>
    <xsl:value-of select="
        files:run(concat(
          'java net.sf.saxon.Transform ',
          '-o ', eg:page-out($id, .),
          ' ', eg:page-src($id, .),
          ' style.xsl',
          ' env=', $env,
          ' images=', if ($id='home') then $images else 'no'
        ))"/>
  </xsl:for-each>
</xsl:template>
```

....

The command line consists of a call to Java with Saxon's class name, output (after `-o`) and input documents' pathnames, stylesheet pathname (`style.xsl`), and stylesheet parameters. Note that the `images` parameter of the current stylesheet process is passed to the subprocess only for the front page, because we don't want to re-create all images again and again for every page of the site.

Other commands, other environments. To make this command line truly portable, you may want to replace all the constant strings with variables and store these variables' values in the corresponding environment in the master document. Another launcher template for Schematron validation (with mode="validate") might be similar to Example 5.17, except that there's no -o parameter in the command line and the compiled schema (**5.1.2**) is used instead of the main transformation stylesheet. See Example 5.21 for a complete stylesheet listing including both transformation and validation launcher templates.

5.6.2   The batch template

Now, all we need to do is apply the launcher templates to the master's page elements from a template matching the root element of a master document, site (Example 5.18).

. . . .

Example 5.18   The main batch processing template calls the validation and transformation launcher templates and logs all the commands they run.

```
<xsl:template match="/site">
  <xsl:result-document
      href="file:///{$src-path}validate-commands.log"
      format="txt">
    <xsl:apply-templates
        select="menu//page" mode="validate"/>
  </xsl:result-document>
  <xsl:result-document
      href="file:///{$src-path}transform-commands.log"
      format="txt">
    <xsl:apply-templates
        select="menu//page" mode="transform"/>
  </xsl:result-document>
</xsl:template>
```

. . . .

Note that each of the `xsl:apply-templates` calls is enveloped in an `xsl:result-document` that redirects the output of the applicable template into a log file. Since the `files:run()` function returns its command-line argument and the launcher template outputs it using `xsl:value-of`, after each batch run you will have two log files listing all commands that were executed for validation and transformation — for your debugging pleasure.

Other site-wide jobs. Besides batch processing, the template for the master's root element might perform other tasks that apply to the site in general but to no specific page in particular. One such task is creating the `robots.txt` file controlling site access by search engine spiders; another is creating a site map page graphically depicting the hierarchy of sections and pages.

Separation vs. convenience. It might be cleaner to place both the launcher templates and the batch template into a separate stylesheet, as they have little to do with the main transformation stylesheet. On the other hand, matching the master document's root element (not matched by anything else) and the unique modes of the launcher templates provide sufficient separation so that adding them to the main stylesheet is convenient and causes no problems.

5.6.3   Problems and solutions

Our batch processing implementation is very simple — yet workable. What are its advantages, aside from the obvious time-saving convenience?

- These templates are absolutely **orthogonal to everything else in the stylesheet**. We didn't have to change anything in our normal processing of a page. You can still use the same stylesheet for transforming single pages as before.

- Compared to other batch processing approaches, such as using shell scripts, batch files, or build tools (**6.5**), the stylesheet-only solution is the most **portable** and independent of the underlying platform. If you can run your stylesheet at all, you can run it in batch mode. Using the `files:run()` extension function spoils the picture a bit; still, copying an extension Java class from one system to another is usually much easier than porting a shell script or a native binary utility.

There are certain problems associated with this approach as well, some of them relatively easy to resolve and some more serious.

- As implemented, the stylesheet processes all pages of the site, which **may take quite some time**. You thus have a limited choice between transforming one page only or producing the entire site. More convenient would be specifying pages (by their identifiers) for transformation in a stylesheet parameter; for example,

```
saxon _master.xml style.xsl process="fb+ home"
```

to process the `fb+` and `home` pages only. Implementing this `process` stylesheet parameter is not in fact difficult and could be a good exercise for a practical XSLT programmer. (Hint: Use `tokenize()` or `xsl:analyze-string`.)

Even more useful would be the possibility of automatically running the stylesheet only on those pages that have changed since the last transformation. This is tricky, and while doable with XSLT, may require an uncommon amount of extension programming. It is where an external build tool might be a better solution (**6.5**).

- Now, **validation errors do not stop batch processing**, which always continues until the last page document (or until a manual user break). If you want processing to stop upon encountering a validation error, you must do some nontrivial programming in a special Java method — catching the validation output, parsing it, and reporting the validation outcome as a single boolean value.

Is this worth the trouble? Probably, if you are planning to run batch processing in an automatic unattended fashion — you don't want it to blindly transform (and possibly even upload to the server!) broken pages. Still, an XSLT stylesheet may not be the best place for implementing validation-dependent transformation.

5.7 **Summary examples**

5.7.1 Shared XSLT library

Example 5.19 is a compilation of code snippets from **5.1.1**, with a few additions and extensions. It is imported by our Schematron schemas (via the `schematron-saxon.xsl` wrapper, **5.1.2**) and by the main transformation stylesheet that follows in Example 5.21.

. . . .

Example 5.19   `_lib.xsl`: A shared XSLT library used by both the schema and the stylesheet.

```
<?xml version="1.0" encoding="iso-8859-1"?>
<xsl:stylesheet
    xmlns:xsl="http://www.w3.org/1999/XSL/Transform" version="2.0"
    xmlns:axsl="http://www.w3.org/1999/XSL/TransformAlias"
    xmlns:xs="http://www.w3.org/2001/XMLSchema"
    xmlns:saxon="http://saxon.sf.net/"
    xmlns:eg="http://www.example.org/">

<!-- Stylesheet parameters: -->
<!-- env specifies the environment where we run the stylesheet -->
<xsl:param name="env" select="'final'"/>
<!-- images=yes turns image generation on -->
<xsl:param name="images" select="'no'"/>

<!-- Master document: -->
<xsl:variable name="master" select="document('_master.xml')"/>

<!-- Are we transforming the master document
   (e.g., in batch processing)? -->
<xsl:variable name="this-master" select="
    boolean(/*[name()='site'])"/>

<!-- Source path for this environment: -->
<xsl:variable name="src-path" select="
    $master//environment[@id=$env]/src-path"/>

<!-- Path to the output directory: -->
<xsl:variable name="out-path" select="
    $master//environment[@id=$env]/out-path"/>
```

```
<!-- Target path, for src and href attributes in HTML: -->
<xsl:variable name="target-path" select="
    $master//environment[@id=$env]/target-path"/>

<!-- Image output directory, for accessing and generating images
    during transformation: -->
<xsl:variable name="out-img">
  <xsl:value-of select="$out-path"/>
  <xsl:value-of select="$master//environment[@id = $env]/img-path"/>
  <xsl:text>/</xsl:text>
</xsl:variable>

<!-- Image target directory, for image src attributes in HTML: -->
<xsl:variable name="target-img">
  <xsl:value-of select="$target-path"/>
  <xsl:value-of select="$master//environment[@id = $env]/img-path"/>
  <xsl:text>/</xsl:text>
</xsl:variable>

<!-- Filename extensions: -->
<xsl:variable name="src-ext">.xml</xsl:variable>
<xsl:variable name="out-ext">.html</xsl:variable>

<!-- Current language, based on the current directory: -->
<xsl:variable name="lang">
  <xsl:choose>
    <xsl:when test="
        substring-after(saxon:systemId(), $src-path) = ''">
      <xsl:message terminate="yes">
        Error: Source file path does not match $src-path
        $env = <xsl:value-of select="$env"/>
        systemId = <xsl:value-of select="saxon:systemId()"/>
      </xsl:message>
    </xsl:when>
    <xsl:otherwise>
      <xsl:value-of select="
          substring-before(
            substring-after(saxon:systemId(), $src-path),
            '/')"/>
    </xsl:otherwise>
  </xsl:choose>
</xsl:variable>
```

```
<!-- Path to the current file (without extension)
    starting from the root dir of the current language: -->
<xsl:variable name="current">
  <xsl:choose>
    <xsl:when test="
        not($master//languages/lang = $lang)
        and not($this-master)">
      <xsl:message terminate="yes">
        Error: Not in a valid language directory
        $lang = <xsl:value-of select="$lang"/>
      </xsl:message>
    </xsl:when>
    <xsl:otherwise>
      <xsl:value-of select="
          substring-before(
            substring-after(
              substring-after(saxon:systemId(), $src-path),
              concat($lang, '/')),
            $src-ext)"/>
    </xsl:otherwise>
  </xsl:choose>
</xsl:variable>

<!-- True if the current page is the site's front page: -->
<xsl:variable name="frontpage" select="$current = 'index'"/>

<!-- Unabbreviation functions: -->

<!-- Unabbreviate external links -->
<xsl:function name="eg:ext-link">
  <xsl:param name="abbr"/>
  <xsl:value-of select="
      if (starts-with ($abbr, 'http://') or
          starts-with ($abbr, 'ftp://'))
        then $abbr
        else concat('http://', $abbr)"/>
</xsl:function>
```

```
<!-- Convert a file:/ URI into Windows native format -->
<xsl:function name="eg:os-path">
  <xsl:param name="s"/>
  <xsl:value-of select="
      if (starts-with($s, 'file:/'))
        then substring-after($s, 'file:/')
        else $s"/>
</xsl:function>


<!-- Return pathname of a page document -->
<xsl:function name="eg:page-src">
  <xsl:param name="abbr"/>
  <xsl:param name="lang"/>
  <xsl:value-of select="
      concat(
        $src-path,
        $lang, '/',
        $master//(page|block)[(@id,tokenize(@alias, '\s+')) = $abbr]
          /@src,
        $src-ext)"/>
</xsl:function>


<!-- Return URI of a transformed HTML page -->
<xsl:function name="eg:page-link">
  <xsl:param name="path"/>
  <xsl:param name="abbr"/>
  <xsl:param name="lang"/>
  <xsl:value-of select="
      concat(
        $path,
        $lang, '/',
        $master//(page|block)[(@id,tokenize(@alias, '\s+')) = $abbr]
          /@src,
        $out-ext)"/>
</xsl:function>

</xsl:stylesheet>
```
....

5.7.2 Advanced Schematron schema

Example 5.20 is a compilation of Schematron rules from **5.1.3**. You
can run this as a separate schema to validate your source (both page
documents and the master document), or you can combine it with
Example 3.3 (page 149) into a single schema. Perhaps the only reason
to keep this schema separate from the simpler schema of Chapter 3 is
that the advanced checks are significantly slower because they search
in many documents to validate all sorts of links and references.

. . . .

Example 5.20   `schema2.sch`: An advanced Schematron schema to be used in conjunction
with Example 3.3.

```
<schema xmlns="http://www.ascc.net/xml/schematron">

<!-- Checks for the master document: -->
<pattern name="master">

<!-- Presence of page documents and orthogonal sources -->
<rule context="menu//page | blocks/block">
  <report test="
      (for $1 in $master//languages/lang
        return boolean(document(eg:page-src(@id, $1))))
      = false()">
    A source document not found for "<value-of select="@id"/>".
  </report>
  <assert test="
      every $i in
        (for $1 in $master//languages/lang
          return (
            if (@select)
              then boolean(document(eg:page-src(@id, $1))
                            //block[@id=current()/@select])
              else true()))
        satisfies $i">
    A block with @id="<value-of select="@select"/>" that the
    "<value-of select="@id"/>" orthogonal block refers to
    is missing.
  </assert>
</rule>

</pattern>
```

```
<!-- Checks for page documents: -->
<pattern name="page">

<!-- Internal links -->
<rule context="int | link[@linktype='internal']">
  <assert test="
      @link = (for $i in $master//(page|block)/(@id|@alias)
                  return tokenize($i, '\s+'))">
    Broken internal link: no 'page' with
    @id="<value-of select="@link"/>" in the
    master document. Valid identifiers are:
    <value-of select="
        string-join(
          (for $i in $master//(page|block)/(@id|@alias)
              return tokenize($i, '\s+')), ', ')"/>.
  </assert>
</rule>

<!-- External links -->
<rule context="ext | link[@linktype='external']">
  <assert test="
      boolean(unparsed-text(eg:ext-link(@link), 'iso-8859-1'))">
    Broken external link: <value-of select="@link"/>.
  </assert>
</rule>

<!-- Language links -->
<rule context="
    lang[not(ancestor::languages)] | link[@linktype='language']">
  <assert test="@link = $master//languages/lang">
    Broken language link: no "<value-of select="@link"/>" language.
  </assert>
</rule>

<!-- Orthogonal references -->
<rule context="page//block[@idref]">
  <assert test="@idref = $master//blocks/block/@id">
    A block with @idref must match the @id of one of the 'block'
    elements in the master document.
  </assert>
</rule>
```

```
<!-- Presence of images -->
<rule context="section[@image]">
  <assert test="
      files:exists(eg:os-path(concat($out-img, @image, '.png')))">
    Image file missing:
    <value-of select="concat($out-img, @image, '.png')"/>.
  </assert>
</rule>


<!-- Side-wide uniqueness of @id in p and head elements -->
<rule context="p[@id] | head[@id]">
  <assert test="
      count(
        for $src in distinct-values($master//(page|block)/@src)
          return
            document(
              concat($src-path, $lang, '/', $src, $src-ext))
              //(p|head)[@id=current()/@id])
      = 1">
    Non-unique @id in a 'p' or 'head':
    @id="<value-of select="current()/@id"/>" is used in:
    <value-of select="
        string-join(
          $master//(page|block)[document(eg:page-src(@id, $lang))
            //(p|head)[@id=current()/@id]]/@src, ', ')"/>.
  </assert>
</rule>


</pattern>
</schema>
```

. . . .

5.7.3 Stylesheet

Learning transformation techniques one bit at a time may be easy, but by now you may feel the urge to see how these bits really fit together. As promised, here's our Big Stylesheet Example (though it is actually small by the standards of many real projects). What is good about this example is that it is working and complete, including all the gory HTML layout details.

Components. This stylesheet builds upon our previous examples. Make sure you have the following software available:

- `_lib.xsl`, our shared library of XSLT code (Example 5.19);

- three of the extension Java classes we've been writing: `files` (Examples 5.6, 5.15), `graph` (Example 5.11), and `text` (Example 5.9); make sure the `*.class` files are in your `CLASSPATH`;

- the master document (Example 3.2);

- a page document (you can use the one in Example 3.1 or write your own);

- `schema-compiled.xsl`, a compiled Schematron schema (see **5.1.2** for compilation instructions); it is only required in the batch mode, and you can modify the template with `mode="validate"` to run a different validator,[32] or disable that template altogether;

- a font in SVG format, if you plan to run the stylesheet with `images=yes`; refer to **5.5.2** for instructions on how to create one, and replace `pushkin.svg` in the stylesheet by the name of your font file.

Processor. You'll also need an XSLT 2.0 processor (the code was tested on Saxon 7.5.1 under Linux and Windows). The `_lib.xsl` library uses one Saxon-specific extension, `saxon:systemId()`; however, similar functions are offered by other processors, so porting the stylesheet away from Saxon should not be a problem. The XSLT 2.0 requirement, on the other hand, is hardly possible to lift, as the stylesheet uses a lot of 2.0 features.

Graphic software. The image creation template uses Batik (tested with version 1.5). Make sure the `batik-rasterizer.jar` file is in your Java `CLASSPATH`. You'll also need Imagemagick (tested with version 5.4.8); its command-line utilities must be in your operating system's executable path.

....

32. If you prefer to rely on a DTD for validation (**2.2.4**), you don't need to do even that — just make sure that your XML parser performs DTD validation before passing the document to the XSLT processor. With Saxon, this is done by specifying the `-v` command-line option.

Windows paths. Unfortunately, under Windows, neither Imagemagick nor Batik recognize Windows pathnames in the URL format (e.g., `file:/C:/Work/Website/image.png`). On the other hand, some browsers on Windows can *only* understand URLs with `file:/` because otherwise they mistake the drive letter for a URL protocol. Therefore, in the master document we store Windows pathnames in the URL format, but in the `create-image` template we need to remove the `file:/` prefix if it is present. This is done by calling the `eg:os-path()` function defined in `_lib.xsl` (Example 5.19). If you don't plan to run your stylesheet on Windows, you can happily drop this function altogether and use the `$svg` and `$png` variables directly.

Deployment. Here's the command used to run this stylesheet on a single page document, using Saxon 7:

```
saxon -o output input style.xsl env=env images={yes|no}
```

Here, `style.xsl` is the name of the stylesheet file, *input* and *output* are the pathnames of the input (XML) and output (HTML) files correspondingly. The default value of the `images` parameter is no. For example, for an English version of `team/index` in the `staging` environment, without image generation, the command would look like this:

```
saxon -o out/en/team/index.html en/team/index.xml style.xsl env=staging
```

The pathnames here are relative, assuming you run this command from the root of the input directory tree (for `staging`, it is `/home/d/web/`, see Example 3.2 on page 143).

To run the stylesheet in batch mode (**5.6**), all you need to do is

```
saxon master style.xsl env=env images={yes|no}
```

where *master* is the pathname of the master document. If everything goes as planned, a batch run of the stylesheet will first display a stream of validation diagnostic messages (including any errors found in individual page documents):

```
Validating /home/d/web/en/index.xml
Validating /home/d/web/de/index.xml
Validating /home/d/web/en/solutions/intro_solutions.xml
Validating /home/d/web/de/solutions/intro_solutions.xml
Validating /home/d/web/en/solutions/life.xml
Line 32:
```

```
    Non-unique @id in a 'p' or 'head': @id="foo" is used in:
    solutions/life, team/hire.
Validating /home/d/web/de/solutions/life.xml
Validating /home/d/web/en/team/index.xml
Validating /home/d/web/de/team/index.xml
Validating /home/d/web/en/team/history.xml
Line 26:
    Broken internal link: no 'page' with @id="bar" in the
    master document.
...
```

After all pages are validated, batch transformation starts with its own diagnostic messages:

```
Transforming /home/d/web/en/index.xml
processing: index
    lang: en
    env: staging
    src-path: /home/d/web/
    out-path: /home/d/web/out/
creating: site.css
Transforming /home/d/web/de/index.xml
processing: index
    lang: de
    env: staging
    src-path: /home/d/web/
    out-path: /home/d/web/out/
creating: site.css
...
```

Layout overview. Compared to the examples scattered throughout the chapter, this stylesheet is more complex in some aspects but simpler in others, as we don't need every trick discussed so far to build a simple web page out of Example 3.1. The stylesheet builds a table-based, stretchable subpage layout (no effort was made to accommodate a different front page layout) with the following areas:

- logo area in the top left corner (static content, fixed width);

- top menu listing the site's top-level sections (built dynamically from the master document data, including image generation for item labels);

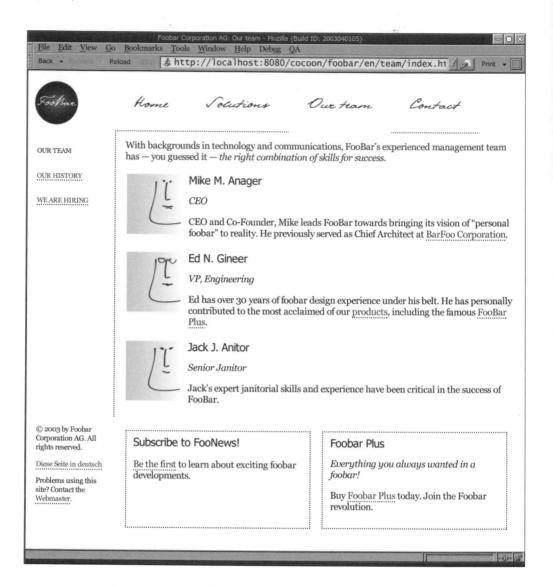

Figure 5.3 The result of transforming the page document from Example 3.1 with the stylesheet from Example 5.21, using Example 3.2 as master document and Example 5.19 as shared library.

- side menu listing the branch of the site's tree to which the current page belongs (generated dynamically from the master document data);

- main content area (generated from the current page document, stretches to fill all available window width);

- footer stuff — copyright notice, etc. (supplied by the master document);

- orthogonal blocks area (orthogonal block references are on the current page; content may be taken from other pages).

In the main content blocks and orthogonal blocks, the `section` template builds a simple structure with a heading, subheading, optionally an image, and a sequence of paragraphs. All formatting properties are expressed via CSS. The browser screenshot of the final transformed page is shown in Figure 5.3.

Don't ask me why. If you want the generated PNG files to be viewable in Microsoft Internet Explorer, add `-bg 254.255.255.255` to the Batik call (after the class name).

. . . .

Example 5.21   `style.xsl`: A summary stylesheet example using many techniques discussed in this chapter.

```
<?xml version="1.0" encoding="iso-8859-1"?>

<!DOCTYPE xsl:stylesheet [
  <!ENTITY copy "&#169;">
  <!ENTITY nbsp " ">
  <!ENTITY mdash "&#8212;">
]>

<xsl:stylesheet
    xmlns:xsl="http://www.w3.org/1999/XSL/Transform" version="2.0"
    xmlns:eg="http://www.example.org/"
    xmlns:files="com.projectname.xslt.files"
    xmlns:graph="com.projectname.xslt.graph"
    xmlns:text="com.projectname.xslt.text"
    extension-element-prefixes="eg files graph text">
```

```
<xsl:import href="_lib.xsl"/>

<xsl:output method="html" encoding="US-ASCII" indent="no"
    doctype-public="-//W3C//DTD HTML 4.0 Transitional//EN"/>
<xsl:output name="txt" method="text" encoding="iso-8859-1"
    omit-xml-declaration="yes"/>
<xsl:output name="xml" method="xml" encoding="iso-8859-1"
    indent="yes"/>

<!-- Page skeleton -->
<xsl:template match="/page">
  <xsl:message>
    processing: <xsl:value-of select="$current"/>

    lang: <xsl:value-of select="$lang"/>
    env: <xsl:value-of select="$env"/>
    src-path: <xsl:value-of select="$src-path"/>
    out-path: <xsl:value-of select="$out-path"/>
    target-path: <xsl:value-of select="$target-path"/>
  </xsl:message>
  <!-- Credits are in XML comments,
    so they can come before the root element: -->
  <xsl:call-template name="credits"/>
  <html>
    <head>
      <xsl:apply-templates select="@keywords | @description"/>
      <xsl:call-template name="title"/>
      <xsl:call-template name="css"/>
    </head>
    <body>
      <table style="table-layout: fixed; width: 100%;">
        <tr>
          <td style="width: 150px;">
            <!-- logo cell -->
            <xsl:variable name="logo" select="
                concat($out-img, 'logo.png')"/>
            <img src="{concat($target-img, 'logo.png')}"
              width="{graph:getw($logo)}"
              height="{graph:geth($logo)}"
              alt="{$master//html-title/translation[@lang=$lang]}"/>
          </td>
```

```
        <td>
          <!-- top menu cell -->
          <xsl:call-template name="top-menu"/>
        </td>
      </tr>
      <tr>
        <td style="width: 150px; vertical-align: top;">
          <!-- side menu cell -->
          <xsl:call-template name="side-menu"/>
        </td>
        <td style="margin: 1em; padding-left: 1em; padding-top: 1em;
          border-left: 2px dotted; border-color: #003399;
          vertical-align: top;">
          <!-- body area -->
          <xsl:apply-templates select="block[not(@idref)]"/>
        </td>
      </tr>
      <tr>
        <td style="width: 150px; vertical-align: top;">
          <!-- page-footer cell -->
          <xsl:call-template name="page-footer"/>
        </td>
        <td>
          <!-- orthogonal content area -->
          <table width="100%" style="border-spacing: 1.2em;">
            <tr bgcolor="#ffffff">
              <xsl:apply-templates select="block[@idref]"/>
            </tr>
          </table>
        </td>
      </tr>
    </table>
  </body>
 </html>
</xsl:template>
```

```xslt
<!-- Static templates -->

<xsl:template name="credits">
  <xsl:comment>
    XSLT programming by Ed N. Gineer, ed at foobar dot com
  </xsl:comment>
</xsl:template>

<xsl:template match="page/@description">
  <meta name="description" content="{.}"/>
</xsl:template>

<xsl:template match="page/@keywords">
  <meta name="keywords" content="{.}"/>
</xsl:template>

<xsl:template name="title">
  <title>
    <xsl:value-of select="
        $master//html-title/translation[@lang=$lang]/text()"/>
    <xsl:text>: </xsl:text><xsl:value-of select="title/text()"/>
  </title>
</xsl:template>

<xsl:template name="css">
  <link rel="stylesheet" href="{$target-path}site.css"/>
  <xsl:message>
    creating: site.css
  </xsl:message>
  <xsl:result-document href="file:///{$out-path}site.css" format="txt">
body {font-family: serif; background-color: #ffffff;}
h1 {font-family: sans-serif; font-size: 120%; font-weight: normal;}
h2 {font-size: 100%; font-weight: normal; font-style: italic;}
.inactive {border: 0em; padding-bottom: 4px; border-bottom: 2px dotted;}
.active {border: 0em; padding-bottom: 4px; border: 0px ! important;}
a {text-decoration: none; border-bottom: 2px dotted; color: #003399;}
.footer {font-size: 80%; margin-top: 1em; margin-left: 0.5em;}
.sideitem {text-align: middle; font-size: 70%; padding-top: 2em;
    margin: 0.5em; text-transform: uppercase;}
  </xsl:result-document>
</xsl:template>
```

```
<!-- Footer stuff -->

<xsl:template name="page-footer">
  <xsl:apply-templates select="$master//page-footer/*"/>
</xsl:template>

<xsl:template match="page-footer/*">
  <p class="footer">
    <xsl:apply-templates select="translation[@lang=$lang]"/>
  </p>
</xsl:template>

<!-- Menus -->

<xsl:template name="side-menu">
  <xsl:apply-templates select="
      $master//menu//item[page/@src = $current]/(page|item)"
      mode="side"/>
</xsl:template>

<xsl:template name="top-menu">
  <xsl:apply-templates select="$master//menu/item" mode="top"/>
</xsl:template>

<xsl:template match="menu/item" mode="top">
  <xsl:variable name="src" select="page[1]/@src"/>
  <xsl:variable name="label" select="
      label/translation[@lang=$lang]"/>
  <xsl:variable name="filename" select="
      concat(
        string(1 + count(preceding-sibling::*)),
        eg:letters-only($label))"/>
  <xsl:if test="$images='yes'">
    <xsl:call-template name="create-image">
      <xsl:with-param name="label" select="$label"/>
      <xsl:with-param name="filename" select="
          concat($out-img, $filename)"/>
    </xsl:call-template>
  </xsl:if>
```

```
<xsl:choose>
  <xsl:when test="$src = $current">
    <span class="active">
      <img src="{$target-img}{$filename}.png" alt="{$label}"
        style="padding: 35px;"
        width="
          {graph:getw(concat($out-img, $filename, '.png'))}"
        height="
          {graph:geth(concat($out-img, $filename, '.png'))}"/>
    </span>
  </xsl:when>
  <xsl:when test="
      ($src != $current) and
      (.//page/@src = $current)">
    <a href="
      {$target-path}{$lang}/{$src}{$out-ext}"
      class="active">
      <img src="{$target-img}{$filename}.png" alt="{$label}"
        border="0" style="padding: 35px;"
        width="
          {graph:getw(concat($out-img, $filename, '.png'))}"
        height="
          {graph:geth(concat($out-img, $filename, '.png'))}"/>
    </a>
  </xsl:when>
  <xsl:otherwise>
    <a href="
      {$target-path}{$lang}/{$src}{$out-ext}"
      class="inactive">
      <img src="{$target-img}{$filename}.png" alt="{$label}"
        border="0" style="padding: 35px;"
        width="
          {graph:getw(concat($out-img, $filename, '.png'))}"
        height="
          {graph:geth(concat($out-img, $filename, '.png'))}"/>
    </a>
  </xsl:otherwise>
</xsl:choose>
</xsl:template>
```

```
<xsl:template match="menu//item/*" mode="side">
  <xsl:variable name="src" select="
      if (self::item) then page[1]/@src else @src"/>
  <xsl:variable name="label" select="
      if (self::item)
        then label/translation[@lang=$lang]
        else document(string(eg:page-src(@id, $lang)))//title"/>
  <xsl:choose>
    <xsl:when test="$src = $current">
      <div class="sideitem"><xsl:value-of select="$label"/></div>
    </xsl:when>
    <xsl:otherwise>
      <div class="sideitem">
        <a href="{$target-path}{$lang}/{$src}{$out-ext}">
          <xsl:value-of select="$label"/>
        </a>
      </div>
    </xsl:otherwise>
  </xsl:choose>
</xsl:template>

<!-- Blocks and sections -->

<xsl:template match="block[@idref]">
  <xsl:variable name="doc" select="
      document(string(eg:page-src(@idref, $lang)))"/>
  <xsl:variable name="select" select="
      $master//block[@id=current()/@idref]/@select"/>
  <xsl:variable name="from" select="
      if ($select)
        then $doc//block[@id=$select]
        else $doc//block[1]"/>

  <td style="margin-left: 1em; vertical-align: top; width: 50%;
    border: 2px dotted; border-color: #003399;">
    <div style="padding: 0.3em;">
      <xsl:apply-templates select="$from//section | $from/p"/>
    </div>
  </td>
</xsl:template>
```

```
<xsl:template match="block[not(@idref)]">
  <xsl:apply-templates select="section | p"/>
</xsl:template>

<xsl:template match="section">
  <table style="margin-bottom: 1em;">
    <tr>
      <td style="vertical-align: top;">
        <!-- image cell -->
        <xsl:if test="@image">
          <img src="{$target-img}{@image}.png" alt="{head}"/>
        </xsl:if>
      </td>
      <td>
        <h1><xsl:apply-templates select="head"/></h1>
        <h2><xsl:apply-templates select="subhead"/></h2>
        <xsl:apply-templates select="p"/>
      </td>
    </tr>
  </table>
</xsl:template>

<!-- Image generation -->

<xsl:function name="eg:letters-only">
  <xsl:param name="s"/>
  <!-- remove punctuation, replace German accented letters -->
  <xsl:value-of select="
      translate(
        lower-case(replace($s, '\ |,|\.|!|\?', '')),
        '&#xc4;&#xd6;&#xdc;&#xe4;&#xf6;&#xfc;',
        'aouaou')"/>
</xsl:function>

<xsl:template name="create-image">
  <xsl:param name="label"/>
  <xsl:param name="filename"/>
  <xsl:variable name="svg" select="concat($filename, '.svg')"/>
  <xsl:variable name="png" select="concat($filename, '.png')"/>
```

```
<xsl:result-document href="file:///{$svg}" format="xml">
  <svg width="500px" height="100px"
     xmlns="http://www.w3.org/2000/svg"
     xmlns:xlink="http://www.w3.org/1999/xlink">
    <defs>
      <font-face font-family="Pushkin">
        <font-face-src>
          <font-face-uri
            xlink:href="{$src-path}pushkin.svg#font"/>
        </font-face-src>
      </font-face>
    </defs>

    <text style="
        fill: #000000; font-family: Pushkin; font-size: 30px;"
        x="10px" y="50px">
      <xsl:value-of select="$label"/>
    </text>
  </svg>
</xsl:result-document>
<xsl:message>
  <xsl:value-of select="
      files:run(
        concat(
          'java org.apache.batik.apps.rasterizer.Main ',
          eg:os-path($svg)))"/>
</xsl:message>
<xsl:message>
  <xsl:value-of select="
      files:run(concat('mogrify -trim ', eg:os-path($png)))"/>
</xsl:message>
</xsl:template>

<!-- Text markup -->

<xsl:template match="p">
  <p><xsl:apply-templates/></p>
</xsl:template>

<xsl:template match="em">
  <em><xsl:apply-templates/></em>
</xsl:template>
```

```
<!-- Links -->

<xsl:template match="link[@linktype='internal'] | int">
  <a href="{eg:page-link($target-path, @link, $lang)}">
    <xsl:apply-templates/>
  </a>
</xsl:template>

<xsl:template match="link[@linktype='external'] | ext">
  <a href="{eg:ext-link(@link)}">
    <xsl:apply-templates/>
  </a>
</xsl:template>

<xsl:template match="link[@linktype='mailto'] | mailto">
  <a href="mailto:{@link}">
    <xsl:apply-templates/>
  </a>
</xsl:template>

<xsl:template match="link[@linktype='lang'] | lang">
  <a href="{$target-path}{@link}/{$current}{$out-ext}">
    <xsl:apply-templates/>
  </a>
</xsl:template>

<!-- Typography -->

<xsl:template match="p//text() | head//text() | subhead//text()">
  <xsl:value-of select="text:typography(.)"/>
</xsl:template>

<!-- Batch processing -->

<xsl:template match="/site">
  <xsl:result-document
      href="file:///{eg:os-path($src-path)}validate-commands.log"
      format="txt">
    <xsl:apply-templates select="menu//page" mode="validate"/>
  </xsl:result-document>
```

```
  <xsl:result-document
      href="file:///{eg:os-path($src-path)}transform-commands.log"
      format="txt">
    <xsl:apply-templates select="menu//page" mode="transform"/>
  </xsl:result-document>
</xsl:template>

<xsl:template match="page" mode="validate">
  <xsl:variable name="id" select="@id"/>
  <xsl:for-each select="$master//languages/lang">
    <xsl:message>
      Validating <xsl:value-of select="eg:page-src($id, .)"/>
    </xsl:message>
    <xsl:value-of select="
        files:run(concat(
          'java net.sf.saxon.Transform -l ',
          eg:os-path(eg:page-src($id, .)),
          ' schema-compiled.xsl',
          ' env=', $env
        ))"/>
  </xsl:for-each>
</xsl:template>

<xsl:template match="page" mode="transform">
  <xsl:variable name="id" select="@id"/>
  <xsl:for-each select="$master//languages/lang">
    <xsl:message>
      Transforming <xsl:value-of select="eg:page-src($id, .)"/>
    </xsl:message>
    <xsl:value-of select="
        files:run(concat(
          'java net.sf.saxon.Transform ',
          '-o ', eg:os-path(eg:page-link($out-path, $id, .)),
          ' ', eg:os-path(eg:page-src($id, .)),
          ' style.xsl',
          ' env=', $env,
          ' images=', if ($id='home') then $images else 'no'
        ))"/>
  </xsl:for-each>
</xsl:template>

</xsl:stylesheet>
```
. . . .

XML software

What wondrous life in this I lead!
Ripe apples drop about my head;
The luscious clusters of the vine
Upon my mouth do crush their wine;
The nectarine and curious peach
Into my hands themselves do reach;
Stumbling on melons, as I pass,
Ensnared with flowers, I fall on grass.

ANDREW MARVELL, *Thoughts in a Garden*

6

XML software

Let's start this chapter by stepping backwards and taking a wide look at our accomplishments so far. We've built a complex system consisting of an XML source definition, a couple of Schematron schemas, and a surprisingly versatile XSLT transformation stylesheet. Now that this basic setup is up and running, we can extend and streamline it with all kinds of XML software.

This chapter describes some software components that will let you build a logistics, management, and support infrastructure around an XML-based web site. This is not core technology; you can do without most of this stuff if you prefer. (Well, you'll probably need an XML editor in any case.) However, carefully chosen auxiliary tools can make your setup more efficient and easier to maintain.

The world of XML software is burgeoning. It's easy to become overwhelmed by claims, puzzled by buzzwords, and doped by hype. Sane, straight, no-nonsense talk is rare, especially in commercial software. I'll try to help.

The products I write about are not always the most popular and may not be the best, but they are usually the most *illustrative*. My goal is to demonstrate concepts and approaches, not specific products. Listing a product here does not imply endorsement, although all products I mention are workable and genuinely useful. Once you get an idea of the possible approaches to (for example) editing XML or debugging XSLT, you will be prepared to look for your own ideal tool.

A no monster zone. I'm a big fan of the well-known Unix motto: "Make your program do one thing but do it well." This means there's a certain slant in this chapter toward small and nifty utilities and away from all-encompassing software behemoths.

Bang for the buck. The XML realm enjoys a healthy mix of proprietary and open source software, and in almost any category, you'll find examples of both. Personally, I prefer the latter simply because a quality open source application is a much more valuable contribution to humanity than a comparable closed source program. Still, the criteria of usefulness and representativeness are paramount.

Where XML and XSLT are concerned, the best things in life really are free! XML and XSLT are free to learn and to use. Most XML parsers and XSLT processors (**6.4.1**) are free and open source, as are Schematron and Cocoon (**7.2**). And do you really need anything else? Generally, only if you want to trade a bit of your programming freedom for some sugar-coated convenience, you'll also need to throw in some money to make the deal.

Standards compliance. All XSLT- and XPath-related programs and utilities described in this chapter support XSLT/XPath 1.0. Those that also provide some support for 2.0 are noted. But software evolves, so be sure to check the current versions.

6.1 Authoring XML

You can hardly name an area in modern computer science where XML is not used. With such a wide applicability domain, the requirements of XML authors are naturally quite diverse. No software, "industry standard" or no "industry standard," can reasonably claim to satisfy all such requirements. Don't feel envious if your authoring tool isn't the latest buzz; chances are you don't need most of the features you are reading about in press releases, but instead need something completely different.

In our own area, web development, we can distinguish at least three very different usage patterns and corresponding sets of requirements. Most users of XML authoring tools will likely belong to one of the following three classes:

- site developers — those who create the site's source definition, schemas, and stylesheets;

- content authors — those who write original content for the web site; and

- site editors — those who maintain the site, update pages, post stories submitted by authors, and so on.

The features that these categories of users want in an XML authoring tool are not only different but in some aspects even contradictory.

Developer's workbench. The ideal XML editor for a site developer is, above all, an *XML* editor. It must be a powerful tool fluent in both XML in general and many XML vocabularies and formalisms in particular. It must not be restrictive in any way; if the tool cannot perform a task automatically, it must at least not prevent the developer from doing it manually. Smart tools are good, but they should not try to be smarter than their user. Usually, source-oriented editors (**6.1.1**), such as Topologi's CME,[1] best suit this category of users.

In short, a developer's XML editor must be a versatile workbench, with all sorts of devices and appliances for any imaginable task — from sophisticated and almost intelligent power tools to a mere screwdriver.

....

1. www.topologi.com

Author's writing desk. An XML editing application for a content author is a different story altogether. Since the job of authors is creating content for web sites, what they need is, above all, a *content* editor aware of XML.

Note the word "aware"; such a tool must not require (or demonstrate) more XML knowledge than absolutely necessary. Authoritative and therefore restrictive, yet friendly and forgiving — these are the qualities that will help such a tool to fulfill its primary purpose: help the author concentrate on content while producing valid and sensibly structured XML documents. For most authors, word processor XML editors (**6.1.4**) such as Morphon[2] work best, although for database-like XML, form-based editors (**6.1.3**) are preferable.

So, if the developer's editor is a workbench, then for the author, a good metaphor would be an austere writing desk with nothing but an ink pot and a sheet of white paper (or an empty form to fill). A dictionary would be handy too.

Editor's assembly line. A small site with occasional updates does not need any specific maintenance software, and this is especially true for an XML-based site whose source is so transparent. If, however, you frequently update a huge site, what you need is not a standalone editing tool but a complete *content management system* (CMS).

CMS software is not specific to XML; in fact, much of it still does not support XML too well. Those systems that are XML-aware (e.g., Lenya[3]) implement one of the traditional XML editing approaches (such as form-based editing, **6.1.3**).

What differentiates CMS tools from regular editors is their ability to work with many documents at once. Ability to combine documents into projects, storage and retrieval automation, versioning, scheduled updates — these features make a CMS similar to an assembly line where long queues of documents are being worked on in a semiautomatic fashion.

....

2. `www.morphon.com`
3. `cocoon.apache.org/lenya`; formerly known as Wyona.

What lies ahead. CMS software is in a world of its own, but it is not directly related to XML and therefore is not analyzed in this book. Instead, we'll start this chapter with an overview of the main categories of XML authoring tools.

Several approaches to XML editing exist today. Some tools implement more than one approach and let you switch between them on the fly; others focus on one approach only. Below we'll examine these approaches, discuss their advantages and disadvantages, and look at some example implementations.

6.1.1 Source editing

It's as simple as that: What you have in front of you is the full and complete source document, the way W3C intended it to be. Nothing but straightforward, uncompromising, truly open source XML — as in, for instance, this book's markup examples.

You can do it too. There's no arguing that XML source editing is more suitable for developers than for authors — but not by much. After all, one of the main goals of XML was to make documents as human-readable — and human-editable — as possible. By properly designing your source definition (choosing logical names, separating site-wide metadata, abbreviating addresses, etc.), you can push this editability even higher. In fact, the entire book you are reading is devoted to the ways of making XML transparent and accessible to anyone, not only developers.

6.1.1.1 Features

Source editing of XML is not the same as plain text editing. Most of the convenience of source-oriented editors is in their XML-specific features. Below is an attempt at classifying these goodies.

- **Generic XML features** are those capabilities that can be useful for any XML document, no matter what schema it conforms to (if any). These are the most basic and frequently used commands, such as closing the currently open element, navigating to the start tag or end tag, commenting or uncommenting a fragment, highlighting well-formedness errors, indentation, and manipulating character data (e.g., replacing all special characters with their numeric character references and vice versa). Some of these features require that the entire document be well-formed, but many will work regardless.

- **Schema-specific features**, often called *guided editing*, take advantage of knowing the schema of the document you're working with. Only a grammar-based schema (**2.2.1**) can be used in this way — Schematron is useless for guided editing (except for simple validation). Guided editing features usually include listing element types or attributes that are valid at a specific point, automatic insertion of required constructs and fixed values, and validation of the edited document (highlighting errors and providing suggestions on how to fix them).

- **Syntax coloring** is a simple but extremely handy feature that can make a world of difference in terms of usability. Unfortunately, many editors treat syntax coloring simplistically, offering separate colors only for generic classes of constructs such as comments, elements, entities, and character data. Such *generic* syntax coloring is the absolute minimum you might require from an XML editor.

  Much more useful is *specific* syntax coloring, which allows you to separately color distinct namespaces, elements, and attributes. Coloring of some element might determine or affect the color of its children or character data. In some situations, even monolithic character data can be usefully parsed and colored — for example, the expressions inside {curly braces} in attribute values in XSLT.

  Traditionally, source editors use a single monospaced font for displays. However, more sophisticated editors can assign not only different colors but also different font sizes and faces to source constructs. This is the approach used for the source code examples in this book (you cannot use color in a black-and-white book anyway); of the editors mentioned in this chapter, XEmacs (Figure 6.1) demonstrates this capability. Such advanced syntax coloring is reminiscent of the word processor XML editing mode (**6.1.4**) — except that it does not attempt to hide anything.

- **XPath tools** are not confined to XSLT stylesheets; they come in handy for various editing operations. Running an XPath expression against the document you are editing to see the result(s) highlighted is a good complement to (or even a substitute for) the traditional plain-text or regexp search. It is especially useful, of course, for writing and debugging XSLT stylesheets; yet after a while, you'll probably learn to "think in XPath" and start using XPath expressions in other XML editing tasks (see also **6.3.2**).

- **External processing** may include XSLT transformation, validation with external tools, and running various previewing or visualization applications. Basically it is just a way to save you switching to a command line to run a command on the document you are currently editing.

- **Project management** is an optional but very useful addition to the feature set of a source-oriented XML editor. It allows you to define a group of documents as a *project*, after which some commands may act on the project as a whole. For example, you might be able to transform or validate all `*.xml` files of the project (similar to the batch processing mode of the stylesheet, **5.6**), or run a text search or an XPath expression against the entire project. Moreover, sometimes you can define various relationships between members of a project, such as dependence (if one document is changed, the one depending on it is also considered changed and should be transformed again; compare **6.5**).

Most of these features are a boon for all three categories of XML users (developers, authors, editors). Developers will especially enjoy XPath tools and external processing. Authors may benefit from syntax coloring (so that the document markup is appropriately subdued in appearance and does not interfere with the text) and, of course, guided editing (so that there's no need to remember the exact names of element types or their usage patterns). Finally, editors will appreciate good project management tools that may make an XML editor comparable to a CMS.

6.1.1.2   Examples

Source XML editors come in two main flavors: generic text editors enhanced for XML and specialized XML editors. It's time for some nice screenshots!

Emacs[4] is a venerable tool. One of the oldest text editors in existence, it is immensely powerful, customizable, and extensible — and as widely used nowadays as ever. If I am to provide only one example of a text editor, it's got to be Emacs.

Along with GNU Emacs, there is a popular variant called XEmacs;[5] it has some benefits compared to GNU Emacs, but overall, the user-visible differences between the two editors are minimal. All information in this section applies to both GNU Emacs and XEmacs, but the screenshot (Figure 6.1) features XEmacs.

The most popular extension for editing XML (and SGML) in Emacs is called PSGML.[6] It implements a validating XML parser that can use a document's DTD (but not a schema in XSDL or any other schema language) for guided editing. Most generic XML editing commands are also available.

Other than that, PSGML has little to offer by itself — but it can work together with other Emacs tools to provide additional functionality. Thus, external processing is not included in PSGML, but you can either program it into Emacs yourself or use other Emacs packages such as XSLT-process (**6.4.3.2**).

Similarly, the syntax coloring provided by PSGML is generic, but you can define your own coloring regexps to cover the namespaces, element types, or other constructs that you use most frequently. XPath is not yet supported by any Emacs tool, but external XPath utilities (**6.3.2**) may be called from within Emacs.

An XEmacs window with our stylesheet (`style.xsl`, Example 5.21) is shown in Figure 6.1. It demonstrates custom, specific syntax coloring

---

4. www.gnu.org/software/emacs
5. www.xemacs.org
6. psgml.sf.net

Figure 6.1 XEmacs: Editing an XSLT stylesheet with generic XML editing commands.
. . . .

(e.g., XSLT instructions are easy to distinguish from HTML literal result elements) using both different colors and different font faces as well as a menu of generic XML editing commands.

Overall, Emacs requires a significant investment in terms of learning time and effort, but the return on this investment may be really good, giving you power and freedom that are hard to achieve with more specialized tools.

For an example of a specialized XML editor, let's look at **\<oXygen/\>**[7] (Figure 6.2). Written in Java, it is pretty typical of this kind of software. Mostly source-oriented, \<oXygen/\> also offers a tree editing mode (**6.1.2.1**). Here's this editor's scorecard:

- The guided editing features of \<oXygen/\> — in particular, context-sensitive element and attribute suggestions — are branded under the name "Code Insight." They can use both DTDs and XSDL schemas as the grammar definitions for a document. The interesting part is that \<oXygen/\> can generate a DTD itself from a well-formed XML document (see also **6.3.3**). This means that a partially written document can "guide itself," helping the author keep its structure consistent.

- Syntax coloring is generic. You can define colors for elements, attributes, attribute values, etc., but you cannot differentiate, for example, XSLT instructions from literal result elements in a stylesheet. Unlike a generic text editor such as Emacs, you cannot implement this functionality yourself — this is the price you pay for the convenience of an all-in-one package.

- The XPath capability is very handy. Right above the document editing window, you type your expression into a text field and hit *Enter*. A frame pops up at the bottom of the window listing the results of the query. As you select one of these results, the corresponding fragment in the editing window is highlighted.

7. `www.oxygenxml.com`

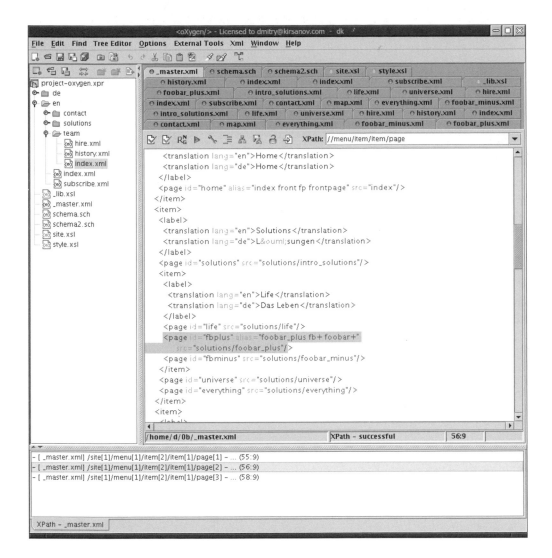

Figure 6.2 <oXygen/> XML editor: Project view, document source, and an XPath expression.

. . . .

- The editor has a built-in XSLT processor that can conveniently be used for transforming the documents you edit, optionally rendering an XSL-FO transformation result into PDF (using FOP[8]). Besides, the external processing feature in <oXygen/> lets

. . . .

8. xml.apache.org/fop

you run any program on your document — for example, you can validate a document with an external Schematron validator (by itself, <oXygen/> does not support Schematron).

- Project management is quite simple — no file dependencies, no batch transformation or validation; <oXygen/> projects are little more than a convenient way to open a group of files at once.

Topologi's **Collaborative Markup Editor**[9] is another source-oriented XML editor written in Java, notable for its extensive code formatting features and groupwork support. Perhaps most interestingly, CME is one of the very few XML editors to support interactive Schematron validation (in addition to other schema types); it highlights offending constructs and displays the corresponding diagnostic messages in the status bar. Like <oXygen/>, CME can deduce a grammar from an existing document using the feature called "Examplotron."

Transforming Editor.   Previous examples of source-oriented XML editors (both generic and specialized) demonstrated some of the ways to combine traditional text editor functionality with XML-specific additions, such as evaluating XPath expressions, for efficient editing of XML documents. However, the powerful concepts of XML and XPath are applicable to more than XML editing. I have written a proposal[10] for a new kind of all-purpose text editor that uses trees of nodes as its data model and an XPath-enabled language such as XSLT for transforming these trees. The two key ideas are representing the document being edited as a number of synchronized trees called *views*, each reflecting a different level of abstraction over document content, and automatic propagation of changes made to any of these views by *transforms* that link the views together.

An XPath interface to all active document views allows the user to program new editing functionality at the appropriate abstraction level, using any XPath-enabled scripting language. Views take much of the boring work out of creating editor commands; for example, you can use XPath to access a view where your document is preparsed into words, or paragraphs, or XML constructs. You can modify, rearrange, or syntax-color any element of any view, and the change will be reflected in all other views of the document down to

---

9. www.topologi.com
10. www.kirsanov.com/te

the lowest-level "characters" view that directly corresponds to the editor's screen display.

Any feedback from readers who find this idea interesting or might be able to help with the implementation will be much appreciated.[11]

6.1.2   Graphical XML editing

The main advantage of source editing is its transparency: Nothing is hidden; the document is visible down to the smallest detail. However, the flip side of this advantage is that too much detail may sometimes distract you from the task you want to perform.

A lot of syntax details of serialized XML (such as the exact layout of whitespace inside tags) do not affect the meaning of the document, yet they take up screen space and require extra keystrokes when editing. On the other hand, the hierarchical structure of an XML document may not be obvious from the mess of names and angle brackets on your screen — even with specific syntax coloring (**6.1.1.1**).

In view of this, several approaches to XML editing have emerged that try to reduce the amount of information that you have to mentally parse when looking at a document. Also, these approaches attempt to make the markup look more consistent, more distinct from the data, and more explicitly hierarchical. One thing that is common to all these approaches is the use of various graphic icons or metaphors to represent the structures described by the XML markup.

6.1.2.1   Tree metaphor

The most obvious graphical representation of an XML document is, of course, a tree. In a source view, the tree structure is not explicit; for example, you have to count the unclosed open elements in order to find out at which level of the tree hierarchy you are standing. Many XML editors therefore offer a separate tree view of the document.

An example of such a tree view is provided by the <oXygen/> editor (Figure 6.3). The branches of the tree can be expanded or collapsed

....

11. dmitry@kirsanov.com

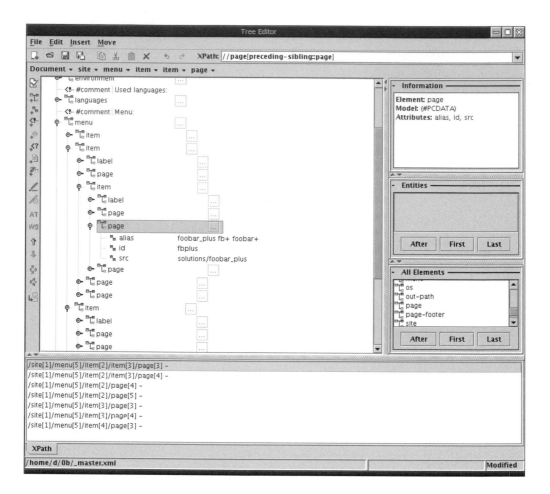

Figure 6.3   <oXygen/> XML editor: The tree view of an XML document and an XPath expression. The information in the panes at right (the current element's content model, lists of all defined elements and entities) comes from the DTD, which in this case was generated automatically by the program from a sample document.
. . . .

as needed. Attributes are represented as separate leaves of the tree, as is the data content of elements. Branches can be copied-or-moved by drag-and-drop or copy-and-paste — and, of course, all names and values are editable without leaving the tree editor.

is a pretty straightforward realization of the tree metaphor. It may be handy for a quick overview of the structure of a document, but it is hardly suitable for real document editing sessions — icons are noisy, and the tree looks kind of awkward. Is there a better alternative?

6.1.2.2   Frames metaphor

Let's have a look at the open source Java-based XML editor called **Pollo**[12] (Figure 6.4). Its display is somewhat tree-like, but the advantages it offers over a traditional tree representation are significant. Instead of icons hanging from the branches of a tree, elements in Pollo are represented by colored frames — which is quite natural if you consider that an element in XML is supposed to *enframe* its content. Instead of drawing connection lines symbolizing tree branches, Pollo simply nests these element frames into one another like matryoshka dolls.

This approach is similar to a tree view in that the nesting level of any node is immediately visible. However, since element frames are painted with different colors, you can get a visual clue as to exactly *which* elements are the ancestors of the current one, not only *how many* of them there are.

All elements of one type are represented by frames of the same color. These colors can be generated by the program randomly, or you can set an exact color for each element type in a "display specification" associated with your schema. Thus, Pollo's implementation of specific syntax coloring (**6.1.1.1**) creates a visually rich but consistent and easy-to-navigate display.

Attributes are conveniently positioned on the top bar of an element's frame. At the bottom of the window, an editing area lets you change the values of attributes and edit text nodes. Just like a branch in a tree, any frame with its content can be collapsed into a plain horizontal bar.

Admittedly, Pollo's XML display is not the best for freeform documents (for example, mixed content looks awkward when inline elements are stacked vertically between two text nodes). However, for

....

12. `pollo.sf.net`

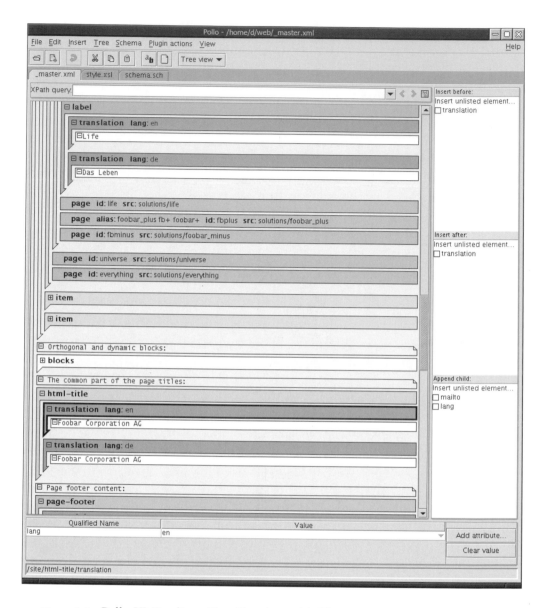

Figure 6.4   Pollo XML editor: Tree-like view with "frames" representing elements. Lists of allowed element types in the panes at right implement guided editing based on a DTD or an XSDL schema. An XPath expression highlights the first match and lets you scroll the list of all matches.

predictably structured XML — such as configuration files, a web site master document, or a Cocoon sitemap (**7.2.3**) — this interface is very intuitive and convenient.

Overcaffeinated! Why is so much XML software written in Java? One reason is Unicode: The XML specification requires that any XML processor must understand Unicode, and Java does that natively. Another reason is that Java, being a nice high-level language, makes it easy to write complex programs (and XML programs are complex, even though XML itself is so simple). But most importantly, it's a snowball effect: The more XML software is already written in Java, the more likely it is that a new XML project will choose this language too (especially contagious in this respect is, of course, open source software). However, other languages' XML snowballs are already rolling (Python shows a lot of potential), and they may one day overtake the Java snowball.

6.1.2.3 Iconic tags

Yet another approach to representing XML graphically is similar to the frames metaphor in that each element is enclosed in a graphical envelope. This time, however, these envelopes are not arranged in any semblance of a tree; instead, the opening and closing tags of each element are shown as icons bearing the name of the element type.

It might be argued that this approach is better — if only marginally — than direct source editing. It helps markup stand out from the text and hides most nonessential syntax details of XML. Also, it removes some of the clutter from document presentation by hiding attributes (they are usually only displayed for one element at a time by a special command).

Iconic tags are a convenient way to edit text-oriented documents — concentrating on the data but keeping the markup structure in sight. This approach to presentation is often combined with CSS-controlled formatting of element content, as in word-processor-like editors (**6.1.4**), for additional visual clues on the roles of element types. The **Morphon**[13] XML editor demonstrates this feature in Figure 6.5.

....

13. www.morphon.com

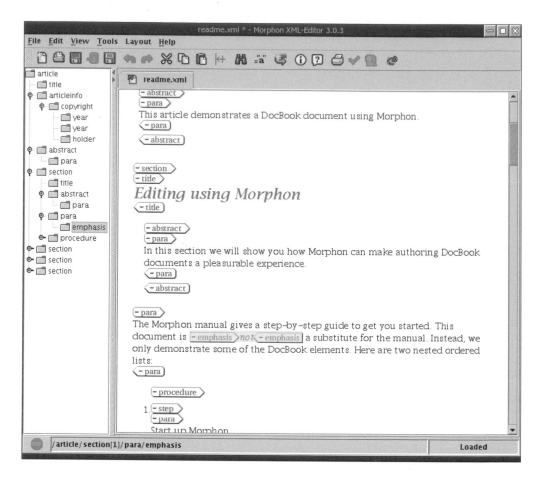

Figure 6.5 Morphon: Editable CSS-controlled presentation of an XML document. Icon
tags let you see what element you are editing, but they can be turned off for
a pure word-processor-like interface.

Microsoft Word 2003 Professional Edition operates similarly, but uses
Word's own style tools rather than CSS.

6.1.3 Form-based editing

Up to this point, all XML editing paradigms we discussed (source
editing, graphical editing) were primarily developer-oriented. An author or editor might use them too, of course; yet, without XML experience, it is easy to be overwhelmed by a rich detailed display (even in

a graphical mode) and a plethora of commands and options (even with guided editing). It may be difficult to fully concentrate on the content when what your editing tool shows you is so in-your-face XML.

The remaining two approaches to XML editing that we'll now discuss are therefore more author-oriented than developer-oriented. Their goal is to hide as many nonessential details as possible, yet not let the user stray from a valid document structure.

The first of these approaches is *form-based* XML editing. It is perhaps the simplest possible interface for the user: no need to know XML, no need to think what is what and how to name anything — just fill out the form. Given the sheer number of forms we have to do in our lives, this must be relievingly easy — provided the form is well laid out and the fields are clearly labeled and commented.

Generally, a form-based XML editing interface is a good idea if:

- you need to manually create lots of similar XML documents (and cannot automate this process);

- the users of this interface have minimal experience with XML or are too numerous to rely on their level of experience (e.g., in a distributed data entry project); and

- your document structure is regular and database-like, not freeform (in particular, mixed content does not usually mix well with forms).

Naturally, to enable an efficient form-based interface, the developer must create a logically laid out, nicely formatted, and helpfully commented form design. Form-based XML editors, such as Ponton XE[14] and Microsoft InfoPath,[15] provide various tools for this task. The starting point is usually a schema or DTD that is transformed into a form with one input field per attribute or element. You can then

----

14. www.ponton-consulting.de/english/xe.html
15. www.microsoft.com/office/preview/infopath

rearrange these fields, format them as appropriate, add explanatory labels, and so on.

All types of interface widgets can be creatively used for a rich but logical form interface. For example, portions of the form sheet may expand or collapse, making it similar to the tree XML view (**6.1.2.1**). Indeed, a form is sometimes accompanied by a parallel tree view of the same document.

Tabular forms. Closely related to form-based editing is the *table* metaphor, often found even in those XML editors that are otherwise freeform text-oriented. When a document contains a sequence of similarly structured elements, a table can be compiled from their content and attributes. This makes it easy to compare and modify parallel structures in predictably structured (database-like) XML.

Smart forms. You may want to embed various validation checks into your form, such as calculations or comparisons triggered by the completion of a field, a group of fields, or the entire form. Note that the *structural* validity of the resulting document is already ensured by the structure of the form itself, so there's little sense in DTD validation. XSDL is more useful, as it can perform data type checks of the form's values. However, XSDL cannot work with an incomplete document and therefore does not support on-the-fly checks in a form being filled in.

There are two main approaches to building "smart forms" capable of controlling their interaction with the user. One is *form scripting*: Just as you use JavaScript with HTML forms, you can use a scripting language in your XML form to perform any interface actions or data processing in response to events (such as the user entering a value). In fact, a simple form-based XML editor might be built out of a plain old HTML form coupled with a script that saves the form input as XML. Another example of a script-based editor is Microsoft's InfoPath (**6.2.3.4**); although it attempts to reduce the amount of programming necessary to create a form and in many cases eliminate it completely, the resulting automatically coded form scripts may be quite entangled.

Another approach to implementing smart forms is more attractive: Instead of *programming* various constraints and dependencies, you can simply *declare* them using a Schematron-like language with XPath expressions for accessing components of a form. For example, if you want a price field to be recalculated when a new currency is chosen from a drop-down list, you just state that the price field (identified by its XPath address within the form) is bound to the currency field with a simple formula. No event tracking, no function calls — just a static declaration. This is the approach of the XForms language, which we'll look at in some detail in the next section.

Using XForms

The W3C XForms[16] standard has emerged as a versatile and powerful — yet not overly complex — technology that enables, among other things, an excellent interface for form-based XML editing. The XForms standard is positioned by the W3C as the next generation of HTML forms, so an XForm must be able to send its input to a web server just as an HTML form does. However, unlike HTML forms, XForms can do lots of other useful things. For our purposes, it is important that:

- The result of filling out an XForm is stored in an XML document that is based on a template, called an *instance*, which is embedded in (or referenced from) the form and may be optionally controlled by an XSDL schema.

- Along with using a schema, an XForm can verify its input with Schematron-like declarative constraints, applying arbitrary calculations to any values in the form.

- The filled-out instance document can be saved to a local file.

- XForms constructs can be embedded into any other XML vocabulary — in particular, into XHTML while using CSS for styling.

Let's see what is involved in building an XForms interface for editing our own predictably structured XML — the master document of our

---

16. www.w3.org/MarkUp/Forms

sample site. Example 6.1 can only display and edit the `environment` elements, but you can expand it to implement an almost complete master document editor. Figure 6.6 shows how this form is rendered by **X-Smiles**[17] — a nice Java-based XML browser offering a fairly complete implementation of XForms (as well as many other XML standards).

. . . .

Example 6.1   `master.xhtml`: An XHTML document with an embedded XForm for editing a master document.

```
<?xml version="1.0" encoding="utf-8"?>
<html
    xmlns="http://www.w3.org/1999/xhtml"
    xmlns:xfm="http://www.w3.org/2002/xforms/cr"
    xmlns:xsd="http://www.w3.org/2001/XMLSchema"
    xmlns:ev="http://www.w3.org/2001/xml-events">
  <head>
    <link rel="stylesheet" type="text/css" href="master.css"/>
    <title>Master Editor</title>
    <xfm:model id="master">
      <!-- Source document to be edited: -->
      <xfm:instance
          src="file:/home/d/web/_master.xml"/>
      <!-- Save edited instance to: -->
      <xfm:submission id="submit1"
          localfile="/home/d/web/_master.xml"/>
      <!-- Constraint: children of 'environment' must not be empty -->
      <xfm:bind
          nodeset="/site/environment/*"
          constraint="string-length() &gt; 0"/>
    </xfm:model>
  </head>
```

. . . .

17. `www.xsmiles.org`

```
<body>
  <p><em>Welcome to the Master Editor!</em> This form interface
  allows you to edit a subset of a master document.</p>

  <h1>1. Environments</h1>

  <p>Each environment defines a set of paths used by the
  stylesheet. In each stylesheet run, the current environment is
  selected by a command-line parameter, e.g.,
  <code>env=final</code>.</p>

  <!-- Repeat for each /site/environment in the instance: -->
  <xfm:repeat nodeset="/site/environment" id="env-repeat">
    <div class="env">
      <div>
        <span>
          <!-- Bind this input field to /site/environment/@id: -->
          <xfm:input ref="@id" class="section">
            <xfm:label class="section">Environment: </xfm:label>
          </xfm:input>
        </span>
        <span>
          <!-- Bind this list to /site/environment/os: -->
          <xfm:select1 ref="os" appearance="full" class="os">
            <xfm:label>   Operating system:</xfm:label>
            <xfm:choices>
              <xfm:item>
                <xfm:label>Linux</xfm:label>
                <xfm:value>Linux</xfm:value>
              </xfm:item>
              <xfm:item>
                <xfm:label>Windows</xfm:label>
                <xfm:value>Windows</xfm:value>
              </xfm:item>
              <xfm:item>
                <xfm:label>FreeBSD</xfm:label>
                <xfm:value>BSD</xfm:value>
              </xfm:item>
            </xfm:choices>
          </xfm:select1>
        </span>
      </div>
```

```
          <!-- Four text fields for *-path elements: -->
          <div>
            <xfm:input ref="src-path">
              <xfm:label>
                Source path (where *.xml are taken from):
              </xfm:label>
            </xfm:input>
            <xfm:input ref="out-path">
              <xfm:label>
                Output path (where *.html are placed):
              </xfm:label>
            </xfm:input>
          </div>
          <div>
            <xfm:input ref="img-path">
              <xfm:label>
                Images path (relative to output and target):
              </xfm:label>
            </xfm:input>
            <xfm:input ref="target-path">
              <xfm:label>
                Target path (for relative links in HTML):
              </xfm:label>
            </xfm:input>
          </div>
        </div>
      </xfm:repeat>


<div>
    <!-- Button to insert a new empty environment: -->
    <xfm:trigger id="insertbutton">
      <xfm:label>New environment</xfm:label>
      <xfm:insert ref="/site/environment"
          at="xfm:index('env-repeat')" position="after"
          ev:event="DOMActivate"/>
    </xfm:trigger>
    <!-- Button to delete the highlighted environment: -->
    <xfm:trigger id="deletebutton">
      <xfm:label>Delete environment</xfm:label>
      <xfm:delete ref="/site/environment"
          at="xfm:index('env-repeat')"
          ev:event="DOMActivate"/>
    </xfm:trigger>
</div>
```

```
<div>
  <!-- Submit saves the instance: -->
  <xfm:submit name="Submit" submission="submit1">
    <xfm:label>Save</xfm:label>
  </xfm:submit>
  <!-- Reset undoes all changes and reverts to loaded values: -->
  <xfm:trigger>
    <xfm:label>Revert</xfm:label>
    <xfm:reset model="master" ev:event="DOMActivate"/>
  </xfm:trigger>
</div>
</body>
</html>
```

This section is not an XForms tutorial, but only a teaser to whet your appetite. Still, comparing the X-Smiles rendering with the source in Example 6.1 might be a good first lesson in XForms. We will now discuss the main components of this XForms-in-XHTML example without going into too much detail.

The role model. Within the head of the XHTML document in Example 6.1, the xfm:model element describes the *model* of the form. An XForms model combines the XML instance that the form will populate with data, its schema (not used in this example), any additional constraints, and the submission action to be taken when the form is completed.

Loading and saving. In this case, the xfm:instance element takes an external document at file:/home/d/web/_master.xml as the instance. This means that the form, when activated, will load this document and distribute its data into the corresponding form controls as default values. You can therefore provide an empty instance document as a template, or you can link your form to an existing master document with real data and use the form to change some of its values.

Conversely, when the form is filled out and the submission action is triggered by the user, the xfm:submission element will save the resulting XML into the local file at /home/d/web/_master.xml. Since this is the same file as that referred to in xfm:instance, the form will effectively edit that document and save it back. If you revisit the form

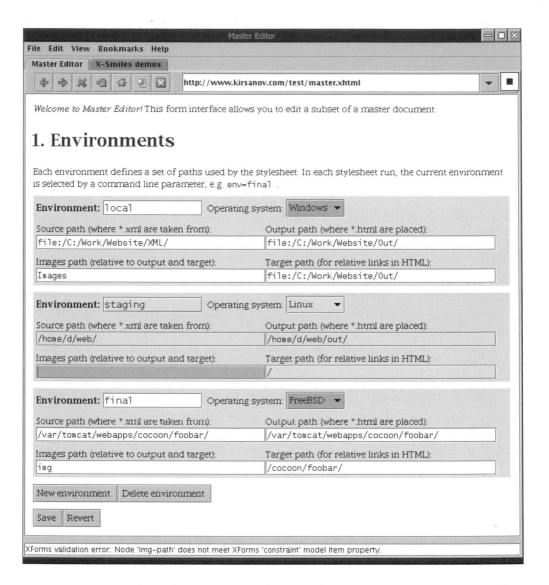

Figure 6.6 X-Smiles: Editing a subset of master document with an XForms interface from Example 6.1.

later, it will load the document again and display it with all the changes you made last time.

Constraining input. An XForms model can also contain arbitrary constraints, exemplified here by the `xfm:bind` element. Such a constraint is very much like a Schematron rule in that it uses XPath to specify its context (the `nodeset` attribute) and the expression that must be true in that context (the `constraint` attribute).

In the example, we declare that all children of an `environment` must be nonempty. A conformant XForms browser will refuse to submit the form until this constraint is satisfied.

The `xfm:bind` element can also be used for many other purposes, such as assigning a data type to the selected nodes, controlling whether these nodes are included into the submission, or calculating values of nodes based on other nodes in the instance.

Please type. In the `body` of the document, interspersed with arbitrary text and XHTML markup, XForms *controls* constitute the visible part of the form. Each control uses an XPath expression in its `ref` attribute to link itself to a node of the XML instance in the form's model. This link works both ways: If a node value is changed by a control or by a calculation inside the model, this change is reflected in all controls that reference that node.

In our example, the `xfm:repeat` element iterates over all `environment` elements in the source. Within it, several `xfm:input` fields and one `xfm:select1` list are linked to the child elements and an attribute of each `environment`.

Growing the document. XForms not only makes it possible to fill in values of elements and attributes that are already present in the instance — you can add new elements, too.

Two button controls after `xfm:repeat` allow you to remove the current environment or add a new empty one after the current. An XForms browser is supposed to keep track of user input and always designate one of the `repeat`ed sections as current. For example, X-Smiles uses yellow highlighting for the section that you are currently editing (in Figure 6.6, it is the `staging` environment in the middle).

When you're done. Finally, the last two buttons do form submission (i.e., saving the document; you will be prompted to confirm if the file already exists) and form reset (i.e., returning to the values loaded from the instance document, losing all changes you've made in this session).

Before the form is submitted, all constraints defined in the model are verified. For example, in the screenshot, the `img-path` field within the `staging` environment is empty, so the browser paints it red and refuses to submit the form until a value is provided.

Limitations.   This example demonstrates how you can quickly and painlessly implement a rich form-based editing interface for your XML documents using XForms. Sure enough, this approach has its share of problems as well. The most important ones are these:

- The locations for the source instance and the document to be saved are hardwired into the form. That means you cannot select an arbitrary document for editing and save it to an arbitrary location (unless your XForms processor provides this functionality as an extension).

  This may actually be an advantage. Remember that the goal of the form-based interface is to make editing *simple*. From this viewpoint, there is nothing wrong with the fact that you don't need to worry about filenames and cannot mess up a document by saving it in the wrong directory. Just select one of the forms from your XForms browser's bookmarks, edit, and press one button to save.

  Are there examples of database-like documents that don't need to be created anew or moved from one place to the other, but only edited where they are? The master document of a web site is one such example; others are various configuration files in XML. Thus, configuring the X-Smiles browser itself is done via an XForms page that displays the options from an XML configuration file and lets you edit and save them.

- As mentioned previously, form editing is hardly appropriate for freeform XML. Unfortunately, XForms cannot handle any mixed content, even if it is but a small part of an otherwise database-like document with a predictable structure. For example, with XForms you can edit the `contact-webmaster` element of our master document (see Example 3.2, page 143) but you will lose its child `mailto` link and any other inline markup.

XForms browsers may provide extensions[18] to overcome this limitation. Another approach might involve using one of the text-to-XML converters (**6.2.1**) to produce mixed content from structured text entered in an XForms `textarea`.

The InfoPath forms editor, which does not use XForms, is one that is capable of handling mixed content, as long as it conforms to XHTML.

6.1.4 Word processor editing

If filling out forms is the fastest and most natural way to author database-like XML, then for freeform XML it is the word processor interface that is most familiar to users. Editing XML with the convenience of a word processor — and yet producing valid and sensibly structured XML documents — is one of the main directions of development in today's XML authoring tools.

Syntax formatting. At first sight, word processor display is in direct opposition to XML editing: The former is largely about appearance, while the latter is strictly about content. However, undiluted abstractions rarely work entirely as intended. The ubiquity of syntax coloring in all sorts of text editors is a clear indication that appearance *does* matter even when you deal with purely abstract structures, because it helps a human reader parse and navigate those structures. From this viewpoint, word-processor-like XML editing is nothing but "syntax coloring on steroids" — or "syntax formatting" if you wish.

Of course, to be applicable to the highly regular XML, the appearance aspect of a document must itself be regular and consistent. Unattached bits of "formatting for formatting's sake" are inadmissible. Do we have a robust technology that would allow us to assign rich formatting properties to XML elements *without* changing the XML document itself in any way? Yes, we do — it's called CSS.[19]

....

18. One such proposed extension is described at `www.dubinko.info/writing/htmlarea`.
19. `www.w3.org/TR/REC-CSS2`

Cascading Style Sheets. Granted, from the design and typography perspective, CSS is less sophisticated than, say, XSL-FO. But we don't need a high level of sophistication for presenting different elements differently. What may be more important is that, unlike XSL-FO which is only good for printed documents, CSS can naturally accommodate various presentation modes, including the screen presentation of information.

This paradigm — whereby you edit a nicely formatted CSS-controlled presentation of your document and get valid semantic XML as a result — is adopted by many XML editors these days. It has its limitations, though.

Memory for faces and memory for names. The most important limitation is that the number of different formatting *styles* that you can reliably remember and recognize is usually much less than the number of element type *names* you can memorize and apply. That is, names attached to markup constructs are easier to remember for many people, even though visual formatting styles may look sexier.

When *creating* markup, you can make use of guided editing — for example, by choosing from a list of markup constructs valid at the current point (such lists may display the names of constructs, or the corresponding formatting samples, or both). However, when *editing* existing markup, you will often find it difficult to guess what element you are in, judging solely by the formatting style at the cursor.

Certainly, distinguishing a heading from a paragraph of text is easy. But some widely used vocabularies, such as DocBook, contain hundreds of element types. Assigning a recognizable set of visual properties to each element type may therefore be difficult if not impossible.

As a response to this problem, many word processor XML editors can optionally display element tags without removing CSS formatting. The tags are usually rendered as icons. You can use them while you are learning a new vocabulary and then switch them off, or you can enable them periodically to remind yourself of the inner workings of your document. The Morphon XML editor is a typical example (Figure 6.5, page 298).

What you see is what you pay for. Other limitations of the word processor XML editing paradigm may seem less important, especially for those who have always used traditional word processors for authoring. Yet they are limitations, and you as a developer should be aware of them in advance.

- **XML comments** are invisible and inaccessible. Consequently, if you want the authors to be able to comment their content, you have to provide a special element type for this (to be ignored or converted into XML comments by the stylesheet).

- **Attributes** are also invisible, although they can affect presentation of content. For example, `element[attr="foo"]` in CSS2 selects an element based on its attribute value, much as `element[@attr="foo"]` matches it in XSLT. An XML editor may of course provide a command to view and modify attribute values for an element, but by the very nature of the word processing approach, this can only be done through a special dialog, and not as a routine editing operation.

- **Nesting of elements** is not obvious. For example, if I see a green sentence inside an italic paragraph, does that mean that the "green" element is a child of the "italic," or is this *two* "italic" elements with a "green" one in between?

  It may be very difficult to combine unambiguously several formatting styles that correspond to several element ancestors of the current text fragment. Despite the "cascading" in "CSS," many editors do not even attempt to visualize nesting in any way, effectively reducing XML to the flat styles of conventional word processors (**6.2.3.3**). On the other hand, as we'll see below (**6.1.5.1**), it is possible to use the CSS frame and background properties to visualize the hierarchical structure of the top-level elements of a document.

6.1.5   Writing CSS for XML visualization

You will need CSS style sheets for visualizing your XML if you want to author your custom-vocabulary XML in a word-processor-like XML editor. But it is also very useful to be able to view your XML documents quickly, without transformation, in an XML/CSS-capable web browser.

But we already have a web site? Creating CSS for XML is not much of a graphic design job; the style sheets may have very little in common with the way this same material looks on the web pages after transformation. Our goal is to render source XML in a consistent and visually unambiguous way so it is easy to review and edit. This means the document structure must be expressive and laconic at the same time.

HTML text in the XML structure. It may, however, make sense for our CSS style sheet for XML to imitate to some extent the *character formatting* of the transformed HTML pages. This imitation will let site authors and editors see at once where elements in their XML editor window will end up on the web page. On the other hand, the visualization of document *structure* cannot and should not be in any way influenced by the layout of the web page, if only because a web page will contain components (such as navigation) that are absent from that page's source XML.

6.1.5.1   Nested boxes

Thus, we have to find a clear yet unobtrusive way to use CSS to reflect the hierarchical structure of XML. The Pollo XML editor (**6.1.2.2**) suggests the idea of using nested rectangular frames with different visual properties. Indeed, with CSS, you can easily present content blocks as boxes with different border types, specify colors of their borders and backgrounds, and adjust margins for better recognizability.

6.1.5.2   Links and images

Compared to XSLT, CSS is very limited when it comes to manipulating data. For instance, you cannot pull information from one place in a document and insert it into another (let alone into a different document). Luckily, we don't need this ability for straightforward XML visualization, especially given that our page documents (Example 3.1, page 141) are so simple.

Thus, you cannot create clickable links from abbreviated link addresses (**3.5.3**) in your XML because CSS lacks facilities for proper unabbreviation. (A simple XSLT stylesheet can be added to handle this — but then, why use CSS at all?) But perhaps you don't *need* the visualized links to be clickable; much more useful for editing is to *see* the link address in its original abbreviated form. However, you'll still want such a link to stand out from the surrounding text so that its link status is clear.

Similarly, CSS cannot be used to fetch images and insert them into the displayed document.[20] Instead, we will simply show the (abbreviated) image references as they are given in the source. Technical validity of both links and image references can be checked by a Schematron schema (**5.1.3**); what we are interested in when editing the document is that these references actually *make sense*, and this is where seeing the original abbreviated addresses can really help.

6.1.5.3   Example and demonstration

A CSS style sheet for visualizing the structure of our sample page documents (such as the one in Example 3.1) is given in Example 6.2. Note that unlike the XHTML+CSS combination, CSS applied to a generic XML document has no default properties associated with any element types. You'll have to define everything explicitly, including the *display:* block property for block-level constructs such as paragraphs.

---

20.   At least not if you use an XML-capable web browser such as Mozilla for displaying XML documents with a CSS style sheet. XML word processors may use special tricks to add this functionality for certain XML vocabularies; for example, Morphon uses special plugins for inserting images referred to from a DocBook document.

. . . .

Example 6.2 A CSS style sheet for visual rendition of an XML page document (see Figure 6.7).

```
page { background-color: white; padding: 5pt; margin: -5pt; }

page title { letter-spacing: 0.5em; margin: 5pt; }

block {
  display: block; padding: 10pt; margin: 5pt;
  border: lightgray 4px solid; }

section {
  display: block; padding: 0pt 10pt 10pt 10pt; margin: 5pt;
  border: black 2px dashed; }

section > head {
  display: block; background-color: #cccccc;
  padding: 5pt 10pt 5pt 10pt; margin: 0pt 0pt 0pt -10pt;
  font-weight: normal; font-size: large; }

section > subhead {
  display: block; background-color: #eeeeee;
  padding: 5pt 5pt 5pt 1cm; margin: 0pt -10pt 0pt -10pt;
  font-style: italic; }

p {
  display: block; padding: 5pt; margin: 5pt;
  border: black 2px dotted; }

block[src]:before {
  content: "[Orthogonal block reference: "  attr(src) " ]";
  color: gray; font-family: monospace; font-size: small; }

section[image]:before {
  content: "[Image: " attr(image) " ]";
  display: block; padding: 3pt;
  color: gray; font-family: monospace; font-size: small; }

int, link[linktype="internal"] {
  color: green; border-bottom: 1px solid; }
```

```
ext, link[linktype="external"] {
  color: blue; border-bottom: 1px solid; }

int:after, link[linktype="internal"]:after {
  content: "[int: " attr(link) "]";
  color: gray; font-family: monospace; font-size: x-small; }

ext:after, link[linktype="external"]:after {
  content: "[ext: " attr(link) "]";
  color: gray; font-family: monospace; font-size: x-small; }

em { font-style: italic; }

code { font-family: monospace; }
```

If your CSS visualization is to be used by content authors or site maintainers, it makes sense to create a "legend" XML document that uses all of your source XML vocabulary and explains the formatting conventions of the CSS visualization. A browser screenshot of such a sample document is shown in Figure 6.7.

6.2 Converting into XML

Apart from authoring directly in XML, the only way to create source documents is by converting them from some other document format. This is not quite analogous to, say, converting from one image format to another. By itself, XML is a simple markup syntax, but the way it is used in semantic vocabularies — such as that of a web site source — is conceptually different from most other document formats used today.

Not a simple algorithm. Transforming a typical document format into XML does not amount to simply renaming, rearranging, or reformatting bits of content; this task always involves certain *rethinking* as well. Unless your other format was developed specifically to provide a one-to-one mapping to your particular source vocabulary, conversion will inevitably be an unreliable, heuristic approximation always requiring manual checks and fixes.

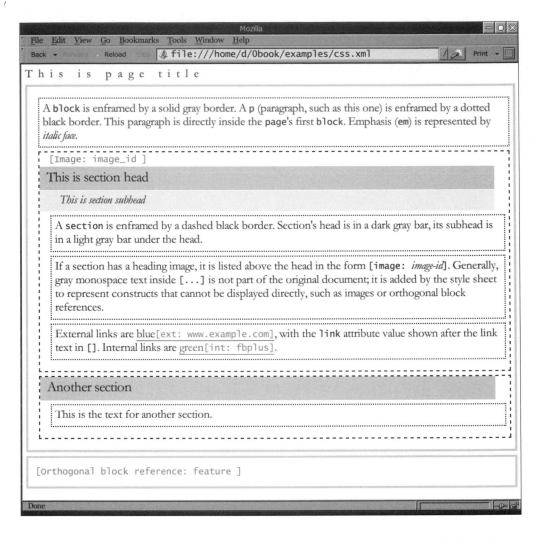

Figure 6.7   A "legend" XML document using most of the element types defined for the page documents, rendered by Mozilla with the CSS style sheet from Example 6.2.

Generally, any document-to-XML conversion may be broken into two stages:

- **Low-level (syntactic) processing** is where you break into the source format's envelope, extract the atoms of content you are interested in (such as words, numbers, or paragraphs), and decode or decipher them if necessary. The difficulty of this stage may range widely, depending on the clarity of the data format and how well it is documented. Its output is best stored in some intermediate XML vocabulary reflecting the structure of the source format, not the target format. Sometimes, however, software limitations leave HTML or even plain text as the only choice for such an intermediate format.

- **High-level (semantic) processing** is the process where the atoms of meaning extracted during the first stage are examined, and educated guesses are made as to what each atom represents and how to mark it up using your target XML vocabulary. This stage may also be very difficult, especially if the source format provides no clues about the semantics of its content atoms or if these clues are not used consistently.

Sometimes, these two stages are combined into a single application. With your custom XML vocabulary, however, this is not likely to happen because existing conversion tools cannot be aware of your vocabulary. This means you'll have to use one of the existing tools for low-level processing, save the result as intermediate XML, and then write your own XSLT stylesheet for high-level transformation of that intermediate format into your target vocabulary.

Multiple inputs, multiple outputs. With this approach, you can have one low-level converter plugged into several high-level transformation stylesheets for different target vocabularies. Or, you can handle several source formats with different low-level converters sending their output to one high-level transformation stylesheet.

6.2.1 Plain text

When you have documents or data in plain text, low-level processing is usually easy to implement. All programming languages, without exception, can read plain text files and break them into lines, words, or other units. Semantic processing, however, is much more difficult because the source format provides no regular markup and scarcely any clues as to what part of the file is meant to be what.

Still, since plain text has long been the only format of Usenet and email, a number of well-known conventions exist that can be used to recognize and mark up a few common semantic elements in a plain text file. Based on these conventions, **txt2html**,[21] an amazingly versatile Perl script, converts plain text into HTML. It attempts to mark up headings, paragraphs, lists, links, inline elements, and even tables. With the `--xhtml` command-line option, txt2html will output XHTML, which you can then convert into your target XML vocabulary with an XSLT stylesheet.

Chaperon[22] is used with Cocoon (**7.2**) as a text-to-XML generator, but it can also be run separately. It is controlled by grammar and lexicon files in a special XML vocabulary and can handle arbitrary structured text as input.

Another project worth looking at is **txt2xml**.[23] This is a Java library that is more database-oriented than freeform-oriented; the example application on its web site is a conversion from a comma-separated plain text spreadsheet. This tool is similar to XSLT in that the mapping from a source text format to the output XML is defined by a set of processors and subprocessors (similar to XSLT's templates), each generating elements of one type when triggered by a regexp match in the source file.

6.2.2 HTML

Even though this book is mostly devoted to the opposite task — converting semantic XML into presentation-oriented HTML — sometimes you may run into a pile of legacy data that is only available as HTML. By this I do not mean modern XHTML, which is actually XML and can be transformed into whatever you want with XSLT, but old, supposedly-SGML-but-really-just-lousy HTML with swamps of

....

21. `txt2html.sf.net`; look at a sample text file, `txt2html.sf.net/sample.txt`, and its conversion to HTML, `txt2html.sf.net/sample.html`.
22. `chaperon.sf.net`
23. `txt2xml.sf.net`

weird formatting code and swarms of markup errors that only a seasoned web browser can make sense of.

Luckily, there is some competition for browsers in this area. **HTML Tidy**[24] (originally written by Dave Raggett) is a wonderful piece of software that knows the entire HTML specification by heart, including its most arcane bits. More importantly, it is smart enough to fix any broken HTML files you throw at it and output them as either valid HTML (you can specify which version) or XHTML.

Common to many toolchains. The importance of Tidy goes beyond handling broken web pages. Many older applications (e.g., some of the office suites discussed in the next section) are totally unaware of XML but can produce some sort of HTML. In most cases, before you can work with this intermediate HTML any further, you have to fix it using Tidy — the only way to rescue valuable data from these dead-end formats and let it flow into the boundless ocean of XML.

Forcibly tidy. Sometimes, an HTML document is so severely broken that Tidy will refuse to process it. In this situation, use the `--force-output yes` command-line option to force Tidy to produce output no matter what, but be aware that some of the original markup may be lost or misinterpreted.

6.2.3 Office formats

Converting from office document formats is perhaps the most important practical scenario, as most content authors tend to use office suites for their work. And more often than not, they assume that everyone else does, too.[25]

Only if they are willing to listen. It would be nice — and profoundly beneficial for everyone involved — to train all your content creators to use semantic XML markup, but in many cases this is simply not doable. User inertia is a force to be reckoned with; don't

---

24. `tidy.sf.net`

25. Sometimes, they even claim it *must* be so because their favored office suite is "industry standard." Explaining to them that the meaning of the word *standard* in that phrase is actually very different from that in *standards-compliant* or *open standards based* may be frustrating.

expect to get many XML converts among people who've spent a good share of their lives mastering Microsoft Word and feel quite comfy with it. Also, there are certain content-oriented tasks, such as collaborative editing, where word processors still have a lead over anything today's XML editors have to offer.[26]

Who is to blame? Unfortunately, converting legacy office formats into XML is also one scenario where even low-level processing may be far from trivial, and high-level processing can easily become a nightmare. An important difference, however, is in *who* is responsible for these two levels of obstacles — and what *you* can do about them.

Low-level processing problems are entirely the responsibility of the office suite's vendor. There is little you can do about it — other than switch to a different office suite with a more open document format. Reverse-engineering a closed office format and creating a low-level conversion utility for it is a daunting task that even large groups of dedicated programmers don't always succeed in accomplishing.

If an office suite cannot *itself* export all of its content and markup into a meaningfully parsable representation, you are stuck with whatever third parties have to offer for this format (**6.2.3.3**).

What is to be done? It is all quite different with the high-level semantic processing of the low-level converter output. Here, both content authors and yourself as the web site developer can do a lot to make your work anything from almost automatic to hard, largely manual, and excruciatingly tedious. Office applications are notoriously feature-bloated, and it is your job to make it known to those who use them what features are acceptable and what are not.

You must be proactive with this if you don't want to be swamped by tons of badly formatted, inconvertible documents. Start by testing the office suite your authors will be using. Search through all of its features (including those you may never have used yourself) to figure out the

---

26. Word 2003 Professional Edition (**6.2.3.4**) offers some relief, with its ability to create valid custom XML using Word's normal WYSIWYG user interface.

best possible approximation of your target XML vocabulary using the program's native formatting tools.

The reference implementation. The selected subset of approved features and the recommendations on how best to use them will be revised repeatedly as you test your chosen low-level converter and write the stylesheet for the high-level transformation. As the result of all this work, you will have created a template document in the office format that demonstrates and explains all the best practices of for-XML office suite authoring. This template must be publicized, and no web site author should begin working on a document without first studying it in detail.

This office-format template for site authors is an important part of your source definition (Chapter 2). Its scope and features will depend not only on your target vocabulary but, above all, on the expressiveness of the intermediate format that you standardize upon. Let's see what intermediate formats we can use and their implications for the setup of your office-format conversion system.

6.2.3.1   Converting via plain text

In the simplest possible case, you can use plain text as your intermediate format. This makes sense if you don't want to trouble your authors with any format or structure concerns at all — that is, if all you want to get from them is the data, not markup. This approach has one big advantage: You don't need any third-party converters because all office suites, without exception, can export their documents as plain text.[27]

Extracting paragraphs.   Plain text is not entirely structureless (**6.2.1**). One structural unit you can almost always identify in a text document is a paragraph (separated from other paragraphs by either newlines or empty lines). Approaching this problem from the other end, you can always ask the authors to structure their output *at the document level* by only producing small documents that correspond,

---

27. Even if they couldn't, you would still be able to use copy-and-paste. In fact, it may sometimes be faster and even give better results.

not to entire web pages, but to high-level constructs within a page (such as sections or blocks, **3.1.2**).

As such block-sized documents are likely to be small, you can parse them simply by guessing the role of each paragraph based on its position within the plain-text rendition of the document. For example, you may assume that the first paragraph of each block document is the heading, the last one is the author byline, and all paragraphs in between are the content of the block. Of course, any such conventions are very limited and relying on them is risky, but they will allow you to build a working word-processor-to-XML toolchain really fast — assuming you can get the necessary cooperation from the authors.

6.2.3.2   Converting via HTML

Using HTML (**6.2.2**) as an intermediate format is the next option to consider after plain text. Like text, HTML does not normally require any external converter; it has been around for so long that all office applications can "Save as HTML" by now.

Microsoft HTML.   HTML exported by Microsoft Office is notoriously bulky, contaminated with Office-specific extensions, and often simply broken. For many projects it is actually easier and more reliable to use plain text. Still, with the help of Tidy (**6.2.2**), Office's HTML can be used as a starting point for high-level processing.

If you need to access MS Word documents but do not wish to touch MS Word itself, I recommend the **wv** library[28] and its accompanying utilities. This open source software runs on many platforms and converts MS Word documents to plain text, HTML, LATEX, and other formats.

Rigidly quirky.   HTML as an intermediate format will likely work only for relatively simple projects. This is because the inventory of structural units preserved in conversion cannot differ much from the inventory of element types in HTML — which pretty much limits you to headings, paragraphs, lists, links, and simple inline elements.

28. `wvware.sf.net`

This approach isn't very flexible either: Generally, you have little control over which styles and formatting in the source get converted to which HTML elements. With some third-party converters, generated HTML will be adorned with CSS `class` attributes storing the names of the corresponding source styles, which helps.

6.2.3.3 Converting via XML

Using XML as an intermediate format for converting Microsoft Office documents is only available with third-party conversion utilities or with Office 2003 or later (**6.2.3.4**). Therefore, a lot of details of your project setup will depend on the capabilities of these conversion utilities. Some commercial XML editors, especially those implementing the word processor paradigm (**6.1.4**), will also import common office formats such as RTF and even Microsoft Word.

Le style est l'homme même. What kind of XML do we want to get from these converters? The key idea is this: When editing a document in an office application, apply named *styles* (such as "paragraph" or "list item") instead of anonymous formatting properties (such as margin width or font size) to the structural units. Then, ask the converter to please translate these styles into XML elements with the same names . . . thanks, we can take it from here. No, we don't need anything else. We'll do the rest in XSLT.

There are several MS Word to XML converters that will do this job. In our testing, **Upcast**[29] proved sufficiently reliable. Other standalone converters include **Logictran**[30] and **Majix**.[31] All of them can handle RTF, but converting directly from a `.doc` file can only be done on Windows and requires that MS Word be installed.[32]

The law of inertia. The biggest problem with this approach is not technical, however — it is user inertia. The requirement that *every* structural unit (including, for example, inline emphasis as in "every"

---

29. www.infinity-loop.de/products/upcast/
30. www.logictran.com
31. www.tetrasix.com
32. Oh the joy of closed formats!

in this sentence) must be assigned a corresponding named style is likely to put off at least some users.

The concept of named styles has been in MS Word for ages, yet it is astounding how many users simply ignore it. They actually *prefer* to format their stuff by manually applying fonts and colors instead of just selecting one of the styles from a drop-down list. It's up for discussion whether Word's interface is to blame for this; in practice, just be prepared to annoy your Word authors for quite some time before you start getting consistent styles-only documents from them.

Styles are flat. There are some technical issues with styles as well. The biggest problem is that unlike XML elements, styles generally *do not nest*.

MS Word styles come in two flavors, *paragraph* (block-level) and *character* (inline-level). A fragment of text may have a character style of its own and be affected by the paragraph style of its paragraph. You cannot, however, mark a text fragment with more than one character style, or make a paragraph belong to two or more overlapping areas with different paragraph styles. Each character has exactly one character style, and each paragraph has exactly one paragraph style.

For example, suppose you want to use numbered programming code examples, each consisting of a preformatted listing and a caption. In Word, you can assign the corresponding paragraph styles to a `listing` and its `caption`, but then you cannot tie them together by applying another common style to both. Alternatively, you can mark both a listing and its caption by a common `example` style — but then you cannot separate the caption from the code.

As a result, your transformation stylesheet will have to be less straightforward, and therefore less reliable than it could be if styles would nest. For instance, your stylesheet could provide that if a `caption` is immediately followed by a `listing`, both are wrapped into an `example`. Such provision, apart from being utterly inelegant, is likely to break often, especially if `captions` or `listings` are allowed to be part of other constructs as well.

Write the Style Bible. It is in situations like these that a comprehensive template document is invaluable, showing samples of all styles that your stylesheet can handle, as well as their most common combinations. Simply creating the new styles and embedding them into the template is not sufficient; you must provide complete instructions on when to use each style, why this is important, and what will happen if the user just clicks on the *I* button instead of selecting the `emphasis` style.

As a part of the complete source definition, this template document has to make the same internal distinction between rules that can be enforced automatically and those that can only be explained (and then reiterated) to the user because they cannot be checked with software (**2.2.1.4**). The only difference is that in a word processor, the boundary between what you can and cannot enforce automatically is much lower than in any schema language.

Minimize the disruption. Here are some additional bits of advice:

- Where possible, authorize the use of standard Word styles, as they have the big advantage of familiarity. You can change their formatting somewhat, to give better visual clues to *what* is being edited (e.g., by making the formatting of paragraphs or headings similar to that of the final web pages).

- If there's no direct analog for what you need in the inventory of standard styles, create a new style with a consistent and descriptive name.

- Keep the number of new styles low. (This one is important: If a user feels daunted by the amount of new stuff he or she has to learn, the motivation to comply with your rules will suffer.)

- Don't forget to remove from the template any standard styles that you don't want to see in the submitted documents.

- Include in the template document all relevant rules concerning special characters and typographic conventions (**5.4.2.3**).

Allow some time for users to adapt to the new word processing rules. Errors will be plentiful at first, but you must be persistent in tracking down each one to either fix what is broken in your software (the template or translation stylesheet) or talk over the error with the user who turns out to be the culprit.

Redefining the "source." After a page document is submitted, converted, transformed, and uploaded to the server, which format is the "master source" of the web page? In other words, will you edit the word processor file or the XML document when you need to make a change to the page?

The answer to this question depends on what kind of changes you will be making and how often, as well as on whether your word-processor-to-XML conversion is completely automatic. Obviously, if your updates are infrequent, small, and mostly technical in nature (i.e., not requiring the author's expertise), it is tempting to treat the word processor source of the page as a shed skin that you will never return to.

On the other hand, if the updates are more or less regular and can only be done by the original author of the page — *and* if your conversion routine is fully automatic, tested, and proved reliable — you should let the author maintain his or her own copy of the word processor file and rerun the conversion to XML (and then to HTML) on each change.

6.2.3.4   MS Office 2003

Microsoft Office 2003 (also known as Office 11) offers XML equivalents of the Word and Excel file formats.[33] For example, the Word format, called WordML, is a direct equivalent of the binary `.doc` format. It includes the data content of the document, the styles associated with it (whether or not used), and the various settings (such as page margins and tabs).

It is substantially easier to parse and use the Word document format with WordML than with `.doc` or RTF. One enterprising company has

---

33. www.microsoft.com/office/xml

even developed an XSLT stylesheet for converting from WordML to XSL-FO.[34]

The Professional editions of Office that also support user-defined custom XSDL schemas (but not DTDs). Word, for example, provides guided editing and the option of saving the document both in WordML and as an instance of your custom schema. The Professional Enterprise edition of the suite also includes the new InfoPath forms-based editor.

6.2.3.5 Other office suites

The increasingly popular open source office suites, such as KOffice,[35] OpenOffice.org,[36] and Sun's StarOffice,[37] also save documents in XML using their own presentation-oriented vocabularies — in fact, this is their native document format. However, no custom schema support and no guided editing are currently available.

These XML document formats are pretty well documented[38] and free of patent or license restrictions. The OASIS consortium has started a project to develop a common XML-based office format[39] to be used by all office suite vendors.[40]

6.2.4 Semantic processing and XML-to-XML conversion

If you expect that I will now reveal a yet-unmentioned XML-to-XML conversion tool comparable to XSLT, I'm sorry to disappoint you. If you want to convert between arbitrary XML vocabularies, XSLT is the most powerful and, perhaps, the only practical solution.

This is one case where the low-level parsing of input is not a problem at all — you get it for free when you run your conversion stylesheet.

---

34. `www.antennahouse.com/product/wordmltofo.htm`
35. `www.koffice.org`
36. With a name like this, who needs a URL?
37. `www.sun.com/software/star/staroffice`
38. For example, see `xml.openoffice.org/xml_specification.pdf` for the OpenOffice.org format documentation.
39. `www.oasis-open.org/committees/tc_home.php?wg_abbrev=office`
40. Microsoft, however, does not participate.

Therefore, the only issue we'll face — but it may be a major one — is the semantic processing (**6.2**) of the source vocabulary and all the rearranging, renaming, and rethinking that may be involved. As we've just seen, most something-to-XML conversions have an XML-to-XML last stage, so this issue is relevant universally.

The right point to fork. Before starting to write a conversion stylesheet, it is worthwhile to check if the particular source XML vocabulary is your only option. If not, alternatives may be more suitable.

The complexity of an XML-to-XML conversion directly depends on how similar the conceptual bases of the source and target vocabularies are. For example, transforming from XSL-FO or SVG into a semantic vocabulary is bound to be hard. Figuring out what is what in XSL-FO's endless stream of `fo:block`s may require complex heuristics that will be very unreliable.

Luckily, any XML vocabulary that has the information you need, but treats it differently or focuses on different aspects of it, is usually but a step of a stairway of abstractions (**1.1.1**) on which you can freely go in either direction. Your goal is therefore to find the most appropriate step from which to jump sideways to your target XML vocabulary.

So, instead of trying to parse your content out of an XSL-FO rendition, check if its semantic source is available and if it would better suit your needs. It is not always the most abstract level (stairway's topmost step) that you're interested in; for example, a document workflow may start by compiling data from several sources, and you will want to grab this data as soon as it is complete, but before it is migrated to a lower-level vocabulary.

Refactoring strategies. When translating between two similar XML vocabularies, a lot of work consists of simple renaming of element types: What was `p` becomes `para`, `img` turns into `image`, and so on. Each such mapping is a one-liner in XSLT. It is also very easy to remove extra markup or extra data (as long as it is marked up unambiguously so it can be separated).

More tricky is adding markup where none existed in the source. This usually involves parsing the source document's character data with regular expressions (see **5.4.2.4** for an example).

Sometimes, markup exists in the source but is less specific than you need. For example, the source XML may mark up list items as paragraphs, but you'll likely have a special element type for list items in your target vocabulary. When you need to infer missing semantics, there are several possibilities:

- You can get clues from the **formatting-related markup** of the source. For example, a paragraph that is actually a list item may have a CSS `style` attribute setting a wider left margin. This is the primary strategy when dealing with XML or XHTML originating from a presentation-oriented tool such as a word processor with few (if any) named styles (**6.2.3.3**) available.

- You can determine the **position** of a source element relative to other known elements and make your conclusions based on that position. For example, a paragraph of preformatted text immediately following a `caption` may automatically be made a `listing`. This is another trick commonly used with word-processor-generated XML, since word processor styles do not nest (**6.2.3.3**).

- As a last resort, you may try to analyze the **content** of an element to determine its role. For example, if a paragraph starts with a hyphen character, you can mark it up as a list item and remove the hyphen (instead, a graphic bullet may be displayed when your XML is formatted for presentation). This is the primary approach for plain text (**6.2.3.1**), but it may turn out necessary for XML-to-XML conversions as well.

6.3 **XML utilities**

6.3.1   XML diff tools

Dealing with plain text or programming in any text-based language is unthinkable without the *diff*[41] and *patch*[42] utilities. Sooner or later, you will find yourself looking for their XML analogs. Automatic diffs might be especially useful for group work: Figuring out exactly what a colleague has changed in the file you're working on, or merging changes to a collaboratively edited document, is much easier if you can extract a diff and then apply it back.

Don't touch what you can't parse. Of course you can use the regular, plain text versions of the diff and patch utilities. This is a less than optimal approach, however.

- One problem is that two XML documents may be the same in the "XML sense" while being worlds apart from the viewpoint of a plain text diff. XML permits a fair amount of syntactic variation that does not change the semantics of a document, such as varying the amount of whitespace in tags or the order of attributes.

- Another problem is that if a document to be patched has changed even slightly since the diff was extracted, a plain text patch may either fail or (worse) produce a non-valid or non-well-formed output. The plain text utilities work with lines, but to keep XML well-formed, you must change it only at the level of elements or attributes. An XML diff utility must therefore include a complete XML parser and produce differences attached to specific locations in the XML tree rather than to line numbers.

Several open source diff projects for XML exist, implementing various approaches to this task. Some of them can only do diff; others attempt patching as well. Formats of diff lists also vary. Commercial products are also available.[43]

....

41. www.gnu.org/software/diffutils
42. www.fsf.org/software/patch
43. www.deltaxml.com

Diffs for viewing

If you are only interested in *seeing* the changes, then the **diffmk** utility,[44] written in Perl by Norman Walsh, might do the trick. Given two XML files, it outputs the second of the two with some additional markup: Revision attributes are added to the elements whose content or attributes changed, and revision elements enclose new or deleted text nodes. (Deleted element nodes are not shown; if you want to see them, simply compare the same two documents in reverse order.)

You can specify different element type and attribute names for this revision markup each time you run diffmk. With the utility's output, it is easy to visualize the differences using CSS (**6.1.5**). Alternatively, you can write an XSLT stylesheet (or modify your existing one) so that the changed fragments are, for example, painted different colors in an HTML rendition.

Overall, the utility is very useful, even though it is not perfect. For one thing, it does not differentiate between elements whose data content has changed and those whose attributes have changed.

A more fundamental problem with diffmk is that its revision markup is only as granular as your source markup. For example, if a long paragraph is a single text node (i.e., has no child elements), then the entire paragraph will be marked as changed even if a single character was modified in it.

6.3.1.2 Diffs for patching

Other XML diff projects promise to do something diffmk cannot — patch an XML document so you can accumulate changes from several independent revisions.

- The two utilities called **diffxml** and **patchxml**[45] were written in Java by Adrian Mouat. They use their own format for diffs called DUL (Delta Update Language). A DUL diff is an XML document where each element (insert, delete, update, etc.)

----

44. www.sun.com/software/xml/developers/diffmk
45. diffxml.sf.net

describes one change. These elements use XPath expressions similar to

```
/node()[2]/node()[1]/node()[22]/node()[19]
```

to uniquely identify the changed nodes. As you can guess, this XPath is rather fragile, as it relies upon the number of nodes of *any* type before the changed node remaining constant. Once you add or remove a node in your document, such an XPath expression will likely miss its target.

- Another utility, called **xmldiff**,[46] is written in Python and uses a similar XML-based diff language called XUpdate.[47] Again, XPath is used for specifying the location of a change, but XUpdate uses a robust syntax that stores element node names of all ancestors of a changed node:

```
/page[1]/block[1]/section[1]/p[2]
```

To merge XUpdate changes, you can use another utility called **4update**, which is a part of 4Suite,[48] a Python-based XML processing platform (**6.4.1.2**).

6.3.2   XPath tools

Many XML editors offer an XPath facility allowing you to see the results of addressing a document with an XPath expression (**6.1.1.1**). A number of standalone XPath tools are worth checking out as well. In some respects, these tools may even be superior to an average XPath engine built into an XML editor.

6.3.2.1   Command line

The simplest tool in this category is a command-line utility that allows you to apply an XPath expression to a document and display the results. Such a utility, called simply **xpath**, was written by Matt

---

46. www.logilab.org/xmldiff
47. www.xmldb.org/xupdate
48. www.4suite.org

Sergeant as part of the XML::XPath Perl package.[49] You'll need an up-to-date Perl installation in order to use this package. Similar utilities, written in Java[50] and in C++,[51] are included with the Xalan XSLT processor.

No matter which XPath utility you choose, the usage is straight-forward. You just give it the document pathname and the XPath expression as command-line parameters, and it displays (in serialized form) a nodeset returned by that expression. For example, the command

```
xpath en/team/index.xml //int
```

applied to our sample page document (Example 3.1, page 141) will display

```
Found 2 nodes:
-- NODE --
<int link="solutions">products</int>
-- NODE --
<int link="fbplus">FooBar Plus</int>
```

Context provided separately.   Note that the version of the utility from Xalan C++ requires two parameters: one is the XPath *context* and the other is the *expression* that is evaluated in that context. Formally speaking, this is unnecessary, because you can always combine the two into an equivalent composite expression evaluating in the "context" of the entire document. However, for an XSLT programmer, this separation makes practical sense: In an XSLT stylesheet, any XPath expression is also evaluated with regard to some context that is set outside of the expression.

6.3.2.2   GUI

If you prefer a GUI to a command-line interface, then the **XPath Explorer** utility[52] (Figure 6.8) may be what you are looking for. It provides source and tree views of an XML document and lets you

....

49. search.cpan.org/dist/XML-XPath
50. xml.apache.org/xalan-j/samples.html#applyxpath
51. xml.apache.org/xalan-c/samples.html#xpathwrapper
52. www.purpletech.com/xpe

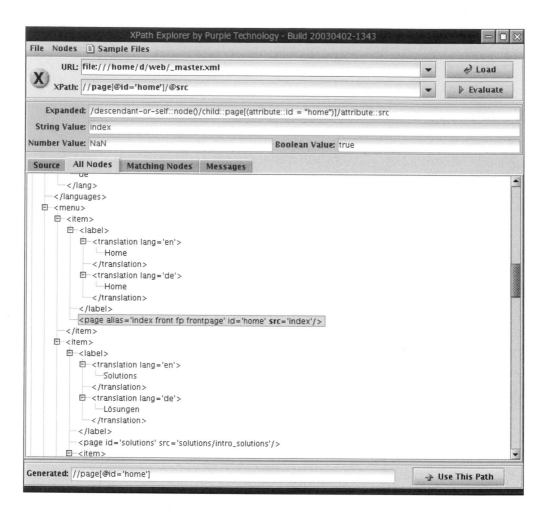

Figure 6.8 XPath Explorer focuses on one thing — evaluating XPath expressions on a document — but does that really well.

....

evaluate XPath expressions against it, highlighting the matching nodes (and listing them on the "Matching Nodes" tab).

Both matching and calculating. Unlike the more simplistic XPath tools we've seen in the previous section, XPE offers some useful extensions to this basic functionality. Most importantly, it not only shows you the matching nodes, but displays the value returned by the expression as a string, as a boolean, and as a number. This makes it possible to run not only match-type expressions but arbitrary calculations and comparisons as well. (You can even use XPE as a simple numeric calculator; type `6*9` in the "XPath:" field and see the result in the "Number value:" field.)

Expression expanded. The "Expanded:" field is another nice touch. It shows you an equivalent of your expression with all XPath abbreviations expanded (e.g., `@` is replaced with `attribute::`, `element` with `child::element`, and so on).

Generated paths. Finally, you can explore the loaded document by clicking on a node and seeing its corresponding XPath in the "Generated:" field below. There is an unbounded number of XPath expressions matching a given node, but most XPath-enabled tools (such as XML diff utilities, **6.3.1.2**) generate XPath expressions similar to

```
/site/menu/item[2]/page[2]
```

XPE uses the same "canonical" form for generated XPath expressions, but with a twist: If the target node is an element with an `id` attribute, XPE assumes that this attribute uniquely identifies the element and uses it as a selector — for example,

```
//page[@id='home']
```

Such an address is more robust — it will still work even if the target node is moved around in the document.

6.3.2.3 Shell

Another nice tool is **xsh**[53] (XML Shell) written by Petr Pajas. It is a full-featured interactive shell that can be used not only for exploring the structure of XML documents with XPath, but also for modifying, transforming, and creating new XML documents. Programs in the xsh command language can thus perform many of the functions of XSLT stylesheets, but look more like traditional Unix shell scripts.

So long as it's hierarchical. The principal metaphor of xsh is that of "XML document as a hierarchical file system." Thus, inside xsh,

....

53. `xsh.sf.net`

the Unix shell commands such as `ls`, `cd`, and `cp` work on nodes or nodesets, and XPath expressions are used in place of file system pathnames. This idea may seem far-fetched at first, but it is very convenient once you are used to it. Manipulating and exploring documents from such a command-line interface may be almost as convenient and fast, and in some cases even faster, than working with the document source in a text editor.

Tab, complete that.   The really nifty capability of xsh is its "tab completion." As in any other Unix shell, you can press the *Tab* key at any time while editing the command line, and the program will fill in as much of the current XPath expression as is unambiguous, or list possible completions otherwise. Thus, at any step of a complex XPath, you can get immediate feedback on what nodes are located along any of the axes, starting from the context of this step (i.e., in terms of XPath 2.0, from the *inner focus*).

Tab completion in xsh speeds up XPath hacking incredibly. With it, you can learn a lot of things about the document structure even before you complete and run your command. For example, getting a list of all element type names at any level in a document is as simple as typing `ls //` and pressing *Tab*. If you think that Unix shells' tab completion is handy (and most people who ever tried it will agree), then you'll probably find the xsh version of this feature addictive.

6.3.3   Grammar generation

As we've seen in the review of XML editors (**6.1**), having a grammar-based schema of your source documents is valuable, if only because it enables guided editing. Schematron rules can only stop you from going in a wrong direction, but they cannot tell you where to go when you are lost. If you're not very familiar with the source definition you must comply with, guided editing is a big boon.

Luckily, if you need a DTD, you don't have to write it from scratch. The idea is to use an existing valid document as input to an algorithm that deduces the DTD from that sample. Some of the XML editors mentioned in this chapter include this functionality, but there also exist standalone tools that will do the job just as well.

Saxon in the 6.* series includes a sample application called **DTDGenerator** that, given a well-formed XML sample, outputs a DTD to which it conforms. This DTD can then be fed to a converter to produce an equivalent schema in XSDL or any other schema language. An example of such a converter is **NekoDTD**,[54] which works by first converting a DTD into an XML representation and then using a bunch of XSLT stylesheets to convert this representation into any of the several supported schema languages.

This procedure cannot be completely automatic. You will have to review the generated DTD and fix its misconceptions, usually by relaxing the restrictions that were deduced from a too small and unrepresentative sample. To make this manual fixup less of a necessity, it's a good idea to aggregate as much material as possible from real-world documents into the sample document that will be used by the grammar generator.

Of course, this aggregation must make sense structurally; for example, you cannot have multiple body elements in your sample if a body is supposed to occur only once per page. Instead, you might be able to take the content from many pages' body elements and insert it into your sample's body.

6.4 XSLT tools

6.4.1 Processors

Saxon and the rest. After an XML editor, an XSLT processor is the first tool any XML web developer needs, and a lot of parameters of your project will depend on the capabilities of your chosen processor. Much of this book focuses on Saxon,[55] the primary reason being its support for XSLT and XPath 2.0. Saxon has many other benefits as well: Java extensibility, exceptional standards compliance, good performance, and active development.

Still, there are many other XSLT processors out there. This section is not intended to be a comprehensive directory; I only mention those

---

54. www.apache.org/~andyc/neko/doc/dtd
55. saxon.sf.net

processors that I tested and found interesting in some aspects. Unless otherwise noted, all tools in this section are open source and support XSLT 1.0.

The speed race. Usually, one of the main concerns of those who shop around for an XSLT processor is speed. This is understandable, given that XSLT is typically orders of magnitude slower than traditional non-XML text processing tools even when their tasks appear comparable in complexity. Unfortunately, it is very hard to tell which processor is the fastest, as the speed very much depends on the stylesheet, source documents, and (for Java- and Python-based processors) the virtual machine used. XSLTMark[56] is a benchmark suite often used to measure the performance of XSLT processors, but its results are to be taken with a grain of salt, so are the notes below — which, nonetheless, might give you some idea of what to expect from major processors.

6.4.1.1   Java

On the Java platform, the Apache XML Project[57] hosts a lot of XML-related open source software, including many products mentioned in this book (Cocoon, Batik, Xindice, FOP). Notably, Xerces[58] is perhaps the most robust and advanced Java-based validating XML parser (it can use both DTDs and XSDL schemas for validation). You can successfully use Saxon with Xerces instead of JDK's default parser (or the Ælfred parser that was included with Saxon up to version 7.1).

Xalan is the XSLT processor of the Apache XML Project. It exists in two versions, one written in C++ and the other in Java, but the C++ version lags behind in version numbers and appears to have stagnated. As for the Java version of Xalan — called Xalan-J[59] — it is actively developed, complete, and well-tested (in part, perhaps, because it is usually the default XSLT processor used in other Apache XML projects).

....

56. www.datapower.com/xml_community/xsltmark.html
57. xml.apache.org
58. xml.apache.org/xerces2-j
59. xml.apache.org/xalan-j

Xalan is extensible in Java and (indirectly) in many other languages, including JavaScript and Python. It offers a growing library of ready-to-run extensions, covering most of EXSLT (**4.4.1**).

Xalan-J is generally slower than Saxon, but it includes an *XSLT compiler*, **XSLTC** (originally developed by Sun), that creates a set of compiled Java classes out of an XSLT stylesheet. Such a compiled version of the stylesheet, called a *translet* ("transformation applet"), runs much faster than the original stylesheet interpreted by Xalan (although a translet still requires Xalan itself to be installed).

XT,[60] originally written by James Clark, is another well-known XSLT processor in Java. XT is quite old and seems to be abandoned; it is small and very fast (definitely faster than Saxon), but its support of XSLT is incomplete. A relatively new processor, **jd-xslt**[61] by Johannes Döbler, is one of the fastest Java processors currently available (in my testing it was faster than XT); it appears to offer solid XSLT support and Java extensibility.

6.4.1.2   Python

4xslt is part of an XML processing framework called 4Suite[62] published by Fourthought. The entire framework is written in Python and includes, along with an XSLT processor, an XML repository (database) and server as well as tools for RDF processing and support for XLink, XPointer, RELAX NG, and other standards. The 4xslt processor supports some EXSLT functions and is extensible in Python; the biggest problem with it is that it is quite slow compared to most other processors.

6.4.1.3   Native binary

You might expect processors that are compiled into native binary executables, and therefore do not require any virtual machine, to be among the fastest. This is not so clear-cut, however.

---

60. www.blnz.com/xt
61. www.aztecrider.com/xslt
62. www.4suite.org

Sablotron,[63] by Ginger Alliance, is a small processor written in C++ and running on many platforms. Surprisingly, Sablotron's performance for large transformations is not top of the class; it can be outperformed by a fast Java processor such as Saxon. However, as a native binary, it starts up much faster than any Java- or Python-based processor. Its quick startup makes Sablotron ideal for projects where simple XSLT transformations (such as filters or format converters) are chained or intermingled with non-XSLT processing. Sablotron supports a few EXSLT functions and is extensible in Javascript.

Another multiplatform native-binary processor written in C++ is Gnome's **libxslt**.[64] It starts up a bit more slowly than Sablotron but easily wins on large input files. It also supports almost all EXSLT extensions and even some Saxon extensions.

6.4.2   Generators

There are tools that claim to generate your stylesheet for you, based on some sort of a simplified description of the desired transformation, or controlled by an interactive interface.

If we ignore for a moment all the advanced XSLT tricks we did in Chapter 5, an XML-to-HTML stylesheet is little more than a simple mapping between source XML elements and areas of the rendered HTML page — that is, a list of instructions like "this thing goes here and that thing goes there." If you already have a sample XML source and a corresponding formatted web page (note that the latter can be built in a GUI without any manual HTML coding), such a basic mapping may be established simply by drag-and-drop.

This is the approach taken by Altova's **Stylevision**,[65] an XML and XSLT editor specifically geared toward web designers interested in "migration of traditional HTML web sites to advanced XML-based sites." This application is one of Altova's suite of Windows-only XML tools, which also includes a well-known XML editor called XML Spy.

---

63. www.gingerall.com/charlie/ga/xml/p_sab.xml
64. www.xmlsoft.org/XSLT
65. www.xmlspy.com/products_xsl.html

It goes without mention that such a "point and drool" interface is unable to create anything more complex than a primitive outline of a stylesheet. Stylevision just tears your HTML into pieces and wraps each piece into an `xsl:template` with a simple `match` attribute (usually, only containing an element type name). Even this simple process may go awry, so you'll have to manually move some misplaced HTML code into another template.

Still, such a tool may be useful for quick XSLT prototyping if you plan to take the automatically generated stylesheet as a starting point for further development (which you can do in Stylevision as well, for it has a mode for editing XSLT and an XPath analyzer). This kind of interface seems to be better suited for database-like XML, since handling mixed content via drag-and-drop is less than intuitive.[66]

6.4.3   IDEs

With most programming languages, you can conveniently program inside an IDE (Integrated Development Environment). XSLT is no exception.

An IDE is, basically, a text editor tweaked for convenient coding in the given language, with a number of specialized functions for running and debugging the program without leaving the IDE. Exactly how much stuff is added to the text editor foundation varies widely from language to language and from IDE to IDE.

6.4.3.1   Processor-neutral

XSLT is special in that to debug a stylesheet, you'll want to simultaneously see two inputs (the source document and the stylesheet) and two outputs (the result of the transformation and the stream of messages produced by the stylesheet). **Treebeard**[67] is a simple IDE that displays the source, stylesheet, and transformation output in the three panes of its window, while the messages are shown in a separate

---

66. *Mixed content < . . . > has always separated the men from the boys in the *ML editing sweepstakes.* — Tim Bray, co-editor of the XML specification.
67. `treebeard.sf.net`

floating window. It also boasts detailed XSLT syntax coloring, with separate colors for functions, variables, axes, and so on.

One area where Treebeard is lacking is debugging. When you run an external XSLT processor from within an IDE, you need to have support from that processor if you want to use facilities like breakpoints, step-by-step execution, and watched variables. XSLT processors vary widely in the amount of such debugging support they provide, and those that provide it do so each in its own special way. Hopefully, this area will be standardized one day.

Since Treebeard is supposed to be processor-neutral and works with many Java-based processors (including, by the way, Saxon 7), it cannot take advantage of any processor-specific debugging capabilities. Therefore, the only debugging features available with Treebeard are those provided by XSLT itself or your chosen processor's XSLT extensions (see **4.4.2.3** for Saxon's debugging features).

6.4.3.2   Processor-specific

More convenient for complex XSLT debugging is the **XSLT-process**[68] package for Emacs. This is a full-featured IDE that adds a lot of XSLT-related features to the already quite good XML editing support in Emacs.

Unlike Treebeard, XSLT-process supports only two processors: Saxon and Xalan, as these are the only ones with a "tracing" interface making it possible to track execution of a stylesheet and query the processor status. By using this interface, XSLT-process can provide a complete array of debugging tools, including breakpoints (both in the stylesheet and in the source document), step-by-step execution of the stylesheet, and display of both local and global variables at any point.

Figure 6.9 shows an XSLT-process session with the source view, stylesheet view, output view, and a debugging console where you can run debugger commands. In any of the panes, you can also view the stylesheet output or diagnostic messages. A vertical sidebar window

68. xslt-process.sf.net

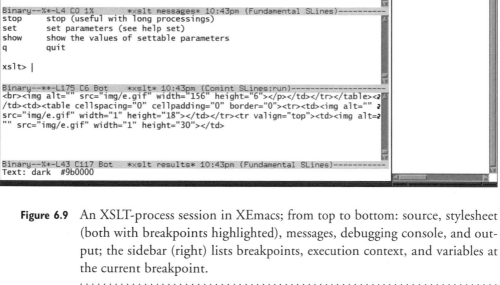

Figure 6.9   An XSLT-process session in XEmacs; from top to bottom: source, stylesheet (both with breakpoints highlighted), messages, debugging console, and output; the sidebar (right) lists breakpoints, execution context, and variables at the current breakpoint.

on the right shows breakpoints, describes execution context (i.e., all the elements that were entered but not yet left) in both the source and the stylesheet, and lists the type and value of all global and local variables.

6.4.4 Profilers

Another good tool that takes advantage of Saxon's and Xalan's debugging interfaces is an XSLT profiler called **catchXSL!**.[69] It was designed to perform a single task: compile an *execution profile* of an XSLT stylesheet — that is, the list of all its instructions with information on how many times each one was called and how much time it took.

True, optimization should not be your priority until the stylesheet is fully debugged and proved stable (**4.4.2.2**). But then, only real bottlenecks need to be addressed, and profiling stylesheet execution is the best way to discover these bottlenecks. Even if you're not really interested in optimization at this time, seeing a detailed analysis of a stylesheet run may be very instructive.

catchXSL! (Figure 6.10) presents its findings both in a tree form and as a table that can be sorted on any column. The tree may reflect either the stylesheet elements' hierarchy ("template view") or the hierarchy of calls ("tree call view"). You can ask the program to run your stylesheet several times and average the results.

6.5 **Build tools**

The larger your project is and the more frequently it is updated, the sooner you will discover that creating a working web site is only the beginning. Maintaining it is just as important and often more time-consuming. If nothing else, running a transformation again and again for each updated page is tedious and error-prone. In Chapter 5, we

----

69. www.xslprofiler.org. (No, I'm not *that* excited about the program — the exclamation mark is part of its name.)

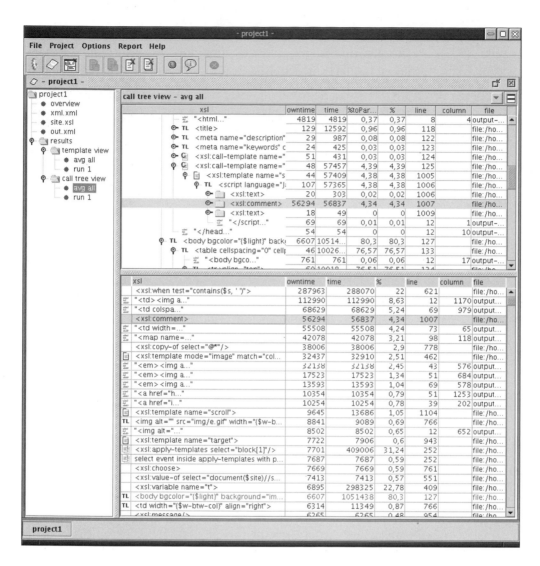

Figure 6.10   catchXSL!, an XSLT profiler, displays execution timings for each instruction in a stylesheet.

addressed this by programming a batch processing mode in the stylesheet (**5.6**).

Housekeeping chores. However, transforming pages is only a part of the web site maintenance routine. Other tasks you will likely want to automate are:

- Deleting stale versions of transformed pages. For pages being updated, this is not necessary because your stylesheet will overwrite the old HTML file. If, however, you have removed a source page document, you'll want its corresponding HTML page to be cleaned up automatically.

- Deleting all sorts of temporary files, such as SVG and intermediate PNG files left over from graphic generation (**5.5.2**).

- Uploading the finished HTML files and graphics to the staging or production server.

- Taking a certain action (e.g., emailing the site admin) in case validation or transformation of a document fails. This may be necessary if the site building process runs unattended.

Process what was changed.   For large sites it would also be nice to transform only those documents that changed since the last transformation, instead of all the documents registered in the master. This can be done by comparing the modification times of the source and output files for each page and running the transformation only if the source is newer than the output. If, however, the master document or the stylesheet was modified, we will need to transform all the pages, regardless of their timestamps.

A hierarchy of tasks.   All these tasks form a natural hierarchy wherein some tasks depend on others. For instance, uploading files only makes sense after some of the pages have been transformed. So, if the user gives the upload command, the system must start by checking whether the transformed files are up to date. If some are stale, validation and transformation must be run for them first; if there is any error in validation or transformation, the entire upload operation must be canceled.

Tools for building projects.   All this is possible with one of the *build tools* that we'll explore in this section. A build tool is basically an interpreter that executes a *build file* — a formalized description of your project that lists all of its tasks and components and specifies how they depend on each other. When a build file is used, the entire project, including all of its primary and auxiliary tasks, can be built by one simple command.

The build file does not need to change during the routine maintenance of a project, but only when you add or remove components (such as web pages) or change the dependency rules. It therefore makes sense to generate the build file automatically from the master document whenever the latter is updated.

6.5.1   make

No doubt the most widely used build tool today is the classic `make` utility. It is the tool of choice for countless programming projects and therefore the first thing to try.

The build file of `make`, called a *makefile*, uses a simple plain text format. It contains definitions of *targets* (tasks that you want to perform), their *prerequisites* (other targets or files that each target depends on), and the corresponding operating system commands that will be run to fulfill each target. A combination of a target, its prerequisites, and its commands is called a *rule*.

The reliance on OS commands is the largest drawback of `make`. This utility is native to the Unix world (it is available by default on almost any Unix system) and therefore takes many conventions of a Unix environment for granted. Nevertheless, you can successfully use `make` on Windows as part of the Cygwin environment.[70]

Let's see how `make` can be used to automate web site building with a Java-based XSLT processor. The examples in this section cover a few basic tasks, but applying these principles to more complex scenarios is straightforward. If you want to dig deeper, a complete manual for `make` is available online.[71]

---

70. www.cygwin.com
71. www.gnu.org/manual/make

6.5.1.1   Validation and transformation script

When processing a makefile, `make` stops and signals an error whenever any of the commands it runs returns a nonzero exit status (a standard Unix convention for indicating a program's failure). We can use this facility to cancel transformation of a page that fails to validate, but we need to make some preparations first.

The problem is that in our setup, the Schematron schema used for validating a page document is nothing but a special-purpose XSLT stylesheet (**5.1.2**). From the processor's viewpoint, the stylesheet is OK and works as programmed even when it displays diagnostics. This means that a zero (no error) exit status is returned by the XSLT processor when validation finishes, *regardless* of its outcome. (And you cannot set the exit status of the processor from within a stylesheet.)

One more layer of logic.   To work around this problem, we'll write a shell script[72] that tries to validate a page document, analyzes the validation output, and runs the transformation only if no errors were detected. Such a script for an `sh`-compatible shell[73] is shown in Example 6.3.

A language for scripting what? As was the case with the Java examples in Chapter 5, you don't need to be familiar with the shell scripting language. You will most likely be able to use this example as is or with trivial changes in XSLT processor invocation.

Variables and parameters.   The script takes three command-line parameters: `$1` is the pathname of the input XML file, `$2` is the pathname of the transformed HTML page, and `$3` is the value of the `$env` parameter of the stylesheet (**5.1.1**; for example, `staging`). The `saxon` variable stores the command to run the XSLT processor — you can change it to whatever works on your system.

---

72. I.e., a small program to be run by the OS command interpreter, called *shell* on Unix systems.

73. Just as does `make` itself, this script runs on any Unix system or on Windows with Cygwin.

Example 6.3   process: A shell script that validates and transforms a page document.

```
#!/bin/sh
saxon="java net.sf.saxon.Transform"
ERR=`$saxon -l $1 schema-compiled.xsl env=$3 2>&1`
ERR=$ERR`$saxon -l $1 schema2-compiled.xsl env=$3 2>&1`
if [ -z "$ERR" ]
then
  echo "Validation successful, transforming..."
  $saxon -o $2 $1 style.xsl env=$3
else
  echo $ERR
  exit 1
fi
```

Two-stage validation. Suppose you have two Schematron schemas (such as those in Examples 3.3 and 5.20) and want to run both schemas against each source document. To make this possible, the $ERR variable first receives the output of one validation command (`back quotes` run the quoted command and return its output) and then appends the output of the second one.

No matter whose problem it is. The 2>&1 construction redirects standard error to standard output so that both output streams are caught by the back quotes. In this case, standard output will contain any Schematron diagnostics, while standard error will be used by the processor itself in case the compiled schema is broken or some other runtime error happens.

If and only if. Then, the value of $ERR is checked. If it is an empty string, no errors of any kind were encountered and we can safely run our transformation. The exit status of the script in this case will be the same as the exit status of the transformation process (which may also fail for a variety of reasons, such as a broken stylesheet or a Java problem).

Note that for this to work, your schema must be absolutely silent unless it finds a serious error. Unsolicited advice such as that in Example 2.2 (page 65) needs to be shut off.

Otherwise, we print $ERR and finish with a nonzero exit status. In this branch of the if statement, you can add any other emergency measures, such as emailing $ERR to the site admin, excessive loud beeping, or going belly up. You can also specify a nonzero exit code other than 1; it will be reported by make so that you can use it to tell a validation error from other kinds of errors.

Makefile

Armed with this script, we can now write a makefile for our web site project. For Example 6.4 to be immediately understandable, some of the hairier stuff, such as image generation, is ignored. This example does, however, demonstrate all the main building blocks of a makefile — targets, prerequisites, commands, and variables. A real project's makefile will therefore be very much like this one, only larger.

Variables. The first part of the makefile contains variable definitions. As in any other programming language, make can use variables to store values used more than once, thereby making the code less verbose and easier to understand. Here,

- saxon is the command that runs the XSLT processor.

  We could store this command in an environment variable and use it both in the shell script and in the makefile.

- env is the environment identifier passed to the stylesheet (**5.1.1.1**). It is assumed that each environment has its own makefile, so we won't try to do any environment switching here.

- out-path is the directory path for output files (same as $out-path in the stylesheet). We don't need to specify the *source* path because the makefile will always be run from the root directory of the site's source tree (where it resides along with the stylesheet, schemas, and the master document).

- upload-path is the URI or pathname of the directory where the final HTML pages will be uploaded after transformation. This is not the same as $target-path in the stylesheet; for example, if you are installing the site in Apache's HTML directory on your system, upload-path may be /var/www/html/ while $target-path may simply be /. If your makefile is generated automatically from

Example 6.4   `Makefile`: A makefile primer.

```
saxon = java net.sf.saxon.Transform

env = staging
out-path = /home/d/web/out/
upload-path = remote:/tmp/upload/

globals = \
  _master.xml \
  style.xsl \
  schema-compiled.xsl \
  schema2-compiled.xsl

files = \
  $(out-path)en/index.html \
  $(out-path)en/team/index.html \
  $(out-path)en/team/hire.html \
  $(out-path)en/team/history.html
  # ... list all of your output files here

upload : build
        rsync -v -t -u -r $(out-path) $(upload-path)

build : $(files)

$(out-path)%.html : %.xml $(globals)
        ./process $*.xml $(out-path)$*.html $(env)

%-compiled.xsl : %.sch
        $(saxon) -o $*-compiled.xsl $*.sch schematron-saxon.xsl

clean :
        rm -f $(files)
```

the master document, you can store the `upload-path` value for each environment, along with all the other paths, in the master.

- `globals` is a list of files that all page documents will specify as their prerequisites. Include here all the files that are used during validation or transformation of a page (except the source of that page): master document, transformation stylesheet, and compiled schema(s). You can add `Makefile` itself to this list to make sure the project is rebuilt when the makefile changes. (The \ at the end of a line means the list is continued on the next line.)

You may also need to include here all static images that are accessed during transformation (e.g., using the `graph:geth()` and `graph:getw()` extension functions, **5.5.I**). Otherwise, your HTML may stray out of sync with the images should they be changed for some reason.

- `files` is the list of all HTML files generated by the project. Each file is given as a complete pathname starting with the `out-path` (to reference a makefile variable, you enclose it in `()` and prepend `$`). Only a few files are shown here for illustration, but in a real makefile, you'll list *all* of your site's pages in this variable.

Upload rule. Following the variable definitions, the makefile lists its *rules*. Each rule consists of a target (before the colon), a list of prerequisites (after the colon), and optional commands (each on its own line starting with a tab character, visible as an eight-space indent).

A target may be a filename or an arbitrary identifier. The target of the first rule in our makefile is called `upload`. This rule depends on another target, `build` (prerequisites of a rule may be either filenames or targets). To fulfill the `upload` target, `make` will run `rsync`[74] to copy the output directory to the upload location (remote or local).

Smart uploading. Note that `upload` specifies another target, and not some file(s), as its prerequisite. This means `make` cannot compare timestamps to determine if this target needs to be rerun or not. As a result, the `rsync` command will *always* run when the `upload` target is activated. Since `make` may be unable to find out the status of uploaded files on a remote server, this "just in case" uploading makes sense: With the options shown in **6.5.I.2**, page 350, `rsync` will itself compare source and destination files and only transfer those that are newer on the source side.

Build rule. The second rule's target is `build`, and this rule runs no commands. It simply refers to the `files` variable to declare that *all* of the project output files must be in place and up-to-date for this

----

74. `rsync` (`rsync.samba.org`) is a file transfer utility that uses a protocol similar to `ftp`, only better.

target to be considered fulfilled. Translated into plain English, this rule says, "Consider `build` done when all of `$(out)/en/index.html`, `$(out)/en/team/index.html`, ... are done."

Page processing rule. Next comes a rule for processing specific files. It is unusual in that its target contains a % character, which works as a wildcard. Rules whose targets contain % are called *pattern rules*; they are supposed to run multiple times on different files.

Thus, when `make` attempts to fulfill the first prerequisite of `build`, `$(out-path)en/index.html`, it first tries to find a rule with exactly this target. If none is found, it checks the available pattern rules to see if one of them matches. Indeed, `$(out-path)%.html` will match if we replace % by `en/index`.

So, `make` fires this pattern rule on this specific file. It first checks the existence of `en/index.xml` and all the `globals`; if no HTML file for this page exists yet, or if some of the prerequisites are newer than the HTML file, it runs the `process` script (**6.5.1.1**) to validate and transform the page document. Within a command in a pattern rule, the `$*` construct means "whatever corresponds to % in the current invocation of the rule." This pattern rule will thus be run again and again for all the HTML files listed in `build`.

Schema compilation rule. The compiled schemas also depend on other files — namely, on their source Schematron (`.sch`) documents. Another pattern rule sees to it that any schema whose filename matches `%-compiled.xsl` is recompiled into XSLT whenever its Schematron source is modified.

Cleanup rule. The last rule, `clean`, does not depend on anything, nor is it a prerequisite for any other rule. It simply removes all `files` so that the next run of `make` will recreate all the HTML from scratch. You can include other tidying-up operations in this rule, such as removing temporary files, generated images, and compiled schemas.

6.5.1.3   Running make

Save **6.5.1.2**, page 350 as a file called `Makefile` in the site source's root directory. Put the `process` script (Example 6.3) there, too.[75] Now, building and uploading the entire web site is as simple as typing

`make`

on the command line. When called without parameters, `make` tries to fulfill the first target in the makefile, `upload` (called the *default target*). This, in turn, triggers `build`, and `build` pushes all the `files` through the corresponding pattern rule. Thus, in the first run of `make`, all project files will be validated, transformed, and uploaded.

On a subsequent run, `make` will validate and transform only those pages whose XML sources were updated. If, however, a change was made to one of the files in `globals` (e.g., the stylesheet or one of the Schematron schemas), all pages will be redone because they all depend on the changed file.

Explicit targets.   When running `make`, you can give it the name of a specific target that you want to invoke. For example,

`make build`

will perform validation and transformation only, but not upload. Or, you can say

`make clean`

to remove all generated files. Since the `clean` target is outside the dependency tree rooted in the default `upload` target, the only way to activate `clean` is by calling it explicitly.

6.5.1.4   Makefile generation

When the project is stable and updates are routine, `make` is a convenient way to keep the web-ready transformed site in sync with any source modifications. It only becomes less convenient when you

---

75. On Unix, you need to make it executable first, e.g., by saying `chmod +x process`.

frequently add or delete pages (which requires adding or deleting corresponding pathnames in the makefile).

In this case, it is preferable to have the makefile generated automatically from the information in the master document. For this, you may need to expand your master document's `environment` element type to store the additional information to be put into the makefiles, such as the commands used to run the processor in each environment and the names of the upload directories.

Once this information is available, however, translating it from the master document's XML into the makefile format is very simple. It may be convenient to include this functionality within the main transformation stylesheet, replacing our batch template (**5.6**), so that makefile generation is triggered when you run the stylesheet on the master document.

6.5.2 Apache Ant

Apache Ant[76] is a Java-based build tool that in many respects is similar to `make`. Ant's main points of difference are these:

- Ant's **build file is XML**, not plain text. The two immediate consequences of this are that the build file (called `build.xml`) is more verbose and easier to read than a makefile.

- To fulfill its targets, Ant runs **Java classes, not OS commands**. This gives Ant its biggest advantage: portability and independence of the underlying OS. You can use any of Ant's collection of predefined classes for performing common tasks, or you can write your own class for the functionality you need. One of the predefined Ant tasks, `exec`, even lets you run an arbitrary program outside the Java virtual machine (this is not recommended, though).

- Unlike `make`, in Ant **targets only depend on other targets**, not on files. This means you can build a hierarchy of tasks, but you

---

76. `ant.apache.org`

cannot expect a task to be run only when its output file is older than the input file. Ant will run a prerequisite task in any case; it is the class called by that task that may decide whether to perform an action based on file dates (or any other information).

Thus, the built-in Ant task `javac` that compiles Java source files does check for file dates and processes only those files whose source (`.java`) is newer than the binary (`.class`). However, an XSLT transformation target that you may define will not have this functionality (unless you write a custom Java class for this), and your build process will therefore always transform all page documents.

Despite this latter limitation, Ant may still be a good choice if you know Java and use other Java-based tools for working with XML.

XML on the server

Towred Cities please us then,
And the busie humm of men,
Where throngs of Knights and Barons bold,
In weeds of Peace high triumphs hold,
With store of Ladies, whose bright eies
Rain influence, and judge the prise
Of Wit, or Arms, while both contend
To win her Grace, whom all commend.

JOHN MILTON, *L'Allegro*

7

XML on the server

Chapter 6 was devoted to XML software in the authoring and development environments; what remains to be discussed is XML-capable software for the web server. This server-side software makes it possible to transform page documents on the fly (in response to requests from web clients) and combine an XSLT processor with a traditional dynamic web site engine.

As we saw in Chapter 1, running XSLT transformations offline (**1.4.1**) or in the user's browser (**1.4.3**) both have serious disadvantages: In the first instance, weak support for dynamic web pages; in the second, a requirement for XML and XSLT support in the browser. This leaves XSLT processing on the server (**1.4.2**) as the most viable setup. It can accommodate any type of site and requires no special software on the user's end.

The sample site we've been building so far was developed and tested offline. This does not mean, however, that it has to remain that way. As we'll see in this chapter, migrating our offline XSLT setup to the server is fairly easy to do. We'll start by determining the minimum software necessary to run a Java-based XSLT processor, such as Saxon, on a web server. The bulk of the chapter, however, is devoted to Apache Cocoon, which is currently the most complete framework for building dynamic XML-based web sites.

7.1 XSLT processor as servlet

7.1.1 Saxon servlet

A Java class written specifically to be run on a web server is called a *servlet*. A software layer that works as an interface between the actual web server (such as Apache) and Java servlets is called a *servlet container* or *servlet engine*. So the two things we need, besides a regular web server, are

• an XSLT processor packaged as a servlet (as opposed to a regular runnable class file); and

• a servlet engine to run this processor servlet.

Saxon includes a basic servlet class called `SaxonServlet` in the `examples/java` subdirectory of the Saxon distribution. This class is fairly simple and is included more as a proof-of-concept demo than a production-ready servlet implementation. For one thing, the only way to pass the names of the source document and the stylesheet to this servlet is via a URL of the form

```
http://example.org/SaxonServlet?source=page.xml&style=style.xsl
```

Can we simplify this? You may want to have the servlet fired for any `.xml` file requested from the server, as in

```
http://example.org/page.xml
```

The stylesheet URI in this case might be taken from the `<?xml-stylesheet?>` processing instruction in `page.xml`. This is possible if you

• configure your server to associate all `.xml` files with the Saxon servlet; and

- modify the Saxon servlet so that it can take the URI it is called with as source and use the processing instruction in the source document to find the stylesheet.

Better yet, install Cocoon (**7.2**) over Tomcat and let the former solve this problem in an elegant and generic fashion.

7.1.1.1 Tomcat servlet engine

A good servlet engine is Tomcat,[1] developed by the Apache Software Foundation. Tomcat is the reference implementation of the Java Servlet and JSP (Java Server Pages) technologies.

Tomcat may work as a servlet engine with another web server, such as Apache or Microsoft IIS, but it also contains a web server of its own. So, you don't have to run a full-featured web server if you want to install Tomcat on your local system to experiment with it. Note that you'll also need to install Tomcat (with or without a separate web server) if you want to run the Cocoon framework discussed in the next section.

Refer to **7.2.6**, steps 1 to 4, for instructions on installing and testing Tomcat. See the Tomcat documentation on how to install web applications (such as the Saxon servlet) into Tomcat.

7.2 **Apache Cocoon**

No book on XML in web design can ignore Cocoon.[2] On the other hand, no book can do Cocoon justice unless it is entirely devoted to this complex piece of software.[3]

Cocoon is not only large; it is also quite unlike other web development platforms. Therefore, be prepared for an avalanche of new terms and concepts. I will try to make this section easier to digest by focusing on those aspects of Cocoon that are the most relevant in the context of this book. In any case, this section is only a starter.

....

1. jakarta.apache.org/tomcat
2. cocoon.apache.org
3. A list of books devoted to Cocoon is at cocoon.apache.org/link/books.html.

Cocoon step by step.   The foundation of Cocoon is the same basic idea you're already familiar with: Mark up the content in XML and transform it into HTML using XSLT. Cocoon adds a lot of new terms to this equation, but you can explore them incrementally when (and if) you need them.

In particular, we can quickly deploy Cocoon to run a static XML/XSLT web site, such as our sample site from previous chapters, with minimum changes (**7.2.7**). You can therefore enjoy the immediate benefits of server-side transformation without delving too deeply into Cocoon specifics. Later, led by curiosity or by the demands of more dynamic web site functionality, you can always extend your setup by adding advanced Cocoon components.

A bit of history.   Cocoon started in 1999 as a simple servlet for server-side XML-to-HTML transformation, similar to the Saxon servlet (**7.1.1**). It quickly outgrew its modest beginnings and has by now turned into a complex framework for building XML-based dynamic sites, where XSLT is only one of the inventory of tools for processing data.

Cocoon version 2,[4] first released in 2001, is now quite mature and runs many web sites around the world. Hosting providers have started providing Cocoon-enabled accounts. Overall, Cocoon is a rich platform with a sound conceptual foundation — and without the code-centric entanglements of ASP or PHP. Cocoon's development community is active and willing to help newbies.

But its feature set and documentation are not quite coordinated. Cocoon usually offers more than one way to perform any single task (reminding of Perl, another famous web development platform), and it may not always be easy to figure out how these different approaches compare.

....

4. Examples in this book were tested in version 2.0.4.

7.2.1 Cocoon applicability

While Cocoon is in many aspects similar to the conventional XML/XSLT setup that we worked on throughout this book, in many aspects it is also different.

Enter logic. The holy grail of Cocoon is a clean separation of *content*, *logic*, and *style*. If you compare that to the content vs. style distinction we discussed in Chapter 1, you'll notice that *logic* (i.e., the programming code that implements the logic of a dynamic site's functionality) is the new item that Cocoon puts on the agenda.

In theory, content, logic, and style are completely orthogonal to each other. In practice, if you have a working two-layer system separating content and style (something we have focused on in this book), adding some programming logic to it is relatively easy: Most probably it will only affect content. On the other hand, traditional web development technologies largely deal with style and logic only (**1.5.1**); there, it may be much harder to cleanly separate content from the other two aspects if it wasn't designed orthogonally from the start.

Even though Cocoon's attempts to separate logic from style are not always successful (as we'll see in **7.2.4.1**, this separation is not always possible), the content-logic-style triad is a natural fit for dynamic web sites. With that in mind, we can identify two situations where using Cocoon has clear advantages: dynamic sites that want to use XML for content markup and XML sites that need to run on the server with acceptable speed and scalability.

7.2.1.1 Dynamic sites with XML

Cocoon lets you combine full-scale dynamic processing (such as interfacing with a database) with XML content markup — without programming the entire system from scratch. Moreover, XML-based technologies such as RSS and SOAP enable new kinds of dynamic web-based applications that are straightforward to implement in Cocoon.

Building blocks. The wealth of prepackaged components available to a Cocoon developer is not so wide compared to the vast libraries of older languages like Perl. Still, the basics of a dynamic web site are well covered; for example, Cocoon provides facilities for session tracking, sending email messages, and site search. Plus, you have the full power of XSLT and Java at your disposal.

Java, again. Being Java-based, Cocoon naturally leans toward programming the logic of a web site in Java. Therefore, if you have a working dynamic web site made with Perl, PHP, or ASP, migrating it to Cocoon may not be trivial. If, however, you are using a Java-based technology such as JSP, or if you are starting a new dynamic site from scratch and are not predisposed against Java, Cocoon is a much more attractive option.

7.2.1.2 Server-side XML

No doubt, the fastest of all XML web site setups is offline transformation (**1.4.1**): Nothing can beat a native-binary, lean and mean web server spewing out plain HTML and graphic files prepared offline. When you burden the server with on-the-fly XML processing, performance cannot but suffer.

The XSLT bottleneck. Still, Cocoon delivers acceptable performance and scalability for medium-duty web sites. Most of the processing time for each request is consumed by XSLT, but Cocoon reduces this time significantly by caching results of transformations. You can further speed things up by using a faster processor (for example, Saxon is notably faster than Xalan, which comes with Cocoon; still faster Java processors exist, **6.4.1**) and by removing all static content, such as images, from Cocoon and serving it with a fast conventional web server.

Size matters. Another important performance factor is the size of documents. Memory requirements for processing grow very fast as your documents get bigger, and the practical document size limit is easily reachable even on capable systems. Cocoon steps around this problem by representing XML data not as static trees but as linear streams of events that go down pipelines. This significantly lowers memory requirements and speeds up processing.

For XSLT processing, however, building a tree representation of XML is inevitable — XPath connotes arbitrary access to the entire document tree. In some cases you can use Cocoon's pipeline tools to break large documents into parts before transformation and reassemble transformed pieces later.

Cocoon's downsides

There are a number of caveats that you should consider before deciding to build your web site with Cocoon:

- It is likely that the main obstacle to Cocoon deployment will be the **server (re)configuration required**. If your web server does not already run Cocoon, you will have to install quite a bunch of software on it: Java runtime, Tomcat servlet engine, and Cocoon itself. Hosting administrators are often reluctant to install new software on their servers because of security and performance considerations. If you control your web server, you are of course free to experiment, but remember that such a drastic change in configuration is risky and should be thoroughly tested before deployment.

- As mentioned before, Cocoon is **big and complex**, with a steep learning curve (even if you are already familiar with XML and XSLT). In my opinion, this complexity is well worth the effort, as the power you get with Cocoon is immense — even though it may take time to implement your first dynamic Cocoon web site. On the other hand, installing a simple static XML/XSLT web site under Cocoon isn't at all difficult (see **7.2.6** for a how-to).

- Besides being big and complex, Cocoon is still an **unstable, evolving** piece of software. Certain architectural aspects may seem awkward to a person coming from either a traditional web development background or an XML/XSLT background. I will detail the most noticeable discrepancies between Cocoon's approach to XSLT and the way we used the language in previous examples. None of these discrepancies is too serious, but they require some getting used to.

The following sections cover the most important architectural principles of Cocoon and present some of its often used components. If you prefer to "learn as you type," you can skip to **7.2.6** for a step-by-step guide to setting up a minimal Cocoon site, or even to **7.2.7** where we'll see what it takes to adapt our sample Foobar site to run under Cocoon.

7.2.2   Pipelines

Cocoon's architecture is based on the concept of a *pipeline*. A pipeline is a device that is triggered by an HTTP request (such as a user browsing to a URL on a Cocoon server) and responds to the request by preparing the corresponding resource. Generally, this preparation consists of *generation* (e.g., reading an XML file), *transformation* (e.g., XSLT processing), and *serialization* (e.g., rendering the XSLT transformation output as an HTML document that is sent to the requesting client).

DOM vs. SAX. With the possible exception of the very first stage (generation), the entire pipeline is dynamic: Data being poured down the pipeline is never frozen in a static file but is always in a state of flux. The linear stream of XML data between pipeline stages consists of the so called SAX[5] events. The first version of Cocoon used DOM[6] trees to represent XML data, but performance considerations forced developers to switch to SAX.

The three main categories of components available to a Cocoon developer are generators, transformers, and serializers.

- **Generators** produce an XML stream and send it down a pipeline. The simplest generator, which is the default in Cocoon, is the *file generator* that parses an XML document stored in a file. Others include the *search generator* (searching files in a given directory with a given query and returning a list of results), the *directory generator* (similar to our `files:dir()` extension function, **5.3.2.I**), and the *status generator* (producing an XML representation of the status of the Cocoon engine, useful for debugging). With the exception of the file generator (which can read arbitrary XML), most generators produce a specific XML vocabulary as output.

---

5. `www.saxproject.org`
6. `www.w3.org/DOM`

- **Transformers** draw in an XML stream, convert it to some other form of XML, and spit it out further down the pipeline. The most widely used transformer is the *XSLT transformer*, which applies a given stylesheet to its input and sends the transformation result to the output. Other transformers can be used for encoding URLs, converting relative paths in `href` attributes to absolute, aggregating content from several documents, filtering, logging, and so on.

  All transformers expect some specific XML vocabulary as input. For the XSLT transformer, the input vocabulary is defined by the stylesheet it uses; for others, it is usually hardcoded into the transformer itself but may sometimes be affected by the parameters of a transformer call.

  For example, the *i18n transformer* translates (parts of) a document from one language to another (using a fixed vocabulary that you must prepare for your data in advance). It expects to see specific elements from the `http://apache.org/cocoon/i18n/2.1` namespace. It reacts by translating the content of these elements as specified in their attributes and passing along the rest of the data unchanged.

- **Serializers** convert a stream of XML data into a stream of bytes.[7] The most obvious way to serialize an XML document is to represent it in the same way as it would appear in a file; this is what the default *XML serializer* does. Similarly, the *HTML*, *XHTML*, and *text* serializers are analogous to the corresponding output methods in XSLT.

  Cocoon also includes serializers for converting the XSL-FO vocabulary (**5.5.3.2**) into PostScript or PDF, as well as a number of serializers for rasterizing SVG (**5.5.2.1**) into various bitmap image formats (these components use Batik, **5.5.2.2**).

....

7. The term *serializer* implies a conversion from a tree-like XML structure into a stream of bytes. Given that inside Cocoon, XML already exists as a *serial* stream of SAX events rather than a tree, this term may be slightly misguiding even if backed by tradition.

- For serving static non-XML content such as images, Cocoon offers **readers**. A reader is an entire pipeline compressed into a one-line instruction; it reads the specified resource and immediately sends it to the client without attempting to parse, transform, or serialize it.

- In addition to these basic components, a pipeline may also include **aggregators** (**7.2.4**), **actions** (**7.2.5**), and other components used less frequently.

7.2.3 Sitemap

A *sitemap* is the control center of a Cocoon-based web site. It is an XML document describing the configuration of the pipelines and specifying when and how these pipelines are to be activated.

A sitemap consists of two main parts. First, it declares all the components it is going to use; second, it builds pipelines from these components and associates them with various types of requests coming from web clients.

The component declaration part is, although important, not too exciting. You just look up the correct syntax for each component in the Cocoon documentation and copy it to your sitemap with appropriate modifications (see **7.2.6** for a complete sitemap example). It is the defining of pipelines and associating them with requests that is much more interesting.

7.2.3.1 Matching requests to pipelines

A sitemap component called a **matcher** wraps up a pipeline definition and associates it with specific requests. The most frequently used matcher is the *wildcard URI matcher*; it responds to URI requests that match a wildcard pattern. When triggered, a matcher launches the pipeline that is defined inside the map:match element,[8] for example:

....

8. In the examples in this chapter, the prefix map corresponds to the namespace URI http://apache.org/cocoon/sitemap/1.0.

```
<map:match pattern="*.html">
  <map:generate src="source/{1}.xml"/>
  <map:transform src="style.xsl"/>
  <map:serialize/>
</map:match>
```

This matcher catches all URI requests that have the form `*.html`. Within the matcher, the expression `{1}` is used to refer to whatever replaces the first asterisk in the request pattern — in this case, the filename without extension.

The `map:generate` element starts the pipeline by reading in the corresponding XML source file from the `source/` subdirectory. Next `map:transform` applies the stylesheet, `style.xsl`, to this source to transform it into HTML. Finally, the default serializer, `map:serialize`, outputs the result as XHTML that is sent to the requesting client.

Different pipelines may use one source document but different transformation stylesheets and serializers. For example, a *virtual URI* of the form `*.pdf` may activate another pipeline ending with the *PDF serializer* that will produce a PDF version of the same web page that is also available as `*.html`.

Pipelining from afar. The generator need not necessarily read a local file. This example is taken from the Cocoon documentation:

```
<map:match pattern="news/slashdot.html">
  <map:generate src="http://slashdot.org/slashdot.xml"/>
  <map:transform src="stylesheets/news/slashdot.xsl"/>
  <map:serialize/>
</map:match>
```

This pipeline is triggered when a web surfer requests the specific URI, `/news/slashdot.html`, from the Cocoon-powered web site. Instead of relying on its own resources, however, Cocoon leeches the XML version of the front page from `slashdot.org`, transforms it with a local stylesheet, and sends the result to the client.

Other types of generators can connect to databases (including remote ones) and retrieve data from them, or simply generate some XML data on the spot (such as search results or a Cocoon status report). A virtual URI may include, in arbitrary syntax, any parameters that the generator will use, such as a query string for document search or a zip code for a database query.

Readers for static content. For static resources, a matcher can use a reader instead of a complete pipeline:

```
<map:match pattern="img/*.png">
  <map:read mime-type="image/png" src="img/{1}.png"/>
</map:match>
```

Other wildcard options. A plain * matches anything *excluding* the directory separator character, /. Conversely, a double asterisk (**) in a wildcard pattern matches a string that *can* include /. Thus,

```
<map:match pattern="**/*.html">
  <map:generate src="source/{1}/{2}.xml"/>
  <map:transform src="style.xsl"/>
  <map:serialize/>
</map:match>
```

will match `news/archive/foobar.html` and take the corresponding source from `source/news/archive/foobar.xml`. Here, {1} refers to the ** in the pattern that matches the entire directory path (`news/archive`), and {2} is the single * which represents the filename (`foobar`).

Other types of matchers can respond to a specific client hostname or hostname mask, HTTP request parameters, etc. More complex URI patterns can be recognized by the *regexp matcher*; see the examples in the Cocoon distribution for ideas on how to use it.

Virtual URIs vs. abbreviated addresses. Note that any pipeline processing remains invisible to the user. If someone surfs, e.g., to `www.example.org/about.html` on the Cocoon server, the browser will display the received HTML document with that same `www.example.org/about.html` in the URL line. The user will have no way of knowing that no static HTML file corresponding to this URI exists on the server and that the XML source of the page may be stored in some very different place or generated on the fly. Such a URI is therefore called a *virtual URI* in Cocoon.

This correspondence between virtual URIs visible from outside the server and the actual locations of source XML documents on the server might remind you of our address abbreviation technique (**3.5.3**). Indeed, Cocoon's virtual

URIs serve a similar purpose, but there is also an important difference: While our abbreviated addresses were only used in source XML markup and remained unseen to the site's visitors, a virtual URI in Cocoon is used by *both* XML content authors and web surfers.

For one thing, this means that if a virtual URI changes, all documents linking to it will have to be updated. Abbreviations, on the other hand, were designed in part to avoid exactly this problem. Besides, a virtual URI is still a URI — even if stripped of the filename extension, it has to carry certain technical baggage such as protocol specification.

These observations suggest that virtual URIs are a complement rather than competition to address abbreviations used in XML markup, and in fact, with Cocoon we can use both (**7.2.7**). For this to work, however, your transformation stylesheet must have a way to know both the virtual URI (for creating links in HTML) and the source location (for accessing the source) for each abbreviated address it encounters.

7.2.4 Aggregation

Aggregation is the Cocoon term for combining data from different sources. It usually refers only to static sources represented by XML documents; inserting dynamic values into templates is another matter (we'll get to it in **7.2.5**). As with most other concepts, Cocoon offers several different approaches to aggregation.

- The **XInclude transformer** is an implementation of the XInclude standard.[9] It filters its input looking for specific inclusion instructions and replacing each one with the content of the external resource referred to in the instruction. Such an instruction must have the form of an element in a designated namespace, as in

```
<x:include
    xmlns:x="http://www.w3.org/2001/XInclude"
    href="header.xml#xpointer(//section/head[2])"/>
```

As you can see from this example, XInclude URIs may use the XPointer language[10] for extracting specific fragments from the

---

9. www.w3.org/TR/xinclude
10. www.w3.org/TR/WD-xptr

referenced resource. XPointer is a superset of XPath, so if you are familiar with XPath you shouldn't have problems with XPointer.

Here's how you might include an XInclude transformer in a pipeline in your sitemap:

```
<map:match pattern="*.html">
  <map:generate src="source/{1}.xml"/>
  <map:transform type="xinclude"/>
  <map:transform type="xslt" src="style.xsl"/>
  <map:serialize/>
</map:match>
```

Now, the XSLT transformer will receive as input an XML document in which the `include` elements from the XInclude namespace are replaced by whatever they refer to.

- The **CInclude transformer**[11] is similar to XInclude. Its sole advantage is that it does *not* support XPointer, which means it does not have to build a complete tree of the included document and can just pour it in as a stream. You can only embed entire documents with CInclude, but it is significantly faster than XInclude. Also, CInclude offers a caching implementation which further speeds it up when the same document is included more than once.

  Here's how a CInclude instruction might look in a document:

```
<c:include
    xmlns:c="http://apache.org/cocoon/include/1.0"
    src="header.xml" element="head"/>
```

  Here, the `element` attribute specifies the element which will envelop the included resource.

- A **sitemap aggregator** works at the pipeline level and therefore, unlike XInclude and CInclude, does not require that any instructions be placed in the source files. Here's an example sitemap fragment:

---

11. cocoon.apache.org/2.0/userdocs/transformers/cinclude-transformer.html

```
<map:match pattern="leaflet.pdf">
  <map:aggregate element="leaflet">
    <map:part element="cover" src="source/cover-page.xml"/>
    <map:part element="page" src="cocoon:/page2.xml"/>
  </map:aggregate>
  <map:transform src="leaflet-style.xsl"/>
  <map:serialize type="pdf"/>
</map:match>
```

Here, the `map:aggregate` element works as a generator; it combines two resources into one and passes the result down the pipeline. As with CInclude, the `element` attributes produce wrapper elements around the included content, so the high-level structure of the created document will be:

```
<leaflet>
  <cover>
    <!-- contents of source/cover-page.xml -->
  </cover>
  <page>
    <!-- contents of cocoon:/page2.xml -->
  </page>
</leaflet>
```

A nice thing about Cocoon is that it allows you to reuse any pipelines as data sources for other pipelines. The `map:part` with the `cocoon:/` URI in the above aggregation example does just that: It searches the current sitemap for a pipeline matching the request `page2.xml`, runs it, and uses its output as the second part of the aggregated document. For this to make sense, the referenced pipeline must produce not HTML, but an XML vocabulary that fits the aggregated document's schema and would be correctly processed by `leaflet-style.xsl`.

7.2.4.1 document()ing in Cocoon

As you may remember from Chapter 5, the `document()` function of XPath is one of the cornerstones of our transformation stylesheet, much used for "aggregation" — that is, for looking up arbitrary values in the master document or in other page documents during transformation of a page. In Cocoon, however, `document()` is a bit of a controversy. What's the problem?

Stay in line. The pipeline metaphor implies that each of the components in the middle of a pipeline has exactly one inflow tube and exactly one outflow tube. This applies to the XSLT transformer as well, which means your stylesheet must only take one document as input and produce one document as output.

Any compilation of data from different sources is supposed to be done either by the dynamic code (**7.2.5**) or by specialized aggregators (**7.2.4**). Both of them usually come before the XSLT transformation stage in a pipeline, which means Cocoon leans towards the "Compile, then transform" scenario as described in **1.5.2** (even though Cocoon is flexible enough to implement any dynamic workflow).

Aggregating entire documents with `map:aggregate` or the CInclude aggregator is too coarse for the tasks where we would normally call `document()` with an XPath nodeset selector. XInclude can use XPointer to extract arbitrarily granular fragments for inclusion, but it requires adding instructions in the source XML which is simply impossible in many cases (where would you XInclude a menu label if there is no menu in a page document?). It looks like nothing in Cocoon can give us quite the functionality of a stylesheet's `document()` call.

Logic or style? Moreover, the authors of the Cocoon FAQ[12] claim that the use of the `document()` function in XSLT breaks the separation between style and logic: The stylesheet must only be concerned with styling (i.e., formatting), while aggregating sources belongs in the realm of programming logic.[13]

....

12. `cocoon.apache.org/2.1/faq/faq-xslt.html`

13. The FAQ goes on to say, "Understand that the `document()` function was designed *before* XInclude with XPointer facilities existed. Had such capabilities been available, perhaps the `document()` function, which essentially mimics XInclude and XPointer, would have never been added to XSLT." Wrong. XInclude and `document()` solve entirely different problems. An XInclude instruction in the source may affect the *content*, while `document()` provides access to arbitrary resources from within the *processing* layer (be that "style" or "logic" processing).

This is at least arguable. For example, if building a menu for a web page is part of styling that page, why isn't fetching data needed for the menu from another document? The fact is, in any sufficiently complex web site, the stylesheet needs to see the context of the entire site in order to format a page — and the master document accessed via `document()` calls is the best way to provide that context.

Another example is the presentation of links. The source of a page can only provide the address for a link — but when creating an HTML rendition, we might want to use some information from the linked document, such as its title, that could be shown in the link's floating tooltip. This is another task best performed in XSLT using `document()`.

On the other hand, inclusion of orthogonal content (**2.1.2.2**) could indeed be removed from the stylesheet into a different processing stage. For instance, in a page document each `block` element with an `idref` attribute (Example 3.1, page 141) might be replaced by an XInclude instruction. Whether XInclude (with its XPointer support) is better than `idref` (with its abbreviated block references) is an open question, though.

Forking trouble. Fortunately, the case against `document()` is purely ideological, not technical. A stylesheet with a `document()` call will work just fine under Cocoon, as we'll see in **7.2.7**. It is the other violation of the "one inflow, one outflow" principle — the `xsl:result-document` instruction — that may cause some trouble under Cocoon.

Forking the output of a stylesheet into multiple result documents effectively breaks the pipeline system by sprouting new branches that are unseen and uncared for from the sitemap perspective. What's worse, `xsl:result-document` may simply fail unless the pathname of the output document is absolute.

This is because an XSLT processor uses the pathname of the main result document to resolve the relative pathnames of all non-main ones. Inside Cocoon, however, the processor is run in "stream mode" without any real input or output files. Therefore, for `xsl:result-document` to work, you must provide an absolute pathname for the output file in its `href` attribute.

This is not a particularly elegant solution, as it forces you to hard-code absolute paths into the stylesheet making it potentially unportable. The bottom line is that it is better to avoid `xsl:result-document` altogether if you are planning to run your stylesheet under Cocoon.

7.2.5   Dynamic processing

Although this book is not about dynamic web sites, it is worth spending a few pages on Cocoon's approaches to dynamic processing, from the viewpoint of integrating XSLT transformations with a dynamic web site engine.

- **Legacy code.** For refugees from other web development platforms, Cocoon offers ways to accommodate the old code. You can use special generators (**7.2.2**) if you want to reuse HTML templates with embedded JSP[14] or PHP[15] code. These generators will launch regular JSP or PHP interpreters to process the embedded scripts and then feed the resulting HTML files down the pipeline.

  This approach is obviously very crude — from an XML-enlightened perspective, anyway. It still produces HTML which is nearly useless for our purposes even if it is coming down a Cocoon pipeline. So, it is provided only as a temporary workaround for those pages that haven't yet been converted to more advanced technologies supported by Cocoon.

- **XSP.** The primary mechanism for programming web site applications in Cocoon is called XSP (eXtensible Server Pages, in line with all the other "Server Pages" out there — ASP, JSP . . .). This is, basically, a syntax for embedding programming code into XML. The programming language used by XSP is usually Java, although Cocoon also supports JavaScript.

  Embedding Java code into an XSP page document is not too different from embedding, say, PHP code into an HTML file. One important difference is that you don't work with messy HTML,

---

14. Java Server Pages, see `java.sun.com/products/jsp`
15. `www.php.net`

but with your clean semantic XML that will be transformed into HTML only after all XSP processing is finished ("Compile, then transform," **1.5.2.1**).

Another difference is that instead of PHP's `<? ?>` or ASP's `<% %>`, bits of embedded code in an XSP document are contained in elements from the XSP namespace. To use an XSP page in Cocoon, you call a special kind of generator that executes the embedded code and sends the resulting pure XML down the pipeline.

- **Logicsheets.** An interesting addition to XSP is the concept of *logicsheets* ("stylesheets for logic"). This is an attempt to apply XML's fundamental concept of separating content from presentation to programming code.

  A logicsheet is an XSLT stylesheet that returns its input unchanged except for specific elements (usually from a namespace unique to this logicsheet) that are replaced by bits of XSP code. Thus, another level of abstraction is introduced: In your source XML, you provide a general outline of what the code must do, and the logicsheet fills in a specific implementation.

  The set of element types that a logicsheet responds to is called the *taglib* ("library of tags") of that logicsheet.[16] Cocoon provides several built-in logicsheets for tasks such as database access, sending emails from a web page, and form input validation.

- **Actions.** Finally, you can implement some of your dynamic functionality at the sitemap level using *actions*. One of the reasons for adding actions to the already rich dynamic landscape in Cocoon was that, quoting Cocoon documentation, other approaches "still mix content and logic to a certain degree." Which is perhaps a polite way of putting it — even with logicsheets, you still often have to edit your *content* (i.e., the XML source) if you want to change some aspects of the site's *logic*.

---

16. A taglib is somewhat similar to an API (Application Programming Interface) in traditional programming.

Actions, on the other hand, require no changes to the page documents whatsoever. An action is a Java class that must be declared in a sitemap just like any other sitemap component (generators, transformers, etc.). After that, you can call your action using the `map:act` element from within any pipeline. An action can set parameters of a pipeline, switch pipeline parts on or off, and perform any actions that are sufficiently external to web pages (such as validating the output of a form).

7.2.6   Cocoon primer

Suppose you have a very simple site consisting of a stylesheet (`style.xsl`) and one or more page documents (say, `page.xml`). No master documents, no graphic generation, no extension Java classes — all of that is left for the next section. You have authored the pages and tested them with the stylesheet offline; all you want to do now is install them under Cocoon so they are transformed on the server.

We will now build a setup without a dedicated web server, with the Tomcat servlet engine working as a server. This is simpler to get going, yet perfectly adequate for experimentation.

1. Install Java.[17] (You've probably done that long ago. It's here just for completeness.)

2. Download and install Tomcat.[18] It's easy: unzip the distribution archive into a directory, set the `JAVA_HOME` environment variable to the location of your Java installation, and run `startup.bat` (Windows) or `startup.sh` (Unix) from the `bin` subdirectory of Tomcat.

3. Check that Tomcat is running. Open up your web browser and go to `localhost:8080`. The front page of your local Tomcat installation should appear.

---

17. Sun's Java implementation is at `java.sun.com`; IBM's is at `www.ibm.com/developerworks/java`; there are others.

18. `jakarta.apache.org/tomcat`

4. Stop Tomcat by running `bin/shutdown.{bat|sh}` and launch it again by `bin/startup.{bat|sh}`. You will have to restart Tomcat with these scripts whenever you change the configuration of Tomcat or Cocoon (updating sitemaps, sources, or stylesheets does not require a restart).

5. Download the latest version of Cocoon.[19] Unzip the distribution archive and place the `cocoon.war` file into the `webapps` subdirectory of Tomcat. Restart Tomcat.

6. Check that Cocoon is running by browsing to `localhost:8080/cocoon`. The first page view after a restart may be slow while Cocoon loads its classes and configures itself.

7. Now, go to `webapps/cocoon` under Tomcat (called "Cocoon directory" from now on) and create a subdirectory for your site, e.g., `eg`.

8. Put your stylesheet, `style.xsl`, into `eg`. Create a subdirectory `eg/source` and put `page.xml` and the rest of the page documents there.

9. Create the file named `sitemap.xmap`, shown in Example 7.1, in `eg`. This is the sitemap of your sample site.

10. We also need to mount our new site in the main sitemap of the Cocoon installation. Ascend to the Cocoon directory and edit the `sitemap.xmap` file there by adding, after the start tag of the first `map:pipeline` element:

```
<map:match pattern="eg/**">
  <map:mount
      check-reload="yes"
      src="eg/sitemap.xmap"
      uri-prefix="eg"/>
</map:match>
```

Now, the sitemap for `eg` will receive all URL requests for files from `eg/`, but with everything up to and including `eg/` removed

---

19. `cocoon.apache.org`

Example 7.1   `eg/sitemap.xmap`: A basic sitemap for a Cocoon site.

```
<?xml version="1.0" encoding="utf-8"?>
<map:sitemap xmlns:map="http://apache.org/cocoon/sitemap/1.0">
  <map:components>
    <map:matchers default="wildcard"/>
    <map:generators default="file"/>
    <map:transformers default="xslt"/>
    <map:serializers default="html"/>
  </map:components>
  <map:pipelines>
    <map:pipeline>
      <map:match pattern="*.html">
        <map:generate src="source/{1}.xml"/>
        <map:transform src="style.xsl"/>
        <map:serialize/>
      </map:match>
    </map:pipeline>
  </map:pipelines>
</map:sitemap>
```

from the URL. That is, if you surf to `/eg/page.html`, the root sitemap will cut out the last part of the URL, `page.html`, and pass it down to the `eg` sitemap for matching.

11. That is all! Direct your browser to

`http://localhost:8080/cocoon/eg/page.html`

Cocoon will transform the page and (after some pause) your browser will show you the resulting HTML. Subsequent loads of the same page will be much faster, thanks to caching.

7.2.7 Foobar under Cocoon

Our sample Foobar Corporation site will not quite run out of the box under Cocoon. However, the changes required to make it work are not too drastic.

- To start, our stylesheet uses many **XSLT 2.0 and XPath 2.0** facilities. You can install Saxon 7 as the default processor under

Cocoon if the Xalan processor that is shipped with Cocoon only supports XSLT 1.0. Instructions for doing this can be found on the Cocoon Wiki web site.[20]

- **Extension Java classes** that we developed in Chapter 5 are also easy to install: just copy the entire `com` hierarchy (**5.3.2.2**) into the `WEB-INF/classes` directory under Cocoon.

  By the way, at least some of our extension functions can be replaced by Cocoon components. Thus, instead of the `files:dir()` function (**5.3.2.1**) you can use the much more powerful directory generator[21] that produces an XML representation of a directory listing. This will require, however, a fair amount of redesign of the stylesheet to remove part of its functionality to the sitemap.

- **Directories and URLs.** You can install the site in a subdirectory under Cocoon, as we did in the primer (**7.2.6**), but you could also remove all the Cocoon samples and documentation and install your site right in the root directory of Cocoon, replacing the default root sitemap with the sitemap of your site. This will get rid of the site's subdirectory name in the URL (i.e., the URL will end with `/cocoon/` rather than `/cocoon/foobar/`). You can also configure Tomcat to make Cocoon its root servlet, thus removing the `/cocoon/` from the URL as well.

- The **master document** (**2.1.2.1**, page 49) does not need to be changed in any significant way. You'll only need to define an `environment` whose `src-path` is the absolute path of the site's root directory (for example, `/var/tomcat/webapps/cocoon/foobar/`), and whose `target-path` is the relative URL of the site as seen from outside of Cocoon (for example, `/cocoon/foobar/`, or simply `/` if you have configured Tomcat and Cocoon as described in the previous item). Make this environment the default (by changing the value of the `$env` parameter in the shared library, `_lib.xsl`) so that you don't have to specify the environment identifier when the stylesheet is run by Cocoon.

....

20. `www.wiki.cocoondev.org/Wiki.jsp?page=Saxon`
21. `cocoon.apache.org/2.1/userdocs/generators/directory-generator.html`

- The **shared XSLT library** (**5.1.1**, page 187) needs to be modified. The `saxon:systemId()` extension function that we used for finding out the pathname of the source document will not work because Cocoon runs its XSLT processor on a stream of SAX events, not on a file. We must devise another way to let the stylesheet know which page of those listed in the master document it is working on.

  Since the stylesheet is run from the Cocoon sitemap, we can pass this information from the sitemap to the stylesheet via a parameter. The pipeline might look like this:

```
<map:match pattern="**.html">
  <map:generate src="{1}.xml"/>
  <map:transform src="style.xsl">
    <map:parameter name="request" value="{1}"/>
  </map:transform>
  <map:serialize/>
</map:match>
```

  Here, {1} refers to the replacement of `**` in the matcher pattern — that is, to the URL fragment without the server part (stripped by the root sitemap) and without `.html`. Thus, for a URL like

```
http://localhost:8080/cocoon/foobar/en/team/contact.html
```

  the `$request` parameter will be `en/team/contact` — which is exactly what we want to have in the stylesheet. All you need to do is rewrite the definitions of the `$lang` and `$current` variables in `_lib.xsl` so that they rely on the `$request` parameter instead of calling `saxon:systemId()`.

- **Schematron validation** only makes sense for offline transformation — server-side validation of each page on each request is too expensive (even with caching). Besides, a developer is supposed to fix any validation problems *before* a document gets to the server. As mentioned in **1.4.2**, you will likely need a working offline setup in addition to the server setup anyway. So, we won't even try to port our Schematron setup to Cocoon; you will have to validate your documents offline before uploading them to Cocoon.

- **Image generation** (**5.5.2**) is another thing you won't want to run under Cocoon. It will work (if you run the stylesheet with the $images parameter set to yes), but it is way too slow for on-the-fly generation on the server. Generate images offline and upload them to Cocoon along with the rest of the files.

As you can see, the changes required for migrating our (initially offline) setup to Cocoon are not too serious, even though we used a number of non-orthodox approaches in our stylesheet. We did drop a few components — not because we could not get them to run, but simply because it made little sense to use them on the server.

There are many ways in which a site can be refactored to make it fit the Cocoon architecture better and to optimize its server-side performance. (One possibility I already mentioned is reimplementing the orthogonal content mechanism using Cocoon facilities.) However, I don't think this refactoring is truly a necessity for a static site, since preserving the ability to run the complete transformation process offline has its benefits. For a dynamic XML site, the situation is different; it is preferable to develop the site from the start on the Cocoon platform, but perhaps to separate some of the auxiliary subsystems (such as validation and image generation) to be run offline.

Bibliography

[1]   Micah Dubinko, *XForms Essentials* (O'Reilly & Associates, 2003, ISBN 0596003692). Available online at www.dubinko.info/writing/xforms.

[2]   Charles F. Goldfarb and Paul Prescod, *Charles F. Goldfarb's XML Handbook*, 5th ed. (Prentice Hall PTR, 2004, ISBN 0-13-065198-2).

[3]   Charles F. Goldfarb and Priscilla Walmsley, *XML in Office 2003: Information Sharing with Desktop XML* (Prentice Hall PTR, 2004, ISBN 0-13-049765-7).

[4]   G. Ken Holman, *Definitive XSLT and XPath* (Prentice Hall PTR, 2001, ISBN 0-13-065196-6).

[5]   Michael Kay, *XSLT: Programmer's Reference*, 2nd ed. (Wrox, 2001, ISBN 0764543814).

[6]   Theodore W. Leung, *Professional XML Development with Apache Tools: Xerces, Xalan, FOP, Cocoon, Axis, Xindice* (Wrox, 2003, ISBN 0764543555).

[7]   Lajos Moczar and Jeremy Aston, *Cocoon Developer's Handbook* (SAMS, 2002, ISBN 0672322579).

[8]   Jennifer Niederst, *Web Design in a Nutshell*, 2nd ed. (O'Reilly & Associates, 2001, ISBN 0596001967).

[9]   Shelley Powers, *Practical RDF* (O'Reilly & Associates, 2003, ISBN 0596002637).

[10] Jeni Tennison, *XSLT and XPath on the Edge* (John Wiley & Sons, 2001, ISBN 0764547763).

[11] Jeni Tennison, *Beginning XSLT* (APress, 2002, ISBN 1861005946).

[12] Priscilla Walmsley, *Definitive XML Schema* (Prentice Hall PTR, 2001, ISBN 0-13-065567-8).

[13] Norman Walsh and Leonard Muellner, *DocBook: The Definitive Guide* (O'Reilly & Associates, 1999, ISBN 156592-580-7). Available online at www.docbook.org/tdg/en.

Index

. . . .

Names of elements, attributes, instructions, and functions are shown without namespace prefixes. Instead, for each name, its source vocabulary is specified. An exception is the custom extension functions (such as `files:dir()`) used in the book's examples; they are listed with their namespace prefixes.